The Vietnam Experience

Words of War

An Anthology of Vietnam War Literature

compiled by Gordon Hardy and the editors of Boston Publishing Company

Boston Publishing Company / Boston, MA

Boston Publishing Company

President and Publisher: Robert J. George
Editor-in-Chief: Robert Manning
Managing Editor: Paul Dreyfus
Marketing Director: Jeanne Gibson

Series Editor: Samuel Lipsman
Senior Editor: Gordon Hardy
Design Director: Lisa Bogle
Senior Writer: Denis Kennedy

Text Researcher: Michael Hathaway

Picture Editor: Wendy Johnson
Picture Department Coordinator/Researcher:
Jennifer Atkins

Special contributors to this volume:
Picture Editor: Kathleen Reidy
Text Researchers: Daniel Abramson,
Francis Finnegan
Picture Researcher: Mary Jenkins
(Photosearch)
Design: Emily Betsch, Sherry Fatla
Editorial Production: Dalia Lipkin,
Patricia Leal Welch

Business Staff: Amy Pelletier, Amy Wilson

About the editors

Editor-in-Chief: *Robert Manning* is a long-time journalist and has previously been editor-in-chief of the *Atlantic Monthly* magazine and its press. He served as assistant secretary of state for public affairs under Presidents John F. Kennedy and Lyndon B. Johnson. He has also been a fellow at the Institute of Politics at the John F. Kennedy School of Government at Harvard University.

Editor for this volume: *Gordon Hardy* is senior editor at Boston Publishing Company. He has written and edited other volumes of *The Vietnam Experience* and was senior editor for *Above and Beyond*, Boston Publishing Company's history of the Medal of Honor.

Cover Photo:

Men of the U.S. 1st Cavalry Division (Airmobile) patrol in Long Khanh Province in December 1971.

Library of Congress Catalog Card Number: 87-73402

ISBN: 0-939526-37-9

10 9 8 7 6

5 4 3 2 1

Contents

Preface

The purpose of this series of books, *The Vietnam Experience*, has been to present, mostly in our own words, a comprehensive, accurate chronicle of America's long and painful involvement in the Indochina war. This volume is a departure, in that it tells about the war in the words of others. It is in great part an anthology of literature, fiction and nonfiction, inspired by that war. It also presents in words and pictures many of the emotions stirred by that ordeal— anger, sorrow, insult, acrimony, bitterness, compassion—whether displayed on bumper stickers, shouted at antiwar rallies, uttered in the halls of Congress, or sent out from the Oval Office of the White House.

Like the conflict itself, the language of the war was often brutal, rude, contradictory, confused, and very often offensive or obscene. That it was intended to be at the time; that is how it reads these many years after. We therefore present it as it is, without bowdlerizing or otherwise tampering with a compelling part of the record.

—The Editors

Enter Here

It started with an airplane flight into one of the big U.S. military airports: Da Nang, Tan Son Nhut, Bien Hoa. The plane rolled down the tarmac, stopped, and opened its door as the soldiers shuffled toward the exit. Stepping out of the plane, the first thing they noticed was the stifling heat, or if the monsoons were in season, the rain. In the air terminal they waited in lines, getting gear, getting processed, getting bored. After that they either waited for other flights to other parts of the country or boarded buses with wire-mesh windows to protect against grenades for the drive to a base. They saw their first sights of the country: peasants walking, young boys on water buffaloes, the unexpectedly beautiful countryside. Everything was new and strange, but except for the uniformed men and military vehicles, nothing bespoke the fact that a war was being fought.

Preceding page. *A soldier arrives at the U.S. air base in Da Nang, South Vietnam, 1967.*

Paul Berlin Goes to War

from *Going After Cacciato*
by Tim O'Brien

Going After Cacciato, *Tim O'Brien's National Book Award-winning novel, detailed the escapades of Private First Class Paul Berlin and his comrades through a surreal Vietnamese landscape as they chased an AWOL soldier headed for Paris. Before joining his squad, Berlin spends a week receiving last-minute combat training at the big U.S. base in Chu Lai, South Vietnam:*

Even before arriving at Chu Lai's Combat Center on June 3, 1968, Private First Class Paul Berlin had been assigned by MACV Computer Services, Cam Ranh Bay, to the single largest unit in Vietnam, the American Division, whose area of operations, I Corps, constituted the largest and most diverse sector in the war zone. He was lost. He had never heard of I Corps, or the American, or Chu Lai. He did not know what a Combat Center was.

It was there by the sea.

A staging area, he decided. A place to get acquainted. Rows of tin huts stood neatly in the sand, connected by metal walkways, surrounded on three sides by wire, guarded at the rear by the sea.

A Vietnamese barber cut his hair.

A bored master sergeant delivered a Re-Up speech.

A staff sergeant led him to a giant field tent for chow, then another staff sergeant led him to a hootch containing eighty bunks and eighty lockers. The bunks and lockers were numbered.

"Don't leave here," said the staff sergeant, "unless it's to use the piss-tube."

Paul Berlin nodded, fearful to ask what a piss-tube was.

In the morning the fifty new men were marched to a wooden set of bleachers facing the sea. A small, sad-faced corporal in a black cadre helmet waited until they settled down, looking at the recruits as if searching for a lost friend in a crowd. Then the corporal sat down in the sand. He turned away and gazed out to sea. He did not speak. Time passed slowly, ten minutes, twenty, but still the sad-faced corporal did not turn or nod or speak. He simply gazed out at the blue sea. Everything was clean. The sea was clean, the sand was clean, the air was warm and pure and clean. The wind was clean.

They sat in the bleachers for a full hour.

Then at last the corporal sighed and stood up. He checked his wristwatch. Again he searched the rows of new faces.

"All right," he said softly. "That completes your first lecture on how to survive this shit. I hope you paid attention."

During the days they simulated search-and-destroy missions in a friendly little village just outside the Combat Center. The villagers played along. Always smiling, always indulgent, they let themselves be captured and frisked and interrogated.

PFC Paul Berlin, who wanted to live, took the exercise seriously.

"You VC?" he demanded of a little girl with braids. "You dirty VC?"

The girl smiled. "Shit, man," she said gently. "You shittin' me?"

They pitched practice grenades made of green fiberglass. They were instructed in compass reading, survival methods, bivouac SOPs, the operation and maintenance of the standard weapons. Sitting in the bleachers by the sea, they were lectured on the known varieties of enemy land mines and booby traps. Then, one by one, they took turns making their way through a make-believe minefield.

"Boomo!" an NCO shouted at any misstep.

It was a peculiar drill. There were no physical objects to avoid, no obstacles on the obstacle course, no wires or prongs or covered pits to detect and then evade. Too lazy to rig up the training ordnance each morning, the supervising NCO simply hollered *Boomo* when the urge struck him.

Paul Berlin, feeling hurt at being told he was a dead man, complained that it was unfair.

"Boomo," the NCO repeated.

But Paul Berlin stood firm. "Look," he said. "Nothing. Just the sand. There's nothing there at all."

The NCO, a huge black man, stared hard at the beach. Then at Paul Berlin. He smiled. "'Course not, you dumb twerp. You just fucking *exploded* it."

Paul Berlin was not a twerp. So it constantly amazed him, and left him feeling much abused, to hear such nonsense—twerp, creepo, butter-brain. It wasn't right. He was a straightforward, honest, decent sort of guy. He was not dumb. He was not small or weak or ugly. True, the war scared him silly, but this was something he hoped to bring under control.

Late on the third night he wrote to his father, explaining that he'd arrived safely at a large base called Chu Lai, and that he was taking now-or-never training in a place called the Combat Center. If there was time, he wrote, it would be swell to get a letter telling something about how things went on the home front—a nice, unfrightened-sounding phrase, he thought. He also asked his father to look up Chu Lai in a world atlas. "Right now," he wrote, "I'm a little lost."

It lasted six days, which he marked off at sunset on a pocket calendar. Not short, he thought, but getting shorter.

He had his hair cut again. He drank Coke, watched the ocean, saw movies at night, learned the smells. The sand smelled of sour milk. The air, so clean near the water, smelled of mildew. He was scared, yes, and confused and lost, and he had no sense of what was expected of him or of what to expect from himself. He was aware of his body. Listening to the instructors talk about the war, he sometimes found himself gazing at his own wrists or legs. He tried not to think. He stayed apart from the other new guys. He ignored their jokes and chatter. He made no friends and learned no names. At night, the big hootch swelling with their sleeping, he closed his eyes and pretended it was a war. He felt drugged. He plodded through the sand, listened while the NCOs talked about the AO: "Real bad shit," said the youngest of them, a sallow kid without color in his eyes. "Real tough shit, real bad. I remember this guy Uhlander. Not such a bad dick, but he made the mistake of thinkin' it wasn't so bad. It's bad. You know what bad is? Bad is evil. Bad is what happened to Uhlander. I don't wanna scare the bejasus out of you—that's not what I want—but, shit, you guys are gonna *die*."

On the seventh day, June 9, the new men were assigned to their terminal units.

The Americal Division, Paul Berlin learned for the first time, was organized into three infantry brigades, the 11th, 196th, and 198th. The brigades, in turn, were broken down into infantry battalions, the battalions into companies, the companies into platoons, the platoons into squads.

Supporting the brigades was an immense divisional complex spread out along the sands of Chu Lai. Three artillery elements under a single command, two hospitals, six air units, logistical and transportation and communication battalions, legal services, a PX, a stockade, a USO, a mini golf course, a swimming beach with trained lifeguards, administration offices under the Adjutant General, twelve Red Cross Donut Dollies, a central mail detachment, Seabees, four Military Police units, a press information service, computer specialists, civil relations specialists, psychological warfare specialists, Graves Registration, dog teams, civilian construction and maintenance contractors, a *Stars and Stripes* detachment, intelligence and tactical planning units, chapels and chaplains and assistant chaplains, cooks and clerks and translators and scouts and orderlies, an Inspector General's office, awards and decorations specialists, dentists, cartographers, statistical analysts, oceanographers, PO officers, photographers and janitors and demographers.

The ration of support to combat personnel was twelve to one.

Paul Berlin counted it as bad luck, a statistically improbable outcome, to be assigned to the 5th Battalion, 46th Infantry, 198th Infantry Brigade.

His sense of place had never been keen. In Indian Guides, with his father, he'd gone to Wisconsin to camp and be pals forever. Big Bear and Little Bear. He remembered it. Yellow and green headbands, orange feathers. Powwows

9

at the campfire. Big Fox telling stories out of the *Guide Story Book.* Big Fox, a gray-haired father from Oshebo, Illinois, owner of a paper mill. He remembered all of it. Canoe races the second day, Big Bear paddling hard but Little Bear having troubles. Poor, poor Little Bear. Better luck in the gunnysack race, Big Bear and Little Bear hopping together under the great Wisconsin sky, but poor Little Bear, stumbling. Pals anyhow. Not a problem. Shake hands the secret Guide way. Pals forever. Then the third day, into the woods, father first and son second, Little Bear tracking Big Bear, who leaves tracks and paw prints. Yes, he remembered it—Little Bear getting lost. Following Big Bear's tracks down to a winding creek, crossing the creek, checking the opposite bank according to the *Guide Survival Guide,* finding nothing; so deeper into the woods—Big Bear!—and deeper, then turning back to the creek, but now no creek. Nothing in the *Guide Survival Guide* about panic. Lost, bawling in the big Wisconsin woods. He remembered it clearly. Little Elk finding him, flashlights converging, Little Bear bawling under a giant spruce. So the fourth day, getting sick, and Big Bear and Little Bear breaking camp early. Decamping. Hamburgers and root beer on the long drive home, baseball talk, white man talk, and he remembered it, the sickness going away. Pals forever.

A Marine convoy in I Corps, the northernmost military region of South Vietnam.

A truck took him up Highway One, then inland to LZ Gator, where he joined the 5th Battalion of the 46th Infantry of the 198th Infantry Brigade. There, in a white hootch surrounded by barbed wire and bunkers, a captain jotted his name and number into a leather-bound log. An E-8 took him aside.

"You look strack," the E-8 whispered. "How'd you go for a rear job? I can fix it for you . . . get you a job painting fence. Sound good?"

Paul Berlin smiled.

"You go for that? Nice comfy painting job? No paddy humpin', no dinks?"

Paul Berlin smiled. The E-8 smiled back.

"Sound good, trooper? You get off on the sound of them bells?"

Paul Berlin smiled. He knew what the man wanted. So, only faintly, he nodded.

"Well, then," the E-8 whispered, "I fear you come to the wrong . . . fuckin . . . place."

Words of Commitment

The two leaders were very different political figures. The first was a youthful, energetic president of the world's most powerful nation. The other was a patient, aged veteran of a Communist insurgency in Southeast Asia. Yet John F. Kennedy and Ho Chi Minh had one thing in common—a rare ability to inspire their countrymen with words of dedication and sacrifice. Below are words of inspiration from each: Kennedy's inaugural address of January 20, 1961, and Ho's independence address, delivered fifteen years earlier in Hanoi.

John F. Kennedy's inaugural address

We observe today not a victory of party but a celebration of freedom, symbolizing an end as well as a beginning, signifying renewal as well as change. For I have sworn before you and Almighty God the same solemn oath our forebears prescribed nearly a century and three-quarters ago.

The world is very different now. For man holds in his mortal hands the power to abolish all forms of human poverty and all forms of human life. And yet the same revolutionary belief for which our forebears fought is still at issue around the globe, the belief that the rights of man come not from the generosity of the state but from the hand of God.

We dare not forget today that we are the heirs of that first revolution. Let the word go forth that the torch has been passed to a new generation of Americans, born in this century, tempered by war, disciplined by a hard and bitter peace, proud of our ancient heritage, and unwilling to witness or permit the slow undoing of those human rights to which this nation has always been committed, and to which we are committed today at home and around the world.

Let every nation know, whether it wishes us well or ill, that we shall pay any price, bear any burden, meet any hardship, support any friend, oppose any foe to assure the survival and the success of liberty.

This much we pledge—and more.

To those old allies whose cultural and spiritual origins we share, we pledge the loyalty of faithful friends. United, there is little we cannot do in a host of cooperative ventures. Divided, there is little we can do, for we dare not meet a powerful challenge at odds and split asunder.

To those new states whom we welcome to the ranks of the free, we pledge our word that one form of colonial control shall not have passed away merely to be replaced by a far more iron tyranny. We shall not always expect to find them supporting our view. But we shall always hope to find them strongly supporting their own freedom, and to remember that, in the past, those who foolishly sought power by riding the back of the tiger ended up inside.

To those peoples in the huts and villages of half the globe struggling to break the bonds of mass misery, we pledge our best efforts to help them help themselves, for whatever period is required, not because the Communists may be doing it, but because it is right. If a free society cannot help the many who are poor, it cannot save the few who are rich. . . .

In your hands, my fellow citizens, more than mine, will rest the final success or failure of our course. Since this country was founded, each generation of Americans has been summoned to give testimony to its national loyalty. The graves of young Americans who answered the call to service surround the globe.

Now the trumpet summons us again—not as a call to bear arms, though arms we need; not as a call to battle, though embattled we are; but a call to bear the burden of a long twilight struggle, year in and year out, "rejoicing in hope, patient in tribulation," a struggle against the common enemies of man: tyranny, poverty, disease and war itself. . . .

In the long history of the world, only a few generations have been granted the role of defending freedom in its hour of maximum danger. I do not shrink from this responsibility; I welcome it. I do not believe any of us would exchange places with any other people or any other generation. The energy, the faith, the devotion which we bring to this endeavor will light our country and all who serve it, and the glow from that fire can truly light the world.

And so, my fellow Americans, ask not what your country can do for you, but what you can do for your country.

My fellow citizens of the world, ask not what America will do for you, but what together we can do for the freedom of man.

Finally, whether you are citizens of America or citizens of the world, ask of us here the same high standards of strength and sacrifice which we ask of you. With a good conscience our only sure reward, with history the final judge of our deeds, let us go forth to lead the land we love, asking His blessing and His help, but knowing that here on earth God's work must truly be our own.

Ho Chi Minh's Declaration of Independence

"All men are created equal. They are endowed by their Creator with certain inalienable rights; among these are Life, Liberty, and the pursuit of Happiness."

This immortal statement was made in the Declaration of Independence of the United States of America in 1776. In a broader sense, this means: All the peoples on the earth are equal from birth, all the peoples have a right to live, to be happy and free.

The Declaration of the French Revolution made in 1791 on the Rights of Man and the Citizen also states: "All men are born free and with equal rights, and must always remain free and have equal rights."

Those are undeniable truths. . . .

A people who have courageously opposed French domination for more than eight years, a people who have fought side by side with the Allies against the Fascists during these last years, such a people must be free and independent.

For these reasons, we, members of the Provisional Government of the Democratic Republic of Vietnam, solemnly declare to the world that Vietnam has the right to be a free and independent country—and in fact is so already. The entire Vietnamese people are determined to mobilize all their physical and mental strength, to sacrifice their lives and property in order to safeguard their independence and liberty.

Hurry up and Wait

from *12, 20, & 5: A Doctor's Year in Vietnam*
by John A. Parrish

Dr. John A. Parrish served in Vietnam with the 3d Marine Division in 1967-1968. In **12, 20, & 5** *he recounts his experiences, including the long and frustrating attempt to report for duty excerpted below. The book's title is military shorthand for the condition of a typical group of wounded men arriving on a medevac helicopter: twelve litters, twenty walking, five dead.*

Our dress khakis went into storage as soon as we arrived in Okinawa. This meant that we had bought these costumes for over one hundred dollars just for our flight. We received two or more injections in each arm, and I had malaise, low-grade fever, and headache for our entire two-day stay on the island. We checked in and out of several places, stood in lots of lines, and filled out more forms in triplicate. I exercised once in the gymnasium, which was full of muscled young men who spent most of their time talking about various theories of muscle building all of which were unscientific and untrue.

Most of the Americans I saw on Okinawa were either going to or coming from the Republic of Vietnam. The prostitutes were experts at making the distinction. They focused their attentions on the wide-eyed, nineteen-year-old boys away from home for the first time, afraid they may

not live to return, and determined to show off their manhood in front of their colleagues. The returning seasoned twenty-year-old men of the world were more interested in drinking and telling war stories. They did not want to risk getting VD so close to homecoming. They would, however, usually get drunk and carefree enough to change their minds by late night.

Dancing with the girls and buying them drinks, the neophytes were considerate, almost courteous. They would pay higher prices for the girls' services, and the clever bargirl could usually fast talk her way into leaving them after one or two fast "tricks" in a small, nearby room (which the GI also paid for). The girls would then return to the bar to be picked up by the veterans who paid less, insisted on "all night," and generally drank enough to sleep for at least most of the night. Most girls could work in one or more "short-timers" before their moderately drunk, "all night" trick. Many of these girls were the major source of income for their family.

Another commercial airliner took us to Da Nang. Miles of runway were surrounded by tin-roofed hangars, concrete blast walls, and sandbag reinforced, wooden-frame buildings. Hundreds of helicopters sat in rows with blades folded. Commercial jets shared the runways with fighter jets and large, propeller-driven, military transport planes.

Beyond the airport was more flat land crowded with huts of wood, plaster, flattened tin cans, bamboo, and straw. A single green mountain rose far in the distance. It was clear, and hot, and so bright that the heat waves created by the baking sun and evaporating fuels gave an unreal quality to the landscape. Americans were everywhere, in jeeps and aircraft, on heavy machinery loading and unloading war materials, and in and about the terminal buildings. A few, short-statured, Vietnamese soldiers were scattered about, standing quietly, smoking Salems, and looking out of place. There were no civilians and no women of any race.

My short-sleeved shirt was soaked before I had carried my seabag the thirty meters from the aircraft to the large open warehouse of soldiers called Marine Air Freight. My instructions sounded easy enough. Go to Marine Air Freight and "muster" to go to a place called Phu Bai.

For the next six hours I stood in various lines, put my name on numerous lists, and waited. And waited. No one knew or cared who I was. No one knew exactly how to help me. It seemed that if I never appeared in Phu Bai, no one would know. Could I go back home? I even tried to call Phu Bai on the wall phone, but since I did not know whom I was calling, the code name of the operator, or the switchboard system, the attempts proved to be another exercise in frustration. I waited.

I finally got to the front of another line. The lance corporal behind the counter was hot, and bored, and tired of answering questions.

"Hi, I'm Doctor Parrish. I'd like to go to Phu Bai."

"No more flights today, Sir." He never looked up from his clipboard.

"But I have to report there."

"Sorry, Sir."

"How can I get to Phu Bai?"

"I don't know."

Silence.

"Maybe there'll be an emergency flight up that way tonight," he resumed. He finally looked up.

"Can I get on it?"

"I don't know."

"Who does?"

"Nobody. You'll have to wait and see."

"How long do I wait?"

"I don't know."

Silence.

"My orders say to go to Phu Bai."

"I guess you'd better go there then, Sir."

"How do I get there?"

"Wait for a flight. No more today though. Your best bet is to be here at 0600 tomorrow. Good chance of getting on an early flight."

"Right here?"

"Line up right where you are now at 0600."

"Where do I sleep tonight?"

"I don't know."

Silence. The lance corporal was finally looking at me. He sensed that my frustration was on the verge of turning to anger. Not that he gave a damn. He did not make the rules. He was gathering up his lists and preparing to leave.

"Most of the marines sleep right here on the floor. There's a Transient Officers' Quarters about a mile and a half down the road."

"How do I get down there?"

"I don't know. Walk. Thumb. Call a navy taxi, Mosbey 100. If you want to wait, a truck comes by here at 1900 to take any officers up there for the night. It'll bring you back at 6 A.M."

"Where does it stop?"

"Right out there on the side of the road."

"Is there a mess hall around?"

"No."

"Is there a men's room?"

"There's a piss tube behind this building. The shitter is across the road."

"I beg your pardon."

"There is a piss tube behind this building. The shitter is across the road."

Sacked out.

"Well, I just have to urinate."

"I guess you'd better do it, then, Sir. Piss tube behind the building."

"Thanks."

"Yes, Sir."

A full seabag propped up against a wall makes a fairly comfortable back rest. I sat and watched the aircraft take off and land. It would be an hour before the truck came by. Nothing to drink or eat since breakfast, and it was almost six o'clock. At least I could sit. No more lines shuffling along at zero pace.

I saw two marines drinking cokes walk out of a small building in the distance. I walked into the building and was overjoyed to find a soldier selling cokes, cigarettes, peanuts, and crackers. I took two warm cokes and a handful of assorted trash to eat.

"Forty-five cents, Sir."

I pulled out a one-dollar bill and handed it to the enlisted man.

"Oh, sorry, Sir. I can't take American green. That's illegal here, you know."

"Well, could I trade it for some military money?"

"Not here, Sir."

"Where, then?"

"I don't know."

"Who does?"

"I don't know. MPC window at the air base is closed by now."

"I really want a coke."

"Sorry, Sir, can't take green."

"May I have a drink of water?"

"There's a water buffalo around behind this building, Sir."

"Yes, but———"

"Right around back."

Behind the building was a small, tank-shaped, two-wheeled trailer with several faucets on one side. I returned to the building. "May I borrow a glass, or cup, or something?"

"I don't have any, Sir. The trash barrel is filled with empty coke cans."

Three coke-cans full of water and one bummed cigarette later, I leaned back against my seabag and felt much better.

I waited.

This day counted! I had started my tour in Vietnam. One day was almost over. I was one day shorter. After months of anxiety, weeks of planning, and hours of travel, my tour was finally underway. War zone. Combat pay. I had

Troops are sorted out and sent to their separate units during their first hours in Vietnam.

earned over thirty dollars today standing in lines. It wasn't worth it, but what was really important was that this day counted.

It seemed to get dark rather suddenly. Then it started raining, but managed somehow to remain hot. I crowded my body and seabag back into the marine forms which filled the Marine Air Freight building. No one seemed to notice the rain. When the truck came, I lifted my seabag and walked out into the rain. Unfortunately, about thirty other soldiers did the same thing, and it appeared obvious to me that we were not all going to fit on the dump-truck sized vehicle.

Without any conversation, the driver and his helper threw the suitcases, seabags, and back packs into the truck. Soldiers climbed in on top of them.

It was raining very heavily, and the roadside had already turned to mud. It was dark enough that the traffic on the road needed headlights to travel. We could have been on any dirt road in the world.

When we stopped, our bodies actually spilled over the sides and out of the back of the truck. All of the gear was thrown off into a giant mud puddle, and the truck was gone.

In the darkness it was impossible to tell which of the mud-covered seabags bore the white ink printing I had so carefully placed there in California. I felt the bottoms of several bags before I found a bulge which felt like a 2,052-page Harrison's fourth edition of *Principles of Internal Medicine*. I carried my gear into a poorly-lighted room that looked identical to the Marine Air Freight building. It was equally filled with waiting soldiers. Some of them had formed a line at the far end of the room.

My first day in Vietnam had not been a total loss as far as a learning experience goes. I immediately got in the line without any idea of where it led and why.

Over the next hour, as the line inched forward, I slowly edged out of the building into the rain again, and then into the front door of a small wooden hut. When I finally reached the front of the line, there was a lance corporal seated behind a table with a clipboard and paper.

"Hi, I'm———"

"Orders?"

"Yes, here they are." I pulled two dripping wet papers from my shirt pocket. "I'm Doctor———"

"Hooch fourteen, rack twenty. We're out of blankets and towels. Next!"

"Which way is———"

"Wooden planks down to your right. Last hooch up against the runway. Next!"

"Thanks."

"Next."

Bed twenty was occupied, so I found an empty cot in the corner of the wooden-framed, screen-enclosed, tin-roofed structure and leaned my muddy seabag against it as a symbol of squatter's rights.

"Hi, I'm Doctor Parrish. I'm new in Vietnam."

"That's too bad. I've only got thirteen days left, and I'm going on R and R tomorrow."

"Where can I get something to eat?"

"Chow hall is closed."

I began removing my wet clothes.

"Hey, Doc, that's my rack you got there."

"Sorry." I moved again to another empty cot.

"Hey, Doc, ya want to go into Da Nang with us? We got a vehicle."

"No thanks. I think I could use some sleep. You see, I———"

"Well, you won't get any here. When the phantoms start . . ."

"The what?"

"The fucking phantom jets. They take off right down this runway all night long."

Dry shorts, T-shirt, and the prone position were so great that I could almost forget my hunger and fatigue. My cot was gritty with moist sand, and mosquitoes were battling over territory on my ankles. People continued to walk in and out of the room without communicating. I closed my eyes hoping that sleep would come before loneliness.

At first, I thought it was thunder. But it lasted too long, and, then, it headed straight toward me. It sounded like a freight train whistling in a tunnel, but it approached at unbelievable speed. Streaking, screaming, rumbling. Just before it hit my bed, it blasted into a controlled explosion which streaked past me and tore at my eardrums. At first, I was just startled. Then I was frozen with a fear that pushed in my neck and head and created a vacuum in my chest and stomach. Suddenly I remembered where I was. I remembered Camp Pendleton. I rolled off the bed onto the floor and covered my head.

I waited. Was that laughter around me now?

"Hey, Doc, you okay?"

"Hey, Doc, that was a phantom jet taking off. An F-4C. When it takes off, it turns on its afterburner and makes a hell of a noise."

"Just a jet taking off, Doc."

"If you roll out of bed everytime a phantom takes off, you'll get sore elbows. That goes on all night long."

"Well, that's kind of embarrassing. I thought we were being hit. I'm new here, and———"

"That's too bad. I've only got thirteen days left, and tomorrow I'm going on R and R."

I was prepared the next time a jet took off. But even then it seemed that the pilot had gotten confused. He was headed right for my bed. I was done for. The afterburners exploded past me. I had survived again. My fingers slowly began to loosen their viselike grip on the sides of the cot. I was ready to go home. Enough war zone. To hell with combat pay.

Cherry's Rucksack

from *The 13th Valley*
by John M. Del Vecchio

*Vietnam veteran John M. Del Vecchio's critically acclaimed and popular novel **The 13th Valley** is a highly detailed account of a fictional August 1970 combat assault into the Khe Ta Laou Valley of northern South Vietnam. Before the assault Specialist Fourth Class James "Cherry" Chelini, a radioman just in-country, joins Company A of the 7th Battalion, 402d Infantry, at Firebase Eagle near Phu Bai. There he is outfitted for combat:*

Chelini waited outside the orderly room shack for the first sergeant to call him. He felt completely lost. This was not a training unit where everyone was new or a replacement station where everyone was transient. This was the infantry, a permanent assignment and he was an outsider. The men were busy in closed groups or loafing in closed groups.

The battalion to which Chelini had been assigned was on the last day of a five-day refitting and training stand-down. Before stand-down the men of the Oh-deuce had spent 105 days in the boonies, up the Song Bo and Rao Trang rivers, on the hills by Firebases Veghel, Ripcord and Maureen, and in the swamps west of Quang Tri City. They were the division reaction force. It was not uncommon for them to be extracted from one jungle only to be inserted into another.

Chelini went to the screen door of the hootch and tried to see inside. He could see nothing. He turned and scrutinized the battalion area. Before him was a quadrangle surrounded on three sides by buildings. On the far side a steep hill rose to a helicopter resupply point.

At the center of the quad there was a boxing ring and a PSP basketball court. By the court the old white soldier was still chewing out the same lethargic black boonierat. From where Chelini stood the words were unintelligible. The black soldier had very dark skin. He was shuffling his feet in the red dust, casting upward scowls from a down-hanging head, bouncing and jiving with his knuckles on his hips. The old white soldier was shorter than the black man and much heavier. His head was round and bald on top with the sparse hair at the side shaved. The skin was very red, as if blood was trying to escape.

Very near Company A's office was a narrow moldy structure with a boat on the roof. Five white enlisted men with deeply tanned arms, faces and necks and pallid torsos carried olive drab towels and shaving gear into the shower house. They joked and fooled and slapped each other with the towels and stepped gingerly over the muck patch which flowed past the four-holer EM latrine toward the drainage ditch. They did not even look in Chelini's direction.

Close to the screen door of the office where Chelini stood two men converged, stopped and commenced a strangely ritualistic clapping and shaking of hands and forearms and slapping of each other's shoulders and tapping of each other's fists. One of the men was black, dark brown, not as dark as the soldier at the quad's center; the other was light brown, the color of wheatbread. The ritualized greeting went on for what seemed a long time.

Chelini turned. A clerk opened the screen door. The first sergeant called him in by methodically curling one index finger. Chelini gulped. The first sergeant fumbled with a stack of papers and forms. His desk was clear of everything except essentials. He dusted the land-line telephone with his hand and directed the clerk to empty the trash containers. Then he handed Chelini the forms and a pencil. "Complete thees," he said and turned away. Chelini nodded. Holy Christ, he thought. I'm lost. I'm stuck. I gotta get out of this unit. Chelini glanced at the forms briefly and began filling in his name on a weapons card. He looked up, out the door. The dark black soldier from the center of the quad had joined the black soldier and brown soldier at the front of the office. The greeting rite of raps and slaps and shakes began again.

"Troop," the first sergeant said. Chelini jumped. "Can't you write any faster? You scared of that pencil?"

"No, I just . . ."

"Troop, you a college graduate, ain't you?" Oh, shit, Chelini thought. Two strikes against me already. "You let pencil run you. T'row that pencil down."

"T'row it down?"

"Yeas. That what I said. T'row it down." Chelini dropped the pencil. "Chee!" the first sergeant shouted. "What it do? It don't jump up and bite you, do it? It's daid, Scholdier. Now pick it up and run it."

Chelini began signing the forms. Oh shit, he thought. How'd I get stuck in an infantry unit? They put all the dumb kids in here. Of all the places to be assigned. I wonder what happened to Kaltern from basic. He had a good head. Or Baez from AIT or Ralston. They were some okay people and now I gotta get stuck with a bunch of high school dropouts.

"Troop," First Sergeant Laguana said, "you getting some very expensive equipment. You getting the best weapon in the world. You know that? When you get here at Eagle no magazine in weapon, hokay?" The first sergeant picked up Chelini's weapons card and brought it close to his face. "When you on berm guard you lock en load. You lock en load on helicopter for CA, hokay? On CA you keep the chafety on. If you on the first chopper you go in on automatic, hokay? I don want none my troops schot." Chelini nodded and nodded. This guy's an idiot, he told himself.

The three men who'd been in front of the office came in. The first sergeant ignored them and they ignored him. Chelini looked up. The nearest one nodded and winked.

Chelini nodded back. The dark soldier saluted Chelini with a clenched fist. Chelini startled, stared. He nodded agreement. He was frightened not to. He knew he'd been assigned to a unit of crazy racist psychopaths. The first sergeant picked up the remainder of the forms and scrutinized each. "You getting the best radio in the world," Laguana said. "You know that? You getting seven hun'red channel. You know that?"

"Hey, Babe, we got us a new RTO," the dark black man said snapping his fingers. "Oh Babe, that fucka gowin kick yo ass." He gave Chelini a second power salute. Chelini smiled dumbly and nodded and made a half-hearted attempt to emulate the gesture and the black man laughed.

"Hey, Top," the brown man laughed. To Chelini the laugh seemed bitter. Oh Man, he thought. These guys would slit your throat for a cigarette. "You got a new wristwatch." The brown man grabbed for the first sergeant's arm but the NCO pulled it back. Shit, Chelini thought. Even the first sergeant's scared of them.

"What choos want?" Laguana snapped. "Jackson. Out," he said to the dark black. "Doc. Out," he added. To the brown man he said, "El Paso. You stay."

The two black men departed after chiding and jiving the first sergeant. The light brown soldier stayed.

"Hokay, now I get a rucksack." Sergeant Laguana reached beneath his desk and with a theatrical flip of the wrist produced an aluminum frame with a nylon bag attached. "Thees," he said, "is rucksack. Thees rucksack weigh one pound. By the time I schow you, we get you a P-R-C twen'y-five, chow, ammo and canteen . . ."

"That motha's goina weigh a hundred pounds," El Paso inserted.

Chelini shifted toward the brown soldier and a bit out of the way. El Paso was older than Chelini had thought when he'd first seen him standing in front of the office.

"Troop," Laguana addressed Chelini trying to ignore El Paso again, "you gon carry everyt'ing you need right here. Here, you try it on." Chelini reluctantly reached for the rucksack.

Laguana scowled and walked into the back storeroom and returned with a PRC-25 radio. Then he left again and returned with a case of C-rations. He dropped that on the floor by the growing pack and disappeared into the back room singing to himself. El Paso fitted and secured the radio inside the ruck's main pocket. He fastened it in such a manner that it could be easily removed and carried separately.

"Hey," El Paso said. "Ask Top to give you two extra pair of bootlaces. He'll be okay to you now cause you're new. You won't be able to get them later."

"Thanks," Chelini said. He wanted to ask the brown soldier questions but he was wary.

Top returned with four one-quart canteens, an empty steel ammo can, an M-16, eighteen empty magazines and

eighteen boxes of cartridges, four fragmentation grenades and two smoke grenades. He dropped the equipment on the pile and whistled his way back to the storeroom.

"Hey," El Paso yelled at him, "get him some more canteens. This aint enough."

"Thas enough," Laguana yelled back.

"Guy's a fuckin shithead," El Paso said. "I won't tell you, though. You can't tell one man about another." El Paso set to work filling the rucksack, carefully ordering items with the attention he would give to his own gear. Chelini watched him. "Shit," the brown man said. "Ham and lima beans. Taste like shit. Worst Charlie Rat there is. You oughta throw it out. Aint worth humpin. These, canned fruit and pound cake, they're worth their weight in gold."

The first sergeant returned with four radio batteries, a machete, an entrenching tool, a claymore with wire and firing device, a poncho and poncho liner, one olive drab towel, a web belt, ammo pouches, helmet with liner and cover, a long and short antenna for the radio, and small bottles of LSA and bug repellent. El Paso continued sorting through the food asking Chelini what he liked and throwing what he himself didn't like to one side. From the heavy cardboard of the C-ration case El Paso cut a broad section and fitted it on the inner side of the ruck so it would lie between the lumpy cans and batteries inside and Chelini's back.

"Look at this shit," El Paso said. "Take the batteries but see that you get somebody else to carry one of em. Fuck the E-T and the claymore. When you hump a Prick-25 you can't carry all that shit. Machete's optional. Top'll have you humpin two hundred pounds if you let him. Make sure he gets you more canteens." El Paso tied the empty ammo can, a small steel box with a watertight seal, to the base of the ruck. "That's where you keep all your personal stuff," El Paso said. "Toothbrush, writing paper, extra socks. Everything that's you and not the army." Then he said, "Dump your duffel bag out." Chelini emptied his duffel bag onto the floor. "You can't carry any of that stuff," El Paso said. "You can maybe take a book and you gotta take your razor. Top'll lock away any personal shit you got. The uniforms go into the company clothes fund. You might want to keep out an extra T-shirt but that's all."

First Sergeant Laguana returned again and handed Chelini an extra pair of bootlaces. "Don let nobody see thees," he smiled. "They always try an take them from me. I gotta keep thees locked up."

"Top," El Paso looked up angrily. "You're an ass."

"Jus go trim that mustache," Laguana shouted.

"Don't harass me. I'll get the Human Relations Office to slap the back of your head. This place is fucked up."

Laguana bent down to check and adjust the straps on Chelini's rucksack. "He Company Senior RTO," Laguana

Laden with gear, off to the war.

said proudly trying to mollify the young brown soldier.

El Paso pushed Laguana away. He grabbed the ruck. "Don't fuck with my RTOs," he said. He turned to Chelini. "Try it on."

"He schow you how to put the ruck together pretty good, eh?" Laguana smiled. "Oooo, you gon cuss me. Now I got somet'ing to do. You go cut that mustache. Now get out."

"Hey, Top?"

"Out."

"If you don't listen to me I'll tell the IG."

"What you want?" The first sergeant feigned exhaustion.

"About my R&R request. I'd like to change it from Bangkok to Sydney. Like Egan's."

"Can't."

"Why?"

"Out."

"I want to talk to the L-T."

"He aint in."

"You aren't going to let me see him."

"Get out of here you chon-of-a-bitch," the first sergeant erupted, jumping out from behind the desk, his eyes bulging and his fists clenched.

El Paso ran out of the hootch. He called back through the screen, "I'm only teasing you, Top. Cut yourself some slack." He walked away mumbling, "That stupid asshole. He doesn't have any right to tell me to trim my mustache. Son-of-a-bitch. Gives us Chicanos a bad name. Can't even speak English."

Chelini staggered out of the office hunched under the weight of the ruck.

Left. On patrol outside Saigon, a soldier carries a heavy load of weapons, water, and ammunition.

First Encounters

The Americans who arrived in Vietnam in 1965 found their firepower and helicopters more than sufficient to turn the tide against the Vietcong guerrillas. Yet until that fall, the soldiers of the North Vietnamese Army remained an unknown quantity. That was to change in November, when the men of the U.S. 1st Cavalry Division (Airmobile) were ordered by MACV commander General William Westmoreland to "find, fix, and defeat the enemy forces that had threatened Plei Me," an isolated Special Forces camp in the central highlands. The resulting battle of the Ia Drang Valley proved the NVA a force to be reckoned with.

Major General Harry W.O. Kinnard, commander of the 1st Cav, combined aircraft and ground troops to form swift reaction teams. He used helicopters to ferry troops and supplies into the remote river valley, while other aircraft fixed enemy positions by flying low and drawing fire. Coordination between air and ground units was designed to concentrate troops where they contacted the enemy.

The NVA deployed three regiments in the Ia Drang Valley, and they fought the U.S. troops far more tenaciously than anticipated. In one key fight at LZ Albany, the NVA proved that by hugging the cavalrymen's position, they could neutralize the American advantage of firepower and render useless their helicopters. Worse, they decimated the Air Cav force trying to hold the LZ, killing 150 men.

Kinnard's scheme eventually worked, but at a cost of 240 men killed. After a month of savage fighting, the 1st Cav drove the NVA from the valley with 1,500 confirmed dead and another 2,000 estimated KIAs.

The photographs of the operation could not capture the savagery of the fighting, but they do show an army coming to grips with its new assignment.

Captain Ed Boyt (right) of the 1st Cav stands before his men while a lieutenant from an advance party briefs them about setting up their first camp for the Ia Drang operation.

Above. *Under a field canopy, Captain Boyt studies snapshots of a young sergeant's new baby.*

Left. *In the misty morning of South Vietnam's jungle highlands, Captain Boyt prepares a C-ration breakfast.*

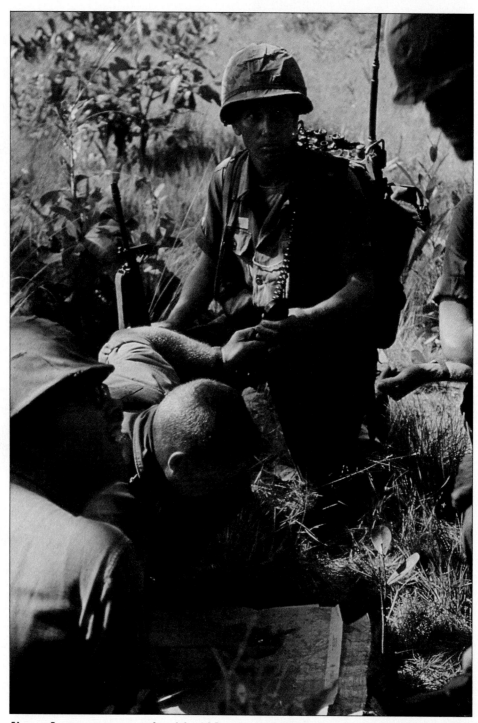

Above. *A company commander of the 2d Battalion, 5th Regiment stationed at LZ X-Ray radios coordinates to his platoons during a combat sweep in the Ia Drang.*

Right. *A patrol moves out through the underbrush from LZ X-Ray.*

Above. *An artilleryman shields his eardrums from the blast of a howitzer as another soldier prepares to fire.*

Left. *Howitzers helicoptered to LZ X-Ray fire at enemy concentrations in the Ia Drang Valley. Artillery battalions fired over 33,000 rounds during the Ia Drang campaign.*

After a battle with NVA units, 1st Cavalry troopers move cautiously into a village in the Ia Drang.

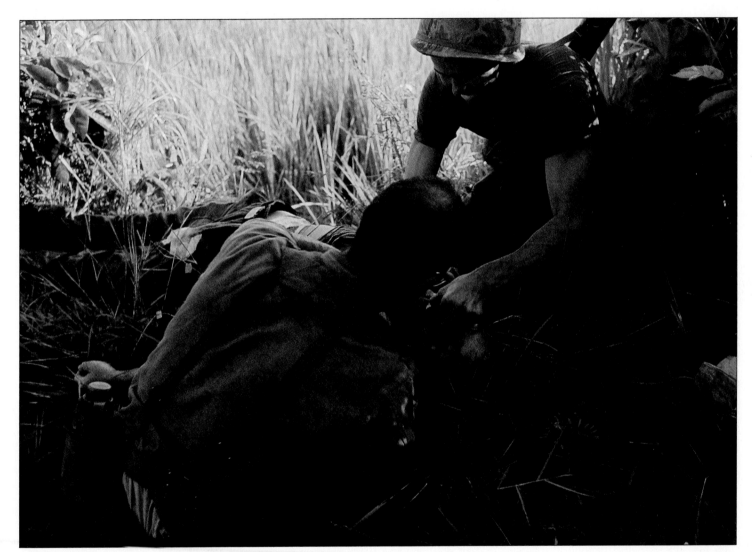

A dying soldier is carried to safer ground by a medic and a comrade.

Above. *Wrapped in a poncho, Captain Boyt stands by a warming fire in the chill of dawn, Ia Drang, November 1965.*

Left. *Men of the 1st Air Cavalry fan out along the perimeter of a landing zone.*

Acts of War

The Vietnam conflict was a clash between the newest and the oldest in warfare. Mechanically and technically, the American military was far more advanced than it ever had been. So much had changed: Helicopters now flew men into battle; firepower was more devastating than ever before; computer print-outs now measured success or failure.

But in combat, war was still war. The military's mission was to destroy the enemy's ability to fight. On a jungle ridgeline that could mean a vicious firefight with an unseen enemy. In a paddy it might mean assaulting a tree line. In a rare moment of city fighting it could mean house-by-house combat against an entrenched foe. Everywhere it meant kill or be killed. In Vietnam it was said there were only two types of men: the quick and the dead.

Preceding page. *U.S. Marines on patrol near Hoa My, June 29, 1965.*

The Longest Day

from *The Offering*
by Tom Carhart

Lieutenant Tom Carhart spent half his one-year tour of duty as a combat infantry officer with the 101st Airborne Division (Airmobile). "The Longest Day" is his recollection of a fierce firefight in the A Shau Valley of South Vietnam's central highlands. "Mad Dog" is Carhart's commander; in military jargon a "dogwood eight" is a wounded man, a "dogwood six" a dead one.

That night Mad Dog is informed of some changes by Battalion. Our company has to move to its initial point (IP) for descent into the A Shau Valley. I look at the map with Doaks and Mad Dog. We have about sixteen clicks to our IP and three days to make it. It doesn't seem to present any problems. Mad Dog wants to avoid any contact that may slow us down, so he outlines roughly the ridgelines he wants to stay on top of. He casually mentions that he wants my platoon to take point for this movement, and I nod.

The next day we move eight or nine clicks by about two-thirty in the afternoon and set up camp on the crest of a thickly jungled ridge.

The following morning, the third of June, one of the ridges on the map tails off into a swamp, and we find ourselves cautiously edging through brackish knee-deep water and rotting undergrowth. The map shows us high on a ridge, and I am starting to get pissed-off. Mad Dog tells

me to move directly west, and within about two clicks it looks as if there is another north-south ridge we can get on that would take us toward our IP. We slog through another hour's worth of swamp. Then suddenly we're mounting a gradual slope.

We move some four or five hundred meters up this slope, our speed slowing as the grade steepens. Then all the undergrowth disappears leaving us scrambling up a steep slope dotted with great gray boulders amid the light brown carpet of dead vegetation.

After a few hundred meters we reach a crest. As I climb over the last boulders, the ground suddenly flattens out, and lush green undergrowth is again all around us. I exhale a pleased, relieved breath, then stage-whisper to Sergeant Johnstone, twenty feet away from me and breathing as hard as I was, "Sergeant Johnstone! Hasty perimeter!" I know everybody's going to want to catch his breath as he comes up. I survey the area. We aren't really on a ridge; rather, we seem to have climbed a single steep hill. Off to my left, it looks as if the hill peaks eight or ten meters higher than we are, thirty or forty meters away, but the vegetation is too thick to see that far. I walk back to the edge and look down. I see twenty or thirty men strung out below me, and the tail of that snake disappears into the jungle some two or three hundred meters down the hill.

They are moving very slowly.

"Hey, sir, there's a gook shitter over here!" I turn around at this hissed warning from Parker, some thirty meters from the edge of the steep slope, my skin suddenly clammy, and take long strides in his direction. There, another ten meters from the crest, is a small clearing. In the center of this open space four bamboo poles are embedded in the bare dirt to form the corners of a small latrine. A woven palm-frond room rests on the four bamboo poles. Squarely in the center of this small, protected plot two small mounds rise six or eight inches from the carefully groomed dirt floor, with holes in the center. No question about it, this *is* a gook shitter! I look quickly around like some frightened bird, then stride over to the latrine and get down on my knees, stick my face directly over one of the mounds and inhale strongly through my nose. A strong odor of fish and shit hits my nostrils, and I know instantly that this is an active latrine.

I stand up and start to turn back when a series of explosions rip the air all around me. I am down on my chest instantly, shaking and scared. Twenty meters away I see the eight or ten men who have made it to the top of the crest scrambling around, shouting at each other or screaming in agony. The fear of God is in my heart now. I look at the top of the hill and see muzzle flashes through the thick vegetation. I hear Sergeant Johnstone screaming, "Up the hill! Get some fire out there!"

I turn and look uphill again. A well-worn footpath leads up the hill from the latrine. Like a zombie, I race up it in a deep crouch, hands sweaty as they grip the rifle stock. I automatically clear the round in the chamber as I run, allowing the heavy metal clunking as the chamber swallows the new bullet to still my heart. Then there is a fork in the path. The path to the left leads directly up the hill, while the path to the right leads around to the right and seems to meander to the top through thicker vegetation. I am only half thinking about anything now, but my heart is leaping inside me.

I take the trail to the right, bending my body low now as I slow my pace. A sudden noise behind me jerks me around. There, close on my heels, is Specialist Fourth Class Kirby Wilson, a sharpshooter from the Carolina hills. I nod to him, and we began to creep forward again. Off to our left and behind us we hear the muffled agony of the men huddling just over the crest of the hill. Then two RPDs open up from the top of the hill, in front of us and off to the left. We hear cries and shouts from down the hill now, and it is clear that the men climbing through the cleared area are getting chopped up. Wilson and I keep creeping anxiously forward. I take the heavy white phosphorus grenade off my web gear and straighten the pin so that it can be thrown quickly and easily. As I peer around the edge of a bush, I see two large overhead-cover bunkers some twenty meters away. We are slightly off to one side of them, the firing slits facing toward the company coming up

the hill. Behind the nearest bunker three gooks are huddled in animated discussion. I turn and signal Wilson to come up on my left, then ease out from behind the bush on my belly and forearms. Wilson comes into the clear next to me. As we lay there, bringing our weapons up to our shoulders, two more gooks appear with AKs, then a third. Now there are six gooks in the clearing, four of them quite close together. My weapon is on semiautomatic, and I don't dare switch to automatic, sure they'll hear the click such an adjustment would require. I open fire, watching the enemy's dark shirts soak up my tracers. I get six or seven rounds off before they are able to get out of sight. I have hit only two of them, maybe three.

My adrenaline is really pumping now. I roll onto my left side, pull the pin of my Willie Peter grenade with my left hand as I heft it in my right, then heave it up toward the rear of those bunkers with all my strength. No gooks in sight. Wilson throws an M-48 hand grenade and is pulling the pin on another one. I grab one off the side of one of the ammunition pouches on my web belt and pull on the pin. The spoon that arms the grenade is held on with a heavy-gauge cotter pin that normally has to be straightened before it can be pulled. I look down in terror at what can be keeping the pin from coming out, then instantly recall the important cotter-pin-straightening exercise you are supposed to go through before you throw a grenade in combat. I have completely forgotten! I grunt, close my eyes, and strain on the pin. Fear gives me the strength of ten men, and the pin slowly slips out. I roll over again and heave the grenade blindly uphill with all I have. When it leaves my hand, I hear a loud thunk as it hits the heavy branch of a vine and ricochets. Where did it go? A chill of terror is rushing through me when suddenly another RPD opens up, this time spraying dirt all over us as the bullets chew the ground. Wilson and I scramble back behind the clump of bushes. There are three sharp consecutive explosions very near us. The last one picks me up off my belly, snaps my head back, and blows my helmet out of sight down the hill. Now that they know where we are, we will do no more good here, and I have to get back to my men.

We start to scramble back the way we had come, and soon we are back at the juncture of the two trails. Then we race back down the single trail to the latrine and the crumpled knot of my men. No one sees us coming until we are among them.

"Sergeant Johnstone! Get a couple of men over here to cover this trail, right now! Where's Speedy?"

"I don't know where he is, sir. Jaune, Waldorf! Get over by Lieutenant Carhart and cover that trail. Move!"

I look around madly. It looks as if we have twelve or fourteen men on top of the hill, many or most of them hit. I need two warm bodies to cover that trail in case the gooks get smart and use it. "Jaune, get over there, right now!" I look quickly over in Sergeant Johnstone's direction. He is yelling at a man huddled on his side in a fetal position. I quickly crawl-scramble over to him. "What's the matter, Jaune, are you hit?"

"It's my knee, sir, an old basketball injury, I can't move it."

"Jesus, a fucking *basketball* injury?"

"Yes, sir, happened in high school, I can't move it." I look into his earnestly pleading face, trembling ever so slightly, terror creeping unwanted up through the cow's lick of milk-white peach fuzz that dusts his throat and jaw. He is frozen with fear, and I suddenly, unreasonably, feel sorry for him. Men are dying all around us, and I need him. But as I look into the cold fright that glazes his eyes, I know that he is absolutely worthless to me this day.

"Fuck! All right, stay where you are. Waldorf, get over there, and cover that trail. Sergeant Johnstone, send somebody else over there with him! Where the fuck is Speedy?"

"He's over here, sir. He's hit; I don't know if he's dead or not."

"Fuck! Sergeant Johnstone, gimme a sitrep. How many men we got up here?"

"Fifteen, sir. The rest of 'em either got back down the hill or else got holed up behind rocks on the hill."

"We got any medics up here?"

"One, sir, but he got hit in the arm. They said Doc Gertsch got caught on the hill, and him and another medic is tryin' to make it up here to us."

"How many Dogwoods?"

"One Dogwood six and seven or eight eights, sir."

"You hit?"

"No, sir, not yet."

"Okay, how many M-sixties we got?"

"Two, sir, but one of 'em got hit, and it don't work no more."

I crawl over to Speedy's body where it lies slumped in a small clearing on the uphill edge of our hasty perimeter. Wilson crawls with me, having hooked on to me. Speedy is lying on his side with his belly toward us. His eyes are closed, and I can see only two large splotches of blood, one on his right calf, the other on the inside of his left thigh.

The gooks are firing RPG bazooka-type weapons into our positions and even throwing hand grenades downhill the thirty or forty meters that lie between us. We are slowly being chopped to pieces, and I have to get on a radio to get some artillery or maybe even some air support. As I approach Speedy, I grab his shoulder and shake him gently. "Speedy, you're okay now, we're gonna take care of you. Where are you hit?"

He opens his bleary eyes and stares vacantly at me. "My legs, sir, my legs."

I look down at his legs, then pull him over onto his belly. The splotches on his legs are large, but I can't even see any big holes in his pants legs. I am sure the medics will be able to take care of him. Shouts inform me that Doc Gertsch, the senior medic in the company, and another medic have made it to the top of the hill. "Relax, Speedy,

you're gonna be okay. Doc Gertsch is on his way over to take care of you." I start to wrestle with his rucksack and try to strip it and the all-important radio from his shoulders. Wilson helps me, and then it breaks free from Speedy's limp body. Inside, I secretly feel good for Speedy. He got hit in the legs, but he is going to be all right. He'll probably even be going home, especially if any bones were broken by the bullets. Lucky guy.

I then begin talking to Mad Dog, who tells me he has sent the first platoon, under Sergeant Harris, around to the left to try to go up the hill from the other side. He has no word from them except that they walked into a real hornets' nest and were stopped, but he doesn't know how far up the hill they got.

As I am listening to this, a medic crawls over my legs and, pulling up Speedy's sleeve, starts to insert the needle attached to a bottle of albumin. Thank God, I think, he's gonna be all right now. But even as those thoughts are flashing through my mind, Doc Gertsch crawls over my legs and up next to Speedy. He puts his fingers on his throat and lays his ear on his chest. Then his voice tears me apart and leaves me stunned. "Never mind this one," he says to the medic inserting the albumin needle. "He's already dead; let's get to the next one."

I turn away from the radio in horror, looking blankly at Speedy as the medics crawl away from him. Dead? Speedy? Christ, I was just talking to him; he got hit in the legs; he can't be dead! I lurch over to him, pick up his limp arm, then thrust my hand around his throat, squeezing hard, desperately looking for a pulse. At first I feel nothing; then I sense a faint, irregular twitching deep in his throat. He's alive! "Doc Gertsch, wait, he's alive, I got a pulse, he's alive, come save him!"

Doc Gertsch is beside me in an instant, his hand quickly replacing mine on Speedy's throat. Silence for a few seconds as I wait expectantly, certain that Speedy will live now. "That's just nerves, sir; that ain't his pulse. He's dead. I'm sorry, sir, but we got other people to keep alive."

I nod blindly, then turn back to the radio, numb and shaken. Speedy dead. I can't believe it. I try to snap out of it and talk to Mad Dog, but I have problems. Only the very real threat of death all around us helps me forget Speedy for the moment. Mad Dog is telling me that we can't get artillery right away because one of the other companies is in a world of shit and in danger of being overrun, but that tactical air support will soon be overhead. I tell him we need some help and am asking whether the rest of my platoon will be able to get up the hill to support us when a sudden explosion lifts Wilson and me off the ground and rips the handset out of my hands. The fear of God churns through my body. Then I open my eyes and realize I am still alive. I look at Wilson, who is also stunned but looks unhurt. The radio is ripped wide open in the center. I depress the key on the handset I still hold. Nothing. Great, now we have no radio. I hear two or three men screaming

Soldiers under fire evacuate a wounded man during the battle of Dong Ap Bia, also called Hamburger Hill.

behind me and to our right. A gook apparently jumped around a tree by the latrine, fired an RPG round at us, then disappeared. One piece of shrapnel from the shellburst hit the radio, but the explosion, some ten meters away, also seriously wounded three men—already hit once and laid behind a big rock to protect them. The RPG round hit right in their midst. At this moment there are three or four enemy soldiers firing AKs from over there.

Now I am mad, and I start yelling to my men to come up and cover our right flank, which is wide open. "Sergeant Johnstone! Where the fuck is Waldorf? I told him to cover that area!"

"He's a Dogwood, sir."

"We'll get some warm bodies over here now."

Suddenly Sergeant Gamel is beside me, just arrived up the hill. "We got two Dogwood eights down there, and I sent 'em down the hill; but I brought eight more men up here with me, including a machine gun. Where d'you want it?"

"Right over there by that gook shitter, they're maneuvering around us there. We've got to stop them."

"Right away, sir!" Then he is yelling and scrambling over me with three or four other men.

"Sergeant Gamel! We need another radio. This one got blown. Can you send somebody down the hill for one?"

"Yes, sir!"

There is a lot of fire coming from our right now, and it looks as if the gooks are massing for a final assault. The

RPDs on the top of the hill are no longer firing down the hill; they have directed their fire on us. Screams from my rear tell me they are finding their mark. Suddenly it is all clear to me: I'm never going to get off this messy little hilltop. This is where it all comes to an end, in an ugly, dirty, grime-encrusted lack of poetry. But even as I recognize this reality of the immediate future, it all seems so unreal, so removed, so anti-climactic. No great thoughts come to me, only the painful regret that I still have half a canteen of lime Kool-Aid, that delicacy of jungle delicacies, and now I'll never get to drink it. Well, they won't get me easily, and I add the fury of my M-16 to the feeble fire being pumped toward the NVA circling to our right. We survivors are all but surrounded now, having only, it seems, the open hillside behind us. We can die here, or we can get pushed over the edge and get killed by the RPDs still raking the open slope.

My naked head feels suddenly bare in the thickening storm of bullets. I reach back over Speedy's body, grab his helmet, and clap it on my head. A sharp explosion directly in front of me lifts my shoulders off the ground, snaps my head back, and pitches Speedy's helmet backward onto my legs. I am stunned and feel only my ears ringing. Then, through a cloud, I hear Jim Parker's voice: "Sir! Sir! Are ya hit, sir?"

"I don't know, I can't—"

"You got hit in the chin, sir, and it's bleedin' a lot; but if you can talk, it doesn't sound like you broke your jaw." I start feeling my jaw with my fingers, reassured as I gingerly move my fingertips, feeling no break. Wilson is fumbling with the bandage he carries on his web gear as Parker examines my chin. I am still numb as he places the bandage Wilson gives him squarely on my chin and wraps the gauze streamers around my neck. "There, sir, it's bleedin' quite a bit, but head 'n' face wounds do that, often look worse 'n they are. That too tight?"

I can only grunt in response. Then a man crawls up and extends a handset to me. "New radio from down the hill, sir. Mad Dog is waitin' to hear from you." A radio! Maybe it isn't all over yet! I press the key.

"Mad Dog, Billy Goat, over."

"This is Mad Dog, what's your situation? Over."

"Billy Goat, our shit is very weak. Do we have any tac air yet? Over."

"This is Mad Dog, roger that. Blue Leader is upstairs right now; he's on the tac air push. Over." I madly twist the dials to the new frequency. "Blue Leader, this is Billy Goat, I am marking my position with smoke at this time. Please identify. Over."

I roll over onto my back, and pull the smoke canister off my LBE [load bearing equipment]. I pop the ring and toss the can behind me. The yellow smoke seems to be moving in slow motion as it coils slowly upward, then begins to pour out of the can in great volume, wreathing up through the trees to the sky above.

"Billy Goat, this is Blue Leader, I see two yellow smokes and one purple. Over."

Fuck! We have four colors of smoke—yellow, purple, green, and red. Green is rarely used because it is difficult to pick out against the jungle, and it is very difficult to find red smoke; that means yellow and purple are the most commonly used. The gooks seem to monitor our radio transmission whenever things are tight, like right now, and they just toss their own smoke, stolen from American supply channels, to confuse things. But I have an ace in the hole. "Roger that, Blue Leader, we are one of the yellows. I am popping smoke again, at this time, please identify. Over." I pull the other canister of smoke from my LBE, pop it, and toss it where the other one was just running out. Soon clouds of bright red balloon out and up through the scrawny trees.

"This is Blue Leader, I see one yellow, one purple, and one red. Over."

"This is Billy Goat. We are the red; other smoke is the bad guys. From our position enemy forces are concentrated some forty meters to our west, azimuth of two seven zero degrees, on the very top of the hill, and some twenty to thirty meters to our north and east azimuth of zero degrees running to ninety degrees. We are in a tight spot. Anything you can put on them will help. Over."

"This is Blue Leader, roger that, Billy Goat, I am now inserting one flight of HE [high explosives]. Where do you want the first strike? Over."

"This is Billy Goat. Put the first one in to our north. Over."

I crawl toward Sergeant Gamel's position. I am just approaching his men when an F-4 goes over like Zeus, close enough to make us all flinch. A second after he has passed, the thunderous explosion rolls over our heads, making me want to crawl inside Speedy's too-tight helmet. I crawl up beside Sergeant Gamel, dragging my radio with one arm. "Whaddya think, Sergeant Gamel?"

"Bring it in another twenty meters, sir."

"Blue Leader, this is Billy Goat, request you move the next one in another twenty meters closer to us. Over."

"This is Blue Leader, roger, wilco, over."

We all bury our heads and hold our breaths as the next F-4 sweeps in. The explosion seems to wash over us, the energy ballooning our shirts around our bodies. Sergeant Gamel is grinning as I looked at him. "That's the one, sir. Couple more strikes there oughta wipe out that assault they were thinkin' about."

I grin back at him, then get back on the radio. "This is Billy Goat, Blue Leader, that last one is on the money. Can you put more strikes in and arc them around to ninety degrees? Over."

"This is Blue Leader, roger that, but how 'bout your other target on top of the hill? Over."

"This is Billy Goat, roger, if you can put anything in there, we'd appreciate it. Over."

"This is Blue Leader. I've got two more strikes of HE, then eight strikes of napalm. Want me to put some burn on top of the hill? Over."

"This is Billy Goat, roger that, torch those fuckers. Over."

"This is Blue Leader, get your men down. Over."

I turn and start to crawl quickly back to my original position. Then to my right a great orange fury blossoms and roars through the jungle, up by the gook bunkers. But as I get on the radio to adjust the napalm, the RPDs on top of the hill seem to open again with a renewed fury. Fuck me! Where the hell are the gooks hiding?

"Sergeant Johnstone, how was that strike?"

"Too far away, sir, gotta move it in."

"How far should I move it in?"

"Another twenty meters at least, sir. But before we move that shit any closer, somebody oughta go get Lesley. He's right up there, and I don't think he's dead."

He is pointing to our front, directly up the hill. Private First Class Lesley was the point man and somehow got about twenty meters uphill from the hasty perimeter when the shit hit the fan. He was hit in the first burst. I see his motionless legs and butt slumped in front of us, and I start to sweat again. I can't ask anyone else to go get him; that is part of my job. I suddenly start tasting acid deep in my throat. "You say he's still alive?"

A voice beyond Sergeant Johnstone answers me. "Yes, suh, Ah heard 'im yellin' two, three minutes ago." I nod grimly, then cup my hands over my mouth and yell in Lesley's direction. "Lesley, I'm comin' to get you, hang tight." I see his shoulder jerk to the side over his hip. I turn to Sergeant Johnstone and murmur the useless "Cover me."

He nods grimly back to me. "We'll cover you, sir."

I lay my weapon down and wipe my soaking, grimy hands on my soaking, grimy shirt. I have two or three dry heaves before I can control my body. I jam Gonzales's too-tight helmet down over my ears, take a deep breath, and burst out over the small rise I have been behind, crawling like a mad fiend for everything I am worth. The underbrush is very light here, and I feel as if I am crawling across an open stage. Gunfire erupts with renewed fury on both sides; but I am unhit, and soon I am reaching out, then touch Lesley's foot with my right hand. I pull myself up over his body, edging up toward his head. Suddenly RPD fire starts to rip through the air and bushes all around us. I mash my weight down on Lesley's body, and he screams in agony. I am rattled and unsure what to do. "Sorry, sorry," I murmur as I try gently to raise my body a few microinches, yet not high enough to get hit.

"Mah helmet," he screams, "gimme mah helmet!"

I glance hurriedly around and see no helmet. Blood is pouring freely out his collar, and his neck is bathed in it, the bright scarlet shining on dark ebony skin. I take Speedy's helmet off my own head and clap it onto his. He immediately seems to relax and drifts into deep moaning. "Okay, Lesley, we gotta get back now. I want you to put your arms around my neck and hang on." I wrench his limp, moaning body over onto his back, then drape inert arms over my shoulders. "Now hang on, Lesley. If you wanna live, hang on!" I feel him weakly clutch me, and I begin to crawl backward the way I had come. Our movement is deathly slow. Then a bullet hits my right forearm and hammers it back against my side. I am frozen in terror for a heartbeat or two but then force my shaking body to start moving again. I can hear automatic bursts from Sergeant Johnstone and several of his men now, and it is a reassuring sound. C'mon, God, I think, just this once get me back. Then I am belted in the butt with a shocking force that slams me down on Lesley and causes us both to yelp in pain. For a moment I lie immobilized, then start the agonizing backward crawl. Lesley falls silent, and his hands fall away from my neck. I drag him with me as I crawl, low and slow and scared. Then Sergeant Johnstone is pulling me and Lesley, other arms are helping, and we are back over the rise.

"You okay, sir?"

"Fuck, I don't know. How's Lesley?"

Doc Gertsch suddenly appears, crawls over us, and starts to open Lesley's shirt. Another medic is there beside me and quickly runs his hands and eyes over my butt.

"You're not bleedin' too bad, sir, but I'll have to rip your pants off to be sure."

"No, let's hold off on that for now. We got stuff to do, and it doesn't hurt so bad now. Let me get the air in." I grab the handset from Parker, who has taken over as my RTO, just as he had been with the Tiger Force, with no need for spoken direction. "Blue Leader, this is Billy Goat, over."

"Billy Goat, this is Blue Leader, waiting for adjustment. Over."

"This is Billy Goat, roger that, we had to clear the stage a little. Request you put another strike in twenty meters closer to our position. Over."

"This is Blue Leader, roger, wilco, over."

There is a sudden roar to our right that throws everyone's face into the ground. I jerk my head quickly back up and look around. I can't tell whether anyone has been hit by this explosion, but as I turn back to the radio, I see there is now a hole in the middle of it big enough to stuff with an orange. I depress the key on the handset, but it is just as dead as I knew it would be. "Hey, Steele!"

"Sir?"

"We need another radio. Can you help us out?"

"On the way, sir."

"When you get down there, tell somebody to tell Blue Leader to repeat that last strike. Do you roger?"

"Roger that, sir."

I turn and edge back over to Speedy's body with Parker. We lie next to him and begin firing uphill on semiautomatic again. I go through two magazines. Then stop and look at what we have left: twelve magazines from Gonzales's bandoliers. After that, we'll have to scrounge from the other Dogwoods. I turn to my right and yell as loudly as I can over the din, "Sergeant Gamel, how you holdin' up?"

His cry comes back instantly: "Okay, sir. Could we get another air strike?" A booming roar to my left and a wave of intense heat tell me as I wince that Steele has reached the bottom and gotten my message through.

"We got no radio. We're waitin' on one. Then we'll get more air strikes."

A sharp outburst of sustained gunfire on the far side of the hill, off to our left and below us, tells me that Mad Dog is at least trying to relieve some of the pressure on us, but without a radio I can't tell what is happening. I turn and begin to squeeze off rounds slowly up hill. With all the Dogwoods we are suffering, every rifle is needed. I am inserting another magazine into my weapon when a band of ten or twelve of our men appears out of the woods to our right rear, racing forward in a deep crouch. One of them sees me, comes streaking over to me, and throws himself flat on his chest next to me. "Sergeant Harold from Lieutenant Doaks's platoon, sir. I brung a squad of men with me. We come around the long way an' up the ridge."

I am elated. "Christ, that's great. D'ja bring a radio?" He shrugs resignedly. "Yes, sir, but it crapped out on us comin' up the hill."

"Shit! All right. Sergeant Gamel is over there on the right. Send half your men over there with him. D'ja bring any M-sixties?"

"Two, sir."

"Good, send one over there; then put the other one over on the left there. Sergeant Johnstone'll show you where."

"Strike Force, sir," and he is gone.

I breathe a heavy sigh of relief; then I hear a plaintive "Sir!" to my left rear. I roll my shoulders over and see Steele on his chest, leaning on his forearms, a radio by his side, the handset in his extended hand. I streak the twenty meters to his side.

"Way to go, Steele, are you hit?"

"Yes, sir, I got hit in the left leg jes' as Ah started back up, 'n' then Ah got one in the right foot jes afo' Ah got here."

"Shit, let's get a medic to look at you. Doc Gertsch! Over here!" I depress the key on the handset. "Blue Leader, this is Billy Goat. Appreciate the last strike. Now we're having some problems back where you put in that first strike. Think we could get some bad stuff in there again? Over."

"This is Blue Leader, roger that, please be advised all I've got is napalm. Do you still want it? Over."

The firefight from Sergeant Gamel's position is reaching a roar now, and both M-60s are hammering full force.

"This is Billy Goat, roger that, we need some help fast. Over."

"This is Blue Leader, roger that. Tell your men to get down; strike going in now. Over."

I raise my head a foot off the ground and yell at the top of my lungs, "Sergeant Gamel, get your men down, napalm going in now!" I hear him echo the warning, then two or three other voices echo his, to be drowned by the all-consuming roar of the huge, ugly F-4 that is suddenly with us, seemingly down in the treetops, its ear-shattering soul-shaking roar paralyzing us. Then as it passes, the second explosion rolls over and through us, the wave of intense heat tightening and burning the skin on my face as I seek desperately to return to earth and feel cool dirt against my belly again. As the roar of the inferno dissipates, Sergeant Gamel is yelling at me, "Tell 'em to drop the next strike back twenty meters, sir; that was too close."

My stomach gnaws at me as I relay the message to Blue Leader and more napalm goes in. Sweat beads unnoticed all over my body, only in part from the heat. The gunfire from the top of the hill is starting to heat up again, but by now everyone has found a position of some refuge, and with the new men Sergeant Harold brought with him, we are answering the fire with more punch. I forgot to call Mad Dog, preoccupied as I was with putting in air strikes, but he hasn't forgotten me. Soon after I put Blue Leader on hold, he comes up on the radio. "Billy Goat, Mad Dog, over."

Left. *An American combat squad rests on a rubble-strewn hillside in the central highlands.*

"This is Billy Goat, over."

"This is Mad Dog. How bad are you hurt? Over."

I glance around, trying to sort my thoughts out. "This is Billy Goat, I think we've got four Dogwood sixes, maybe a couple more, ten or twelve Dogwood eights, maybe more, all kinds of wounds, and we're kinda locked into one small position, can't move around much. Over."

"This is Mad Dog, roger that. Have you seen Pepper Dog and the squad I sent up there with him? We have lost radio contact with him. Over."

Hmph. Pepper Dog must be Sergeant Harold.

"This is Billy Goat, affirmative on that. He arrived in our position about one-five ago. Over."

Sergeant Gamel's yell takes over. "We're ready for another strike, sir, and we need it bad."

I turn and yell to Sergeant Gamel, "Everybody down, Sergeant Gamel, here it comes!" I hear him start to echo the warning to his men, but then he is drowned out by that great ugly, roaring green and black winged beast that thunders through the trees and leaves behind another billowing fire egg. This time it is just a touch farther away. "Sergeant Gamel, want another one?"

"Yes, sir, make this one another twenty meters farther away. We'll get 'em in the trees."

"On the way!" I depress the key again. "Blue Leader, Billy Goat, that was beautiful. Can you put another one in twenty meters farther down the hill? Over."

"This is Blue Leader, roger that. Be advised that I only have two strikes left. If I put one in where you requested it, that will leave us only one. Over."

"This is Billy Goat, roger that, request you put the last one in squarely on the top of the hill, where you were putting in the first napalm strikes. Over."

"This is Blue Leader, roger that, both on the way at this time. Over."

I yell to Sergeant Gamel again, "Sergeant Gamel, here comes the last strike, get your asses down!" Again the great ugly roar of death streaks in from the sky.

Mad Dog is back on the horn. "Billy Goat, Mad Dog, over."

"Billy Goat, over."

"This is Mad Dog, we've got to get clear of this mess. Can you break contact and come down the way Pepper Dog went up? Over."

"This is Billy Goat, negative, we're hurt too bad to move until we get some help. Over."

"This is Mad Dog, roger that. I just sent about twenty men; they should reach you soon. Are you in any danger of being overrun? Over."

"This is Billy Goat, I don't know. I don't think so since those air strikes, but our shit is very weak. Over."

"This is Mad Dog, roger that, help is on the way. As soon as you can, break contact and come down the hill the way Pepper Dog went up, out."

Noise behind me turns me over. Forty meters away I see

green forms loping toward us from the long end of the hill where Sergeant Harold appeared. Thank God! I raise my arm and wave. "Up here! Up here!" I turn over toward Sergeant Johnstone's position. "Sergeant Johnstone, how many Dogwoods you got over there?"

"I think we got two Dogwood sixes, sir, and about twelve Dogwood eights. Some of 'em bad."

"Okay, help on the way; then we've got to break contact and get back down the hill." I pass the same word to Sergeant Gamel.

Doc Gertsch is working on men right next to me, and I hear a couple of muffled moans. Then the reinforcements are among us and edging uphill past us, forming a protective umbrella that will allow us to lick our wounds and struggle back down hill. I am confused and stunned, mired in guilt and self-pity and numbness. I roll over onto my back and see that men who were over with Sergeant Gamel are being guided, at a slow crawl, by some of the men who came up with Sergeant Harold. I turn and grab Speedy by his shoulders, then firmly grab the middle of his shirt with my left hand and begin to snake my way along the gentle downgrade. Parker moves silently with us, helping the body along. After a short eternity and sixty or eighty meters, the steep slope blocks the top of the hill and we are in defilade, now protected from the still-active gunfire. Men begin to stand up.

I stop, soaked with sweat, and stretch my back as I stand up. I lean down and slip my right arm under Speedy's left shoulder, then gradually wedge my left arm under his thighs. With a lurch I lean sharply back, heft his dead weight off the ground, and clasp his limp body firmly to my chest. As I do so, his body seems somehow, mysteriously, to break in half at the waist, and his knees are suddenly jammed into his face as his body starts to collapse in my arms. I grasp desperately at his legs, stumbling off-balance and fall heavily forward onto my face and Speedy's uncaring body. I release Speedy's body and turn to my right, trying to pull my feet free. Speedy's body slumps slowly away from me, his shirt riding up over his back. Where the bottom of his rib cage should have been on the left is an ugly red hole. Out of it ooze pink, red, and yellow glistening tubes and entrails. They cascade down indiscriminately, steaming and slowly uncoiling. I stand up again and bend over Speedy reverently. I pull his shirt back down over this unsuspected death wound and again slip my right arm under his back, lower this time. His head lolls back limply on my shoulder. I slip my left arm under his butt and again lurch to my feet, clasping his body to my chest.

I stumble numbly downhill, following the green figure in front of me. The tears that fill my eyes run down and mix with the snot sprayed over my lower face. I felt a hot, fresh trickle running over my chin and down my throat onto my chest, and I realized that the bandage has slipped off my chin and now hangs cold and stiff around my neck like an outlaw's bandanna after the stickup. I feel a hot spot on my belly and my crotch and realize that Speedy is passing his life's blood down the front of my body.

Soon there is no more gunfire behind us, then we move down a steeper stretch, and link up with more filthy, bearded green monsters that drift out of the weeds. No one speaks. I see people gesticulating up in front of me, but I just keep walking, looking neither right nor left, sobbing softly over the dead body of the son of America I carry in my arms. My blood runs over my chin, down my body, mixes with his somewhere on my chest, runs in rivulets down my legs, into and over my squishing boots, and leaves bloody tracks in the Vietnamese jungle floor. We stumble what seems to be ten thousand endless miles, then stop.

I lay Speedy on an open poncho next to other poncho-wrapped bodies, then stand back up, my aching back screaming unheeded. I look down at his slack, open-mouthed innocent face. His eyes are closed. Then, before I can say good-bye, the poncho is quickly and neatly folded over his face, and he is gone. I look down unthinking as I move away. After ten or fifteen steps I stop and lean against a tree. I don't know where I am or what is happening. I close my eyes and breathe deeply. Gradually order begins to seep back into my mind.

I open my eyes and stand up straight, lean back and arch my back, blink hard, and take slow, deep breaths. Off to my right some twenty meters I see ten or fifteen wounded men stretched out on their backs. Twenty meters beyond them an LZ is being chopped out of the jungle for a dustoff. I walk slowly over to the group. I see Sergeant Johnstone bending over one of the bodies as I approach. Then I remember. "Sergeant Johnstone, did Jaune get hit back there?"

"No, sir, I don't think so."

"Find him and get him over here to me."

He stands up and moves off silently. I slowly cast my gaze back at the bodies wrapped in ponchos. Only three Dogwood sixes. The medics are amazing at keeping men alive. Then I begin to count the wounded stretched on the jungle floor before me. I get to twenty-two when I hear someone behind me. I whirl around and stare into Jaune's ashen, shaking face.

"Well, good job, Jaune, see what you done?" I don't know what I am going to say to Jaune, but I want to chew him out good, humiliate him in front of the wounded. Then a storm of rage comes over me, and I suddenly hit him in the face with my right fist with every ounce of strength in my body. He goes down like a sack of wheat, and I am after him, yelling like thunder. "You killed Speedy, you sorry mother-fucker, because you weren't man enough to do your job, and by God, you're gonna pay!" Through my fury I hear

---

Right. *A soldier of the 25th Infantry Division carries the corpse of a comrade killed in the Ho Bo woods, 1968.*

Doc Gertsch yelling. As he wedges his body between mine and Jaune's, I swing at Jaune again, around Gertsch, and hit his shoulder. Then I suddenly stop pressing and back off. As I turn to my right, there, thirty meters away in the jungle, is Mad Dog, staring at me in shocked, open-mouthed disbelief. Then, quickly, he lowers his gaze and turns away. My fury is still coursing through my body, although I know that I have just broken every rule in the army by striking an enlisted man. I am worse even than George Patton when he slapped that enlisted man in the hospital in World War II. I will probably end up court-martialed for my actions. Mad Dog saw the whole thing, but I don't care. Jaune was a coward and shirked his duty, and I blame all the casualties we suffered, especially Speedy's death, on him. I steam with fury as I walk around. I stop and lean against a tree, gritting and grinding my teeth.

Suddenly I see Sergeant Johnstone's face. "Sergeant Johnstone, how many men we gonna have left in the platoon that didn't get hit bad enough to be evacuated?"

"I don't know, sir, but I'll find out. The guys that was strung out on the hill and never made it up to our position got chopped up pretty bad, too."

"Okay, let me know ASAP." I turn and start to walk away, then stop, trying to breathe slowly and recover my bearings.

Sergeant Johnstone is back before I expect him. "Five, sir."

"Huh?"

"Five men will be left in the field, including me, unless you stay, sir, then we got six, but you got it in the chin."

"Hunh. Yeah, but I'm goin' in a couple days anyhow, and I don't wanna leave Mad Dog out here with just Doaks." The thought of Doaks makes me seethe with anger again. I wonder where his candy-ass was when his platoon came up to rescue us. "Besides, Mad Dog saw me hittin' Jaune, and I gotta show him I'm on his side so he doesn't court-martial me."

"Shit, sir, we're gonna get you a medal of honor for what you did on that hill, savin' Lesley 'n' all. Mad Dog ain't gonna do nothin' about this, 'n' besides, Jaune had it comin', we all know that."

"Yeah, well, I don't wanna take any chances. I don't really know him, and I think he could really hang my ass now if he wants to."

"Well, if you're gonna stay out here, you oughta let Doc Gertsch take a look at your chin, sir."

"Yeah, I will. Thanks, Sergeant Johnstone."

"Strike Force, sir."

I move back over toward the wounded now, see Specialist Gertsch bent over one of them. There are four or five other medics working with him, but he is the senior medic in the company and the one I trust the most. "Hey, Doc Gertsch."

"Sir?"

"When you got a minute, I wanta talk to you."

"Be right with you, sir." I walk back into the trees, and he is there behind me. "Sir?"

"Hey, listen, Doc, I'm not hit too bad, and I can't afford to go to the rear now, so could you take a look at my chin?"

"Sure, sir, lemme get my stuff."

I sit down and lean against a tree, and he is back. He starts poking at my chin with his fingers. Suddenly it hurts. "Unh!"

"Sorry, sir. Looks like you need some stitches there, and I'll have to give you a couple shots; but it won't take long. Whyn't you lay your head back on the ground so's I can work on you?" I lie down and close my eyes, and then he is sewing my chin together. I am amazed that it doesn't hurt as much as I expected. Doc Gertsch cleans the wound on my right forearm and bandages it up, then checks my ass. Some cooling salve is all I get on a thousand tiny wounds.

The dustoff slicks are now hammering in and out, and I see all the wounded have been evacuated; it is time for the dead to be taken out. I walk over to Speedy's body wrapped in a poncho, bend down, and heave him up.

The poncho starts to slip off, and I feel it drag between my legs as I walk. I wrestle with it, kick at it, and it finally falls clear. I step into the knee-deep swampy area that has been cleared for an LZ and begin to wade unencumbered, holding Speedy close. His calmly sleeping face softly nuzzles my shoulder.

Oh, Speedy, Speedy, Speedy, you son of a bitch, I hardly even know you, but I know you too well. Just a few days ago you stepped in front of me as we neared the crest of that hill, so that you'd get hit by the expected RPD burst instead of me—to give your life that I, your platoon leader, might live. And now you really are dead.

You should never have been carrying my radio, you dumb shit, with that heavy Mexican accent. Why the hell did I let you stay on? I should have gotten somebody else, you'd still be alive. . . .

I hug him to me as I wade. Wise guy. Smart ass. Kid. The tears well up as his blood resoaks my chest and stomach.

I look up at the dustoff slick dropping from the sky in a blur, the rotor wash ballooning my shirt. I lean back and lift Speedy up, my arms aching.

I am just an American soldier lifting the body of a fallen brother-in-arms up into a helicopter. But at another level I am offering him back to America for all of us over here, as evidence of our selfless commitment. This is, finally and undeniably, the Offering of those in my generation of Americans serving in Vietnam: our lives offered for our country. Speedy's offer has been accepted.

More bodies are being loaded into the other side of the hovering helicopter, and I strain to lift Speedy up to the reaching hands. Then, suddenly, his weight is taken from me, and the dustoff rises, leaving me cold and shaken, a shiver stirring my legs. Good-bye, Speedy. Good-bye.

I stare after the dustoff until it disappears.

Hell Sucks

from *Dispatches*
by Michael Herr

In 1967 and 1968 correspondent Michael Herr covered the Vietnam War for **Esquire** *magazine. His reports from Saigon and the field captured in memorable style the ugliness and insanity of war. "Hell Sucks" is his account of the battle for Hue during the Tet offensive of early 1968:*

During the first weeks of the Tet Offensive the curfew began early in the afternoon and was strictly enforced. By 2:30 each day Saigon looked like the final reel of *On The Beach,* a desolate city whose long avenues held nothing but refuse, windblown papers, small distinct piles of human excrement and the dead flowers and spent firecracker casings of the Lunar New Year. Alive, Saigon had been depressing enough, but during the Offensive it became so stark that, in an odd way, it was invigorating. The trees along the main streets looked like they'd been struck by lightning, and it became unusually, uncomfortably cold, one more piece of freak luck in a place where nothing was in its season. With so much filth growing in so many streets and alleys, an epidemic of plague was feared, and if there was ever a place that suggested plague, demanded it, it was Saigon in the Emergency. American civilians, engineers and construction workers who were making it here like they'd never made it at home began forming into large armed bands, carrying .45's and grease guns and Swedish K's, and no mob of hysterical vigilantes ever promised more bad news. You'd see them at ten in the morning on the terrace of the Continental waiting for the bar to open, barely able to light their own cigarettes until it did. The crowds on Tu Do Street looked like Ensor processioners, and there was a corruption in the air that had nothing to do with government workers on the take. After seven in the evening, when the curfew included Americans and became total, nothing but White Mice patrols and MP jeeps moved in the streets, except for a few young children who raced up and down over the rubbish, running newspaper kites up into the chilling wind.

We took a huge collective nervous breakdown, it was the compression and heat of heavy contact generated out until every American in Vietnam got a taste. Vietnam was a dark room full of deadly objects, the VC were everywhere all at once like spider cancer, and instead of losing the war in little pieces over years we lost it fast in under a week. After that, we were like the character in pop grunt mythology, dead but too dumb to lie down. Our worst dread of yellow peril became realized; we saw them now dying by the thousands all over the country, yet they didn't seem depleted, let alone exhausted, as the Mission was claiming by the fourth day. We took space back quickly, expensively, with total panic and close to maximum brutality. Our machine was devastating. And versatile. It could do

U.S. Marines take shelter behind heavily damaged homes in Hue during the Tet offensive in February 1968.

everything but stop. As one American major said, in a successful attempt at attaining history, "We had to destroy Ben Tre in order to save it." That's how most of the country came back under what we called control, and how it remained essentially occupied by the Viet Cong and the North until the day years later when there were none of us left there.

The Mission Council joined hands and passed together through the Looking Glass. Our general's chariot was on fire, he was taking on smoke and telling us such incredible stories of triumph and victory that a few high-level Americans had to ask him to just cool it and let them do the talking. A British correspondent compared the Mission posture to the captain of the *Titanic* announcing, "There's no cause for alarm, we're only stopping briefly to take on a little ice."

By the time I got back to Saigon on the fourth day a lot of information from around the country had settled, and it was bad, even after you picked out the threads of rumor: like the one about the "Caucasians," obviously Americans, fighting for the VC, or the one about thousands of NVA executions in Hue and the "shallow graves" in the flats outside the city, both of which proved true. Almost as much as the grunts and the Vietnamese, Tet was pushing correspondents closer to the wall than they'd ever wanted to go. I realized later that, however childish I might remain, actual youth had been pressed out of me in just the three days that it took me to cross the sixty miles between Can Tho and Saigon. In Saigon, I saw friends flipping out

almost completely; a few left, some took to their beds for days with the exhaustion of deep depression. I went the other way, hyper and agitated, until I was only doing three hours of sleep a night. A friend on the *Times* said he didn't mind his nightmares so much as the waking impulse to file on them. An old-timer who'd covered war since the Thirties heard us pissing and moaning about how *terrible* it was and he snorted, "Ha, I love you guys. You guys are beautiful. What the fuck did you think it was?" We thought it was already past the cut-off point where every war is just like every other war; if we knew how rough it was going to get, we might have felt better. After a few days the air routes opened again, and we went up to Hue.

Going in, there were sixty of us packed into a deuce-and-a-half, one of eight trucks moving in convoy from Phu Bai, bringing in over 300 replacements for the casualties taken in the earliest fighting south of the Perfume River. There had been a harsh, dark storm going on for days, and it turned the convoy route into a mudbed. It was terribly cold in the trucks, and the road was covered with leaves that had either been blown off the trees by the storm or torn away by our artillery, which had been heavy all along the road. Many of the houses had been completely collapsed, and not one had been left without pitting from shell fragments. Hundreds of refugees held to the side of the road as we passed, many of them wounded. The kids would laugh and shout, the old would look on with that silent tolerance for misery that made so many Americans uneasy, which was usually misread as indifference. But the younger men and women would often look at us with unmistakable contempt, pulling their cheering children back from the trucks.

We sat there trying to keep it up for each other, grinning at the bad weather and the discomfort, sharing the first fear, glad that we weren't riding point or closing the rear. They had been hitting our trucks regularly, and a lot of the convoys had been turned back. The houses that we passed so slowly made good cover for snipers, and one B-40 rocket could have made casualties out of a whole truckload of us. All the grunts were whistling, and no two were whistling the same tune, it sounded like a locker room before a game that nobody wanted to play. Or almost nobody. There was a black Marine called Philly Dog who'd been a gang lord in Philadelphia and who was looking forward to some street fighting after six months in the jungle, he could show the kickers what he could do with some city ground. (In Hue he turned out to be incredibly valuable. I saw him pouring out about a hundred rounds of .30-caliber fire into a breach in the wall, laughing, "You got to bring some to get some"; he seemed to be about the only man in Delta Company who hadn't been hurt yet.) And there was a Marine correspondent, Sergeant Dale Dye, who sat with a tall yellow flower sticking out of his helmet cover, a really outstanding target. He was rolling his eyes around and saying, "Oh yes, oh yes, Charlie's got his shit together here, this will be *bad*," and smiling happily. It was the same smile I saw a week later when a sniper's bullet tore up a wall two inches above his head, odd cause for amusement in anyone but a grunt.

Everyone else in the truck had that wild haunted going-West look that said it was perfectly correct to be here where the fighting would be the worst, where you wouldn't have half of what you needed, where it was colder than Nam ever got. On their helmets and flak jackets they'd written the names of old operations, of girlfriends, their war names (FAR FROM FEARLESS, MICKEY'S MONKEY, AVENGER V, SHORT TIME SAFETY MOE), their fantasies (BORN TO LOSE, BORN TO RAISE HELL, BORN TO KILL, BORN TO DIE), their ongoing information (HELL SUCKS, TIME IS ON MY SIDE, JUST YOU AND ME GOD —RIGHT?). One kid called to me, "Hey man! You want a story, man? Here man, write this: I'm up there on 881, this was May, I'm just up there walkin' the ridgeline like a movie star and this Zip jumps up smack into me, lays his AK-47 fucking right *into* me, only he's so *amazed* at my *cool* I got my whole clip off 'fore he knew how to thank me for it. Grease one." After twenty kilometers of this, in spite of the black roiling sky ahead, we could see smoke coming up from the far side of the river, from the Citadel of Hue.

The bridge was down that spanned the canal dividing the village of An Cuu and the southern sector of Hue,

blown the night before by the Viet Cong, and the forward area beyond the far bank wasn't thought to be secure, so we bivouacked in the village for the night. It had been completely deserted, and we set ourselves up in empty hootches, laying our poncho liners out over broken glass and shattered brick. At dusk, while we all stretched out along the canal bank eating dinner, two Marine gunships came down on us and began strafing us, sending burning tracers up along the canal, and we ran for cover, more surprised than scared. "Way to go, motherfucker, way to pinpoint the fuckin' enemy," one of the grunts said, and he set up his M-60 machine gun in case they came back. "I don't guess we got to take *that* shit," he said. Patrols were sent out, guards posted, and we went into the hootches to sleep. For some reason, we weren't even mortared that night.

In the morning we crossed the canal on a two-by-four and started walking in until we came across the first of the hundreds of civilian dead that we were to see in the next weeks: an old man arched over his straw hat and a little girl who'd been hit while riding her bicycle, lying there with her arm up like a reproach. They'd been lying out like that for a week, for the first time we were grateful for the cold.

Along the Perfume River's south bank there is a long, graceful park that separates Hue's most pleasant avenue, Le Loi, from the riverfront. People will talk about how they'd sit out there in the sun and watch the sampans moving down the river, or watch the girls bicycling up Le Loi, past the villas of officials and the French-architected University buildings. Many of those villas had been destroyed and much of the University permanently damaged. In the middle of the street a couple of ambulances from the German Mission had been blown up, and the Cercle Sportif was covered with bullet holes and shrapnel. The rain had brought up the green, it stretched out cased in thick white fog. In the park itself, four fat green dead lay sprawled around a tall, ornate cage, inside of which sat a small, shivering monkey. One of the correspondents along stepped over the corpses to feed it some fruit. (Days later, I came back to the spot. The corpses were gone, but so was the monkey. There had been so many refugees and so little food then, someone must have eaten him.) The Marines of 2/5 had secured almost all of the central south bank and were now fanning out to the west, fighting and clearing one of the major canals. We were waiting for some decision on whether or not U.S. Marines would be going into the Citadel itself, but no one had any doubts about what that decision would be. We sat there taking in the dread by watching the columns of smoke across the river, receiving occasional sniper rounds, infrequent bursts of .50-caliber, watching the Navy LCU's on the river getting shelled from the wall. One Marine next to me was saying that it was just a damned shame, all them poor people, all them nice-looking houses, they even had a Shell station there. He was looking at the black napalm blasts and the wreckage along the wall. "Looks like the Imperial City's had the schnitz," he said.

The courtyard of the American compound in Hue was filled with puddles from the rain, and the canvas tops of the jeeps and trucks sagged with the weight of the water. It was the fifth day of the fighting, and everyone was still amazed that the NVA or the Cong had not hit the compound on the first night. An enormous white goose had come into the compound that night, and now his wings were heavy with the oil that had formed on the surface of the puddles. Every time a vehicle entered the yard he would beat his wings in a fury and scream, but he never left the compound and, as far as I knew, no one ever ate him.

Nearly 200 of us were sleeping in the two small rooms that had been the compound's dining quarters. The Army was not happy about having to billet so many of the Marines that were coming through, and they were absolutely furious about all the correspondents who were hanging around now, waiting until the fighting moved north across the river, into the Citadel. You were lucky to find space enough on the floor to lie down on, luckier if you found an empty stretcher to sleep on, and luckiest of all if the stretcher was new. All night long the few unbroken windows would rattle from the airstrikes across the river, and a mortar pit just outside fired incessantly. At two or three in the morning, Marines would come in from their patrols. They'd cross the room, not much caring whether they stepped on anyone or not. They'd turn their radios on and shout across the room to one another. "Really, can't you fellows show a bit more consideration?" a British correspondent said, and their laughter woke anyone who was not already up.

One morning there was a fire in the prison camp across the road from the compound. We saw the black smoke rising over the barbed wire that topped the camp wall and heard automatic weapons' fire. The prison was full of captured NVA and Viet Cong or Viet Cong suspects, the guards said that they'd started the fire to cover an escape. The ARVN and a few Americans were shooting blindly into the flames, and the bodies were burning where they fell. Civilian dead lay out on the sidewalks only a block from the compound, and the park by the river was littered with dead. It was cold and the sun never came out once, but the rain did things to the corpses that were worse in their way than anything the sun could have done. It was on one of those days that I realized that the only corpse I couldn't bear to look at would be the one I would never have to see.

It stayed cold and dark like that for the next ten days, and that damp gloom was the background for all the footage that we took out of the Citadel. What little sunlight there was caught the heavy motes of dust that blew up from the wreckage of the east wall, held it until everything you saw was filtered through it. And you saw things from unaccustomed angles, quick looks from a running crouch, or up from flat out, hearing the hard dry rattle of shrapnel scudding against the debris around you. With all of that dust blowing around, the acrid smell of cordite would hang in the air for a long time after firefights, and there was the CS gas that we'd fired at the NVA blowing back in over our positions. It was impossible to get a clean breath with all of that happening, and there was that other smell too that came up from the shattered heaps of stone wherever an airstrike had come in. It held to the lining of your nostrils and worked itself into the weave of your fatigues, and weeks later, miles away, you'd wake up at night and it would be in the room with you. The NVA had dug themselves so deeply into the wall that airstrikes had to open it meter by meter, dropping napalm as close as a hundred meters from our positions. Up on the highest point of the wall, on what had once been a tower, I looked across the Citadel's moat and saw the NVA moving quickly across the rubble of the opposing wall. We were close enough to be able to see their faces. A rifle went off a few feet to my right, and one of the running figures jerked back and dropped. A Marine sniper leaned out from his cover and grinned at me.

Between the smoke and the mist and the flying dust inside the Citadel, it was hard to call that hour between light and darkness a true dusk, but it was the time when most of us would open our C rations. We were only meters away from the worst of the fighting, not more than a Vietnamese city block in distance, and yet civilians kept appearing, smiling, shrugging, trying to get back to their homes. The Marines would try to menace them away at rifle point, shouting, "Di, di, *di*, you sorry-ass motherfuckers, go on, get the hell away from here!" and the refugees would smile, half bowing, and flit up one of the shattered streets. A little boy of about ten came up to a bunch of Marines from Charlie Company. He was laughing and moving his head from side to side in a funny way. The fierceness in his eyes should have told everyone what it was, but it had never occurred to most of the grunts that a Vietnamese child could be driven mad too, and by the time they understood it the boy had begun to go for their eyes and tear at their fatigues, spooking everyone, putting everyone really uptight, until a black grunt grabbed him from behind and held his arm. "C'mon, poor li'l baby, 'fore one of these grunt mothers shoots you," he said, and carried the boy to where the corpsmen were.

On the worst days, no one expected to get through it alive. A despair set in among members of the battalion that the older ones, the veterans of two other wars, had never seen before. Once or twice, when the men from Graves Registration took the personal effects from the packs and pockets of dead Marines, they found letters from home that had been delivered days before and were still unopened.

Two Marines assist a comrade who has been shot in both legs by a sniper in Hue.

We were running some wounded onto the back of a half-ton truck, and one of the young Marines kept crying from his stretcher. His sergeant held both of his hands, and the Marine kept saying, "Shit, Sarge, I ain' gone make it. Oh damn, I'm gone die, ain't I?" "No you ain't gonna die, for Christ's sake," the sergeant said. "Oh yeah, Sarge, yeah, I am." "Crowley," the sergeant said, "you ain't hurt that bad. I want you to just shut the fuck up. You ain't done a thing except bitch ever since we got to this fucking Hue City." But the sergeant didn't really know. The kid had been hit in the throat, and you couldn't tell about those. Throat wounds were bad. Everyone was afraid of throat wounds.

We lucked out on our connections. At the battalion aid station we got a chopper that carried us and a dozen dead Marines to the base at Phu Bai, and three minutes after we landed there we caught a C-130 to Danang. Hitching in from the airfield, we found a Psyops officer who felt sorry for us and drove us all the way to the press center. As we came in the gate we could see that the net was up and the daily volleyball game between the Marines assigned to the press center was on.

"Where the hell have *you* guys been?" one of them asked. We looked pretty fucked up.

The inside of the dining room was freezing with air-conditioning. I sat at a table and ordered a hamburger and a brandy from one of the peasant girls who waited tables. I sat there for a couple of hours and ordered four more

hamburgers and at least a dozen brandies. It wasn't possible, just not possible, to have been where we'd been before and to be where we were now, all in the same afternoon. One of the correspondents who had come back with me sat at another table, also by himself, and we looked at each other, shook our heads and laughed. I went to my room and took my boots and fatigues off and got into the shower. The water was incredibly hot, for a moment I thought I'd gone insane from it, and I sat down on the concrete floor for a long time, shaving there, soaping myself over and over. I dressed and went back to the dining room. The net was down now, one of the Marines said hello and asked me if I knew what the movie was going to be that night. I ordered a steak and another long string of brandies. When I left the correspondent was still sitting alone. I got into bed and smoked a joint. I was going back in the morning, it was understood, but why was it understood? All of my stuff was in order, ready for the five-o'clock wake-up. I finished the joint and shuddered off into sleep.

By the end of the week the wall had cost the Marines roughly one casualty for every meter taken, a quarter of them KIA. 1/5, which came to be known as the Citadel

Litter bearers pull a wounded man to safety amid the ruins of Hue, 1968.

Battalion, had been through every tough battle the Marines had had in the past six months, they'd even fought the same NVA units a few weeks before between Hai Vanh Pass and Phu Loc, and now three of its companies were below platoon strength. They all knew how bad it was, the novelty of fighting in a city had become a nasty joke, everyone wanted to get wounded.

At night in the CP, the major who commanded the battalion would sit reading his maps, staring vacantly at the trapezoid of the Citadel. It could have been a scene in a Norman farmhouse twenty-five years ago, with candles burning on the tables, bottles of red wine arranged along damaged shelves, the chill in the room, the high ceilings, the heavy ornate cross on the wall. The major had not slept for five nights, and for the fifth night in a row he assured us that tomorrow would get it for sure, the final stretch of wall would be taken and he had all the Marines he needed to do it. And one of his aides, a tough mustang first lieutenant, would pitch a hard, ironic smile above the major's stare, a smile that rejected good news, it was like hearing him say, "The major here is full of shit, and we both know it."

Sometimes a company would find itself completely cut off, and it would take hours for the Marines to get their wounded out. I remember one Marine with a headwound who finally made it to the Battalion CP when the jeep he was in stalled. He finally jumped out and started to push, knowing it was the only way out of there. Most of the tanks and trucks that carried casualties had to move up a long straight road without cover, and they began calling it

Rocket Alley. Every tank the Marines had there had been hit at least once. An epiphany of Hue appeared in John Olson's great photograph for *Life*, the wounded from Delta Company hurriedly piled on a tank. Sometimes, on the way to the aid station the more seriously wounded would take on that bad color, the gray-blue fishbelly promise of death that would spread upward from the chest and cover the face. There was one Marine who had been shot through the neck, and all the way out the corpsmen massaged his chest. By the time they reached the station, though, he was so bad that the doctor triaged him, passed him over to treat the ones that he knew could still be saved, and when they put him into the green rubber body bag there was some chance that he was clinically alive. The doctor had never had to make choices like that before, and he wasn't getting used to it. During the lulls he'd step outside for some air, but it was no better out there. The bodies were stacked together and there was always a crowd of ARVN standing around staring, death-enthralled like all Vietnamese. Since they didn't know what else to do, and not knowing what it would look like to the Marines, they would smile at the bodies there, and a couple of ugly incidents occurred. The Marines who worked the body detail were overloaded and rushed and became snappish, ripping packs off of corpses angrily, cutting gear away with bayonets, heaving bodies into the green bags. One of the dead Marines had gone stiff and they had trouble getting him to fit. "*Damn*," one of them said, "this fucker had big feet. Didn't this fucker have big feet," as he finally forced the legs inside. In the station there was the youngest-looking Marine I'd ever seen. He'd been caught in the knee by a large piece of shrapnel, and he had no idea of what they'd do with him now that he was wounded. He lay out on the stretcher while the doctor explained how he would be choppered back to Phu Bai hospital and then put on a plane for Danang and then flown back to the States for what would certainly be the rest of his tour. At first the boy was sure that the doctor was kidding him, then he started to believe it, and then he knew it was true, he was actually getting out, he couldn't stop smiling, and enormous tears ran down into his ears.

It was at this point that I began to recognize almost every casualty, remember conversations we'd had days or even hours earlier, and that's when I left, riding a medevac with a lieutenant who was covered with blood-soaked bandages. He'd been hit in both legs, both arms, the chest and head, his ears and eyes were full of caked blood, and he asked a photographer in the chopper to get a picture of him like this to send to his wife.

But by then the battle for Hue was almost over. The Cav was working the northwest corner of the Citadel, and elements of the 101st had come in through what had formerly been an NVA resupply route. (In five days these outfits lost as many men as the Marines had in three weeks.) Vietnamese Marines and some of the 1st ARVN Division had been moving the remaining NVA down toward the wall. The NVA flag that had flown for so long over the south wall had been cut down, and in its place an American flag had been put up. Two days later the Hoc Bao, Vietnamese Rangers, stormed through the walls of the Imperial Palace, but there were no NVA left inside. Except for a few bodies in the moat, most of their dead had been buried. When they'd first come into Hue the NVA had sat at banquets given for them by the people. Before they left, they'd skimmed all the edible vegetation from the surface of the moat. Seventy percent of Vietnam's one lovely city was destroyed, and if the landscape seemed desolate, imagine how the figures in that landscape looked.

There were two official ceremonies marking the expulsion of the NVA, both flag-raisings. On the south bank of the Perfume River, 200 refugees from one of the camps were recruited to stand, sullen and silent in the rain, and watch the GVN flag being run up. But the rope snapped, and the crowd, thinking the VC had shot it down, broke up in panic. (There was no rain in the stories that the Saigon papers ran, no trouble with the rope, and the cheering crowd numbered thousands.) As for the other ceremony, the Citadel was thought by most people to be insecure, and when the flag finally went up there was no one to watch it except for a handful of Vietnamese troops.

Major Trong bounced around in the seat of his jeep as it drove us over the debris scattered across the streets of Hue. His face seemed competely expressionless as we passed the crowds of Vietnamese stumbling over the fallen beams and powdered brick of their homes, but his eyes were covered by dark glasses and it was impossible to know what he was feeling. He didn't look like a victor, he was so small and limp in his seat I was afraid he was going to fly out of the jeep. His driver was a sergeant named Dang, one of the biggest Vietnamese I'd ever seen, and his English was better than the major's. The jeep would stall on rubble heaps from time to time, and Dang would turn to us and smile an apology. We were on our way to the Imperial Palace.

A month earlier the Palace grounds had been covered with dozens of dead NVA and the burned-over leavings of three weeks' siege and defense. There had been some reluctance about bombing the Palace, but a lot of the bombing nearby had done heavy damage, and there had been some shelling, too. The large bronze urns were dented beyond restoring, and the rain poured through a hole in the roof of the throne room, soaking the two small thrones where the old Annamese royalty had sat. In the great hall (great once you'd scaled it to the Vietnamese) the red lacquer work on the upper walls was badly chipped, and a heavy dust covered everything. The crown of the main gate had collapsed, and in the garden the broken branches of the old cay-dai trees lay like the forms of giant insects seared in a fire, wispy, delicate, dead. It was rumored during those days that the Palace was being held by a unit of student volunteers who had taken the invasion of Hue as a sign and had rushed to join the North Vietnamese. (Another rumor of those days, the one about some 5,000 "shallow graves" outside the city, containing the bodies from NVA executions, had just now been shown to be true.)

But once the walls had been taken and the grounds entered, there was no one left inside except for the dead. They bobbed in the moat and littered all the approaches. The Marines moved in then, and empty ration cans and muddied sheets from the *Stars and Stripes* were added to the litter. A fat Marine had been photographed pissing into the locked-open mouth of a decomposing North Vietnamese soldier.

"No good," Major Trong said. "No good. Fight here very hard, very bad."

I'd been talking to Sergeant Dang about the Palace and about the line of emperors. When we stalled one last time at the foot of a moat bridge, I'd been asking him the name of the last emperor to occupy the throne. He smiled and shrugged, not so much as if he didn't know, more like it didn't matter.

"Major Trong is emperor now," he said, and gunned the jeep into the Palace grounds.

Congress Backs the War

The Southeast Asia Resolution, passed by Congress August 7, 1964, gave Lyndon Johnson the freedom to escalate American military involvement in Vietnam. Sometimes called the "Tonkin Gulf Resolution," it arose from a series of actual and supposed clashes between North Vietnamese patrol boats and the U.S. destroyers Maddox and Turner Joy in the Gulf of Tonkin on August 2-4, 1964. The resolution's language was so broad and open-ended that the president said it was "like grandma's nightshirt—it covered everything."

The resolution passed both houses of Congress overwhelmingly: 416-0 in the House and 88-2 in the Senate. Only two lawmakers were opposed: Senator Ernest Gruening of Alaska called it a "predated declaration of war." Oregon senator Wayne Morse also attacked it. Below is a portion of the resolution, followed by excerpts from President Johnson's message to Congress and Senator Morse's speeches on the Senate floor.

To Promote the Maintenance of International Peace and Security in Southeast Asia

Whereas naval units of the Communist regime in Vietnam, in violation of the principles of the Charter of the United Nations and of international law, have deliberately and repeatedly attacked the United States naval vessels lawfully present in international waters, and have thereby created a serious threat to international peace; and

Whereas these attacks are part of a deliberate and systematic campaign of aggression that the Communist regime in North Vietnam has been waging against its neighbors and the nations joined with them in the collective defense of their freedom . . .

Resolved by the Senate and House of Representatives of the United States of America in Congress assembled.

That the Congress approves and supports the determination of the President as Commander in Chief, to take all necessary measures to repel any armed attack against the forces of the United States and to prevent further aggression.

President Johnson's Message to Congress, August 5, 1964

Last night I announced to the American people that the North Vietnamese regime had conducted further deliberate attacks against U.S. naval vessels operating in international waters, and that I had therefore directed air action against gunboats and supporting facilities used in these hostile operations. This air action has now been carried out with substantial damage to the boats and facilities. Two U.S. aircraft were lost in the action.

After consultation with the leaders of both parties in the Congress, I further announced a decision to ask the Congress for a resolution expressing the unity and determination of the United States in supporting freedom and in protecting peace in Southeast Asia. . . .

Our policy in Southeast Asia has been consistent and unchanged since 1954. I summarized it on June 2 in four simple propositions:

1. America keeps her word. Here as elsewhere, we must and shall honor our commitments.

2. The issue is the future of Southeast Asia as a whole. A threat to any nation in that region is a threat to all, and a threat to us.

3. Our purpose is peace. We have no military, political, or territorial ambitions in this area.

4. This is not just a jungle war, but a struggle for freedom on every front of human activity. Our military and economic assistance to South Vietnam and Laos in particular has the purpose of helping these countries to repel aggression and strengthen their independence. . . .

As I have repeatedly made clear, the United States intends no rashness, and seeks no wider war. We must make it clear to all that the United States is united in its determination to bring about the end of Communist subversion and aggression in the area. . . .

Senator Morse's comments on the Senate floor, August 5, 1964

Mr. President, I rise to speak in opposition to the joint resolution. I do so with a very sad heart. But I consider the resolution, as I considered the resolution of 1955, known as the Formosa resolution, and the subsequent resolution, known as the Middle East resolution, to be naught but a resolution which embodies a predated declaration of war.

Article I, section 8 of our Constitution does not permit the President to make war at his discretion. Therefore I stand on this issue as I have stood before in the Senate, perfectly willing to take the judgment of history as to the merits of my cause. . . .

I yield to no other Senator, or to anyone else in this country in my opposition to communism and all that communism stands for.

In our time a great struggle, which may very well be a deathlock struggle, is going on in the world between freedom on the one hand and the totalitarianism of communism on the other.

However, I am satisfied that that struggle can never be settled by war. I am satisfied that if the hope of anyone is that the struggle between freedom and communism can be settled by war, and that course is followed, both freedom and communism will lose, for there will be no victory in that war.

Because of our own deep interest in the struggle against communism, we in the United States are inclined to overlook some of the other struggles which are occupying others. We try to force every issue into the context of freedom versus communism. That is one of our great mistakes in Asia. There is much communism there, and much totalitarianism in other forms. We say we are opposing communism there, but that does not mean we are advancing freedom, because we are not.

The Big Battle

from *Brothers: Black Soldiers in the Nam*
by Stanley Goff and Robert Sanders with Clark Smith

Brothers *recounts the Vietnam tours of duty of two black infantrymen who befriended each other during basic training. Robert Sanders was a machine gunner in the 173d Airborne in II Corps. Stanley Goff served in the southern area of I Corps in the 196th Light Infantry Brigade; he also carried a "pig" (M60 machine gun). Their collaborator, Clark Smith, a historian, founded the Winter Soldier Archive, a repository for Vietnam veterans' recollections of their wartime experiences. On August 25, 1968, Stan Goff earned the Distinguished Service Cross for extraordinary heroism in action. This is his account of that day:*

That day, as I remember, we started going real, real slow. We were riding along in a thick woody area, and all of a sudden, out of a clear blue sky, we heard a "boom bam . . . DIDIDIDIDI . . . " The APC stopped and we jumped off and got down beside the tanks. We were looking, trying to figure what was happening. It was way in the back. When you had thirty-five mechanized vehicles, you had to figure this entourage was a huge thing—like a wagon train, it was so damn long. Of course, they knew we were coming. What happened was that one of the carriers got hit. It wasn't a bad hit, but the five guys on top of it got blasted by a shell that hit the side of the carrier. So we had to stop and wait; my squad just stayed put. We didn't know whether we were going to get hit with another rush or not. We just

stayed behind the thing. We sat there and waited until the medivac came in and carried the five guys away.

Slowly we found out what happened. One guy got his arm almost torn off; another guy got hit in the eye. Damn! So we said, "Well, this is the shit. This is what we've been riding so God damn long for." We were moving toward the major conflict. By this time, we were all ready for it. "Let's get it on. Fucking bastards." We were cussing them out, all of us, because it was mostly brothers that got it that day, guys we knew. "Eugene got it man?" "Yeah, man, he got half his fucking arm torn off." "Anyway, he's going home?" "Yeah." "He got outa here . . . " Throughout the war, no matter how you got out, even if you got a leg blown off you, you got out alive. Your time was up. But it was the *way* you got out that was the significance. That was what the American people didn't realize, how tough it was. To be hit and have his arm torn off, that was like somebody giving him two hundred thousand dollars. That was how much his life was worth. His arm. To get out of the war, his contract was his arm.

I guess the caravan stopped about an hour. Then we started moving again. We knew we had to get the assault in the backs of our minds, because the next tank to get hit could be us. So we rode along and I thought about what we were going to do if we got hit. If they came out of the bushes right now, what was I going to do? I had the pig in

53

a ready position and I was going to sling it right down and start spraying. That was all I was thinking. The carriers were lined up at the edge of this one huge rice paddy. They started coming alongside each other, but we weren't told to dismount. So we still stayed on them while they were getting into position. Nobody told us that anything was over across the paddy at all. Nobody said, "OK, there's an NVA regiment over there. Go get 'em." All we knew was that there was a woodline over there.

I never will forget how we approached it, the tanks and APCs quietly lining up in parallel formation. The rice paddy was about two times the length of a football field and about a football field in width. I heard guys mumbling, but I was just listening for a command, which could come from anyone, like the driver. Everything was moving so fast. Within a fifteen-minute interval we stopped and lined up at the rice paddy. Then the word came, "All right, dismount and stay at the back of the carriers." So the men started to climb down the sides of the vehicles. All of a sudden, the carriers started reconning by fire. They just started firing at this woodline, "Boom, boom," with all these big tank guns, just tearing that fucking woodline all up. Man, the whole damn woodline opened up, "BOOM dididid wham WHAM . . ." Rockets. I heard guys getting hit from over to my left. I heard a tank get hit. I didn't know how bad.

Now my mind was jumping. By this time everbody was reconning by fire. I was firing back automatically even while this barrage was coming in. Everybody was standing up there doing nothing but firing like hell. Pretty soon we were told, "Back up, back up, back up, we're going to be backing up, pull back." So we started pulling back. I thought to myself, "God damn. Shit. Fuck it, it's hell over there . . . " This regiment probably had left a suicide battalion over there to knock shit out of us, so that the rest of the enemy could go on and do what they had to do. We pulled back into the opposite woodline.

While I pulled myself together, I was looking around for my men. They were really shaken up. I could see the shock in their faces—no blood at all in their faces. They said, "Hey, man, are we gonna go across to that woodline?" I said, "Yup, I think we are." "Oh, man, that's suicide." "Could possibly be, man." I didn't know what was going on toward the other end of the column. There was our whole fucking company here, 125 men; add the cav unit, and there were three hundred men, easily. Our company was beefed up and now I knew why. After we pulled back into the woodline, I made sure that my weapon was clean. That was what my squad saw me doing.

I never will forget Piper looking at me and shaking his head. It looked as if he was almost ready to cry, because he knew we might be looking at each other for the last time. And I guess there was a sort of unity between Piper and me, because politically he had tried to make every man see the full thing of what our country was doing. Here

it was, just taking us to our death. We were nothing but bodies, that was all; out for a huge body count. And this was it; just setting us up for this race across that paddy. I saw the hurt in his face as he looked at me. Because I had the pig, I guess he thought his brother might get blown away. I took my eyes away from him, because I said to myself, "I'm not going to think about that, I don't want to think about that. I'm not going to get blown away." But I knew the look—he looked at me as though I was a dead man. I guess he figured he would stand a chance of surviving—but the pig—everybody was going to shoot at the pig.

Soon we heard a helicopter come in. They were medivacking guys. One of the tanks was blown away; it took a direct hit. I think we lost that tank and a carrier in the fighting, so they evacuated that team. Somebody asked, "When are they going to send in the planes?" A lot of guys thought they were going to send in planes.

And then we found out that we were actually going to assault that woodline. "Assault on the woodline?" a lot of guys were saying. I wasn't saying anything. "Oh, man, these motherfuckers—" guys were bitching. Then all of a sudden we heard the CO say, "SHUT UP, and that's an order! I mean it, God damn it. Now, we're going to assault this fucking woodline and that's that." An order. Other than the original recon by fire, there was no artillery on the woodline. The CO said the next man that opened his God damn mouth would be court-martialed. We got ready to assault the woodline.

I got my weapon all cleaned and made sure that all my guys were around me, and I didn't do too much talking. I said, "OK, men. Primarily what I want you to do is just stick by me, OK? Emory, when I call for that ammo, I want you to have your ass right here—you got it?" "I got it, Goff, OK." "OK, fine, just keep your head down, man." "OK." And I thought to myself, "This little fucker sure has a lot of balls." I mean, never once, all the time he'd been in-country did I ever see him blink. I sort of favored him over the rest of the guys, even Carl, because I knew what Carl would do. Emory would never have any type of fear or apprehension. I never did even see him swallow hard. He'd only been in-country about six, eight weeks. Here he was, about to see the biggest battle of his whole life—and he was just sitting there, drinking in every word I told him. He stared me right in the eyes, as I stared him right back, and he just drank in every word I told him. I don't know, I guess some of the other guys thought that I was gung ho, and, to a certain degree, they were trying to stay away from me. But he didn't. And then again, Carl, and the other three guys knew that I was vulnerable with the pig, too. When I found out that Emory wasn't gun-shy like that, wasn't so paranoid, I really took to him. He had most of my ammo.

You see, a gunner needed an ammo bearer that was not so worried about his own head that he couldn't effectively feed the gunner the ammo. I would be blowing lead out of that pig so quick I'd go through a belt in ten seconds, needed a man to be able to hand me the ammo. He didn't have to stick it in the weapon. I did that. He just simply handed it to me, and I flopped it in there. I could do it faster than he could, anyway.

As we got ready to go back up to the woodline, the NVA stopped firing, waiting for us to charge. It was very quiet over there. Then the tanks moved out and started firing as they went, the NVA returning their fire. We all started moving out too, walking at first, just walking behind the tanks, letting them do all the firing. As the fire came in, I heard it hit on the top of the tank that I was behind—ding, dang, ding. As the tanks started going faster and faster, they cut us loose as they got ahead of us. Obviously, as that cover pulled out about ten feet ahead, we started lowering ourselves and we started firing. As they finally pulled away from us, we all hit the dirt, out in the middle of the rice paddy, and started inching our way toward the dike. Then we were all running toward the first dike with the tanks forty feet ahead. We couldn't fire too much because they were still too close to us. So we mostly kept our heads down and moved toward that first dike, about two feet high—high enough for protection. As infantry, our job was to take care of the NVA who might have moved on foot to attack the tanks and the personnel carriers from the rear.

As the tanks moved forward, they were shooting like hell, burning up the people in the woodline. My squad was to my immediate right. We were getting all kinds of pig firepower from that brush and all the way to the left. I couldn't see what was happening at the other end of the company; I only knew what was going on in the 2nd platoon.

Now, what were they going to do? The NVA were sitting back there and waiting for us to actually try and attack them head on. What were we going to do? The NVA's sole intent was to have us try to attack them, and they were going to circle us and cut us off from the rear. That was the whole trip.

I was at the dike, firing like hell with Emory right with me, just handing me that lead. He said, "Hey, Goff, I'm out of lead. What do you want to do?" "Don't worry, I got enough right down here," and I was still firing. "What I want you to do is go and get all the ammo from the other guys down at the other end of the company. Find anybody that's got ammo, just get it."

So this kid, on his hands and knees, crawled along in back of the dike, collecting ammo and bringing it back up to me, and I was firing like hell. I probably went through two thousand rounds. Everybody was depending on Goff right then; Goff was the firepower. And I knew I was quieting that area, because my firepower was very effective. As I was running I was steadily blowing out lead. I saw these guys moving around in the woodline. But primarily I wasn't looking at the guys; I was only looking at

An M551 Sheridan leads a column of M113 ACAVs on patrol in South Vietnam.

the angling of my weapon and where my firepower was going. That was the only thing I was worrying about. And as I was going, I was steadily laying down my firepower so effectively that I was just not getting hit myself. That's the only explanation I can come up with.

Emory and I were running up and down this rice paddy firing. The guys would tell me, "Hey, Goff, right here, right in there, man." I would sit down between two guys and blow out where they thought they were getting heavy concentration of fire. Then Emory and I would run into another area along the dike. When Sergeant Needham hollered, "Goff, Goff, over here man, I got thirty or forty of them, right there, right there," I'd fire right where he told me to fire. Those were the thirty or forty NVA I am accredited with in that area. Emory was not with me. I told him to stay while I ran over and was firing my ass off in this particular area, so he started firing his M-16, too.

We were in the middle of the paddy at the first dike, which we went over. We cut down that body of men so well, knocked out their firepower, that we could move now on toward the second dike at the end of the paddy, firing steadily. After we got to the second dike, I went on firing for about fifteen more minutes, but then my pig fell apart. It just blew up in the air like it did earlier at the creek. This time the barrel did fine, but the pins came out of the side of the weapon. It just got too hot, and when it expanded, the pins and the locks and the keys that held it in place were no longer workable, and the pig just came apart. It came apart in my hands. The top of the tray popped up; it was sprung, and I couldn't keep it down. I couldn't fire without the tray being down. By that time there was hardly any activity. I was still staring at the woodline, and the guys saw how it was. "Goff, are you all right?" Emory said, "Are you all right, man?" "Yeah, I'm fine, man." Just exhausted as hell, I could hardly talk, my whole mouth was so dry. I was slumped on my knees at the second dike, just staring. The second dike was almost at the woodline. With us being at the woodline and me sitting there exhausted, and with the area completely quieted, a few of the other squads started to run into the woodline, crouched, searching, looking, weapons at the ready.

They started taking a body count. That was when the CO went into the woodline—to see if they could find any prisoners or whatever. But I'd done most of the work. The rest of the guys were sitting. I'd been doing all the running, so I was dead to the world. The guys just told me to sit there, because my pig was out of action. They got me Juju's pig; he was the other gunner. They told me to sit there while they went to take a body count, which they did. I just sat there with my men and held down the rest of the platoon.

So after that, the main body of men were told to pull out of the dike area and move on up to the grounds of this plantation. We were still firing, taking in rounds over on our right as we moved up. It was coming out of the woods on the right flank. I never will forget this area. Did you ever see grading crews on the road? That's how the whole area looked, obviously from the tanks that went into this area. I was on my knees sweating profusely.

Then we started moving toward another dike about two or three feet high. As I went, I sort of lost my head; I mean I wasn't thinking too clearly. My helmet had fallen off and I knew it was off, but I didn't try to stop and get it even though rounds were still coming in. I didn't see anything in front of me, but I heard the tanks yards and yards ahead of us, way down on the right flank. We were told to wait at the little wall, that the tanks were going to come back for us. Three tanks came back for us. During the battle they were way in front of us. They had gone into the woods only so far and decided to come back and pick up the company. We assumed that our orders were to move after the retreating NVA. That was why they came back and picked us up. We'd blown away their line, so we were going in after them.

I was groggy, but we had to move out; so what if I was groggy! I could hardly get up on top of the God damn tank, I was so weak. Sitting up there, I saw all these bodies, or parts of bodies—hands, arms—so much that it was making me sick to see all these bodies lying on the ground. I realized that it could have been me down there. That was what I kept thinking. I'd just look off into the woods and see rows of bodies, NVA soldiers with backpacks on, T-shirts, parts of uniforms. Obviously, the NVA had tried to strip the bodies as much as they possibly could, to try to prevent us from knowing what rank they were. They'd taken anything of value. There were all kinds of dirt marks dug into the ground. From where my tank was it was hard to tell the tank gashings in the dirt from streaks where bodies had been dragged away. But you knew they had dragged away as many bodies as they could. There were blood marks in the dirt. I got tired of looking. I thought to myself, "See, that's what we were doing."

We moved on the pursuit then. We drove about twenty minutes, traveled about a click down into this deep gulley. Then the orders changed. I don't know why. We turned around and came back to the plantation house on the outskirts of the original rice paddy. We dismounted and I walked about ten or fifteen feet up to the porch and collapsed. "I can't move." It was no laughing matter then. I was conked out on the ground. And I stayed there. My sense at that time was that I had just been in a helluva battle, and that I had done nothing more than anybody else did; that I had done nothing outstanding, but that I was alive; I had survived. I hadn't even gotten hit. And at the same time, I was wondering how many people were hit, how many men had we lost? I was laying down there on this ground, and I was looking up at the sky. Finally I just closed my eyes and thought, man, if somebody came along right now and shot the shit out of me, he'd just have to do it, cause aside from the fact that I was breathing, I was dead anyway. I just had to lay there, just try to get myself rejuvenated. I was completely wasted. I was shaking, just out of it.

Then I heard the medic walk up. Doc took a look at me, said, "Goff, are you all right?" I said, "Yeah, yeah, I'm all right. I'm all right, Doc, just tired." "Yeah, we all are." He walked away. Then I heard the sergeant and the CO come up. I thought I heard them say something like, "This guy did a hell of a job." I thought to myself, "CO says I did a hell of a job." It made me feel good, like any compliment to somebody for working hard. At that particular time I didn't care, except that I did a good job according to the company commander. That the company commander would notice you, out of a hundred men, that would make you feel good. So after that, the medivacs were coming in and carrying guys that had been hit out of the field. I heard pros like Piper saying, "Oh, man, another fucking Khe Sanh." I knew that I had survived a major battle.

Defending the War

Along with a majority of the American public, many of the nation's most prestigious newspapers and journals supported President Lyndon Johnson's big 1965 military build-up in Vietnam. In the February 25, 1966, issue of LIFE magazine, Time Incorporated's editor-in-chief Hedley Donovan opened a special section on the war with an editorial that summarized reasons for U.S. involvement and charted a course for "victory." Here are some excerpts.

Vietnam: The War Is Worth Winning

. . . In this article LIFE offers its own general judgments and guesses about Vietnam. What might it take to end the business? What would be "victory?" What *is* this strange war all about?

—For all the war's strangeness and difficulty, and for all the dangers and uncertainties ahead, our side in fact is doing fairly well.

—The war need not last "a generation," or 10 years, or "six or seven years" (to cite one curiously precise guess that recent press stories attributed to unnamed Pentagon "observers"). There is a reasonably good chance the present phase of the war can be successfully wound up in 1967, or even in late 1966.

—President Johnson's "peace offensive" was well worth trying, and there is still a remote possibility that the diplomacy he set in motion could lead to a satisfactory negotiated settlement of the war.

—The likeliest ending is not around a conference table, however, but in a quiet withdrawal of main-force North Vietnam-ese units, after they have been hurt enough, back to the North, and a gradual tapering off of the Vietcong military effort in the South.

—This would not leave South Vietnam fully pacified by any means; there would still be strong V.C. pockets, and sporadic violence and terrorism. But the war of battalion and regiment-size battles, and big air strikes, would be over.

—In the next phase of the struggle, though there would still be shooting, the war would be essentially economic, political, psychological. Heavy U.S. economic aid would still be required, and some continuing U.S. military presence. This phase might indeed last for some years.

—We are not "bogged down" in Asia. We are deeply, inescapably *involved* with Asia and have been for decades. The involvement has its perils; it also holds high promise.

—The war in Vietnam is not primarily a war about Vietnam, nor even entirely a war about China. It is a war about the future of Asia. It is very possibly as important as any of the previous American wars of this century.

In fact this ugly, maddening, big-little war may some day be remembered as a historic turning point. Many peoples of the West as well as Asia could have reason for gratitude to the extraordinary generation of Americans now serving in Vietnam (their harassed chiefs in Washington might even rate a word or two of thanks), and to the long-suffering troops and people of South Vietnam.

In the U.S. the most persistent question about Vietnam is why the injection of 200,000 Americans has seemingly made so little difference.

The injection of the 200,000 has in fact made an enormous difference. It prevented what otherwise might have been the collapse of the South Vietnam government and army, late last spring, and the defeat of all the previous years of American effort. . . .

Barring a negotiated settlement, nobody will ever be able to name the exact date when the present phase of the war came to an end. But the day should come, late this year or next, when it will be possible to add up some such set of facts as this: dwindling southbound traffic on the Ho Chi Minh Trail for several months; increase in northbound traffic; no firm contact with a full V.C. regiment or bat-talion for several weeks; occasional capture of V.C. or North Vietnam "regulars" now operating with small local guerrilla units; extension of government control to territory containing 75% of the population; decline of V.C. "incidents" within this territory. This would be the end of the big-unit war, and the first instalment of "victory," and this the U.S. does tacitly recognize. To turn the South over to Communism, which would almost certainly be the consequence of a peace negotiated from a few enclaves, would be "defeat." . . .

South Vietnam itself could be a dazzlingly successful country. It has immense food and timber resources, limitless water, hydroelectric possibilities, rubber, superb beaches and scenery, energetic, attractive people. Along with the tragic destruction of war, it is also acquiring, willy-nilly, the best port facilities between Hong Kong and Singapore, and half a dozen first-class jet airfields. It shares the great Mekong Valley system with Cambodia, Thailand and Laos. President Johnson, in one of the few really affirmative specifics he has ever put before Asia, made a generous offer of U.S. aid for a big Mekong Basin project in his Johns Hopkins speech of last April. In a situation which permitted some degree of trust among these countries, an international effort to harness the Mekong could be one of the most exciting engineering and political ventures in the world. . . .

In the past 25 years Asia has experienced three epochal changes that would have filled up several centuries' worth of slower-paced, old-fashioned history. World War II, the first war ever to sweep all of Asia, brought all of Asia irrevocably into the main currents of world politics. The breakup of the British, French, Dutch and Japanese colonial empires created a dozen new nations—total population 800 million—of meager civil experience but powerful aspirations for a better life. Meanwhile the Communist take-over of China gave the earth's most populous country the most strongly centralized government it has known since the Ch'in dynasty fell in 207 B.C. Out of all this upheaval a new Asia will form. The pattern is not yet set. Vietnam is one of the places, at the moment the most crucial place, where the next Asia is being shaped.

WIA

There was one medal very few American soldiers looked forward to receiving: the Purple Heart. It was a hard-won decoration, symbolizing a passage through pain, uncertainty, fear, and sometimes death. If a soldier was WIA—wounded in action—he might live to wear the Purple Heart. If he was killed in action, it was sent to his family.

But wounded soldiers stood a good chance of surviving. The medical evacuation and treatment facilities for American troops in Vietnam were the best in the history of warfare. Men whose lives would surely have been forfeited just a few years earlier were saved by miraculous equipment and superbly trained medical personnel. For the medics, doctors, and nurses who saved young men's lives, though, the war had its own terrible face: a daily grind of easing pain and fighting death.

Preceding page. *A medic treats a wounded soldier in the A Shau Valley, 1969.*

Mas-Cal

from *Home Before Morning*
by Lynda Van Devanter

Lynda Van Devanter served as an operating room nurse in South Vietnam from June 1969 to June 1970. "Mas-Cal" is her recollection of a military hospital as it receives a sudden, heavy influx of casualties:

"This kid's in shock. Get a couple of IVs into him."

"Somebody want to check that tourniquet? His limb's discolored."

"We need more plasma. Where the hell is it?"

"If we don't get his ass into the OR in the next five minutes, he's had it."

"This one's got no reflexes. Shove him over with the expectants."

"Goddamnit, I knew it was going to fucking happen. Those fucking fucked-up fuckers in the fucking mess hall ought to be fucked. I told them not to serve any more fucking fruit cocktail. I don't care how fucking stupid it sounds, every fucking time they serve fruit fucking cocktail, we end up with more fucking wounded than we can handle. I warned those fuckers."

"Snow him with morphine. He's going to die within the hour."

"Got a big belly wound here."

"Call Bubba to look at that head and order five pints of AB negative blood from the lab."

It was my first Mas-Cal, short for mass casualty situation, and although the instructors back in basic had warned us what to expect, no amount of warning could have ever prepared me for the sheer numbers of mutilated young bodies that the helicopters kept bringing to the 71st. "Now you'll see how we really earn our money," Slim said. The emergency room floor was practically covered with blood. Dozens of gurneys were tightly packed into the ER, with barely enough space for medical people to move between them. And the helicopters were still bringing more. Dead bodies in Glad bags were lined up outside the ER doors, to be moved to the morgue as there was time. The moans and screams of so many wounded were mixed up with the shouted orders of doctors and nurses. One soldier vomited on my fatigues while I was inserting an IV needle into his arm. Another grabbed my hand and refused to let go. A blond infantry lieutenant begged me to give him enough morphine to kill him so he wouldn't feel any more pain. A black sergeant went into a seizure and died while Carl and I were examining his small frag wound. "Duty, honor, country," Carl said sarcastically. "I'd like to have Richard Nixon here for one week."

I started to prepare another soldier for surgery. He grabbed my arm. "I can't feel my foot," he kept saying. He was cold. Somebody had covered him with a blanket to keep him from slipping into shock. I put a couple of IVs into his arms. "Nurse, I can't feel my foot!" I glanced down at the lower part of his blanket. "Your foot's still there," I said. "We'll have you fixed up in no time." I pulled the blanket back from his chest and cut his fatigue shirt off. When I removed the blanket from his legs so I could cut away his pants, I was shocked to see the lower part of his left leg lying on its side, separated from his knee by a bloody jagged wound. The medic in the field had applied a tourniquet to keep it from bleeding out.

I had to get that foot out of the way so I could cut the boot off his other leg. But I kept thinking that if I picked up the lower leg and carried it off, he would scream. I knew I would then lose my grip and scream, too. I didn't want to break down. I let it lay for the moment.

Coretta came to give me a hand. "You okay?" she asked. "You look like you're going to get sick."

"I'm fine," I answered.

We removed the old field tourniquet and put a pneumatic tourniquet around his leg so we could relieve the pressure once in a while to keep the stump from becoming gangrenous. He kept asking about his leg and we tried to distract him while we doped him up with pain medication. Later, when we brought him back to the OR, we lifted him from the litter to the operating table. I stood next to the empty litter, looking down at the lower leg. "What am I supposed to do with this?" I asked nobody in particular.

"Throw it in the trash," somebody said. "It's no good to him now."

I wrapped the leg in a pillow case and sent it to the pathology lab.

After I put on my surgical suit and scrubbed, I found myself working again with Carl Adams on the first of many cases that we would handle together during the next seventy-two hours. Our initial soldier had a gunshot wound. The bullet had entered the left chest wall at the nipple line. Someone in ER had put in chest tubes to drain the wound and get the lung expanded again.

"Let's get him on his side," Carl said.

We turned him onto his right side and lifted his left arm over his head. Carl made the incision and together we tied off the bleeders. With a pair of large retractors I held the ribs apart while he went in and removed the bullet. He repaired the rest of the damage in the chest cavity, irrigated with sterile saline, and closed. "That was an easy one," he said. "Don't start getting cocky on me."

The next case was far more complicated. The soldier had been wounded through the stomach, but at an angle where the metal fragments went up from the stomach into the chest. Apparently, the guy had just finished eating a big meal before he was hit. Partially digested lima beans and ham were splattered throughout his chest cavity. "Sometimes it's easier," Carl said, "if you tell yourself they're not people you're working on, but merely bodies.

We're not in a hospital, Van. This is a factory. If you look at it any other way while you're working, you might make yourself crazy." When we got into the chest and started cleaning the wound, we found more than food. There were dozens of worms crawling around. We tried to get all of them out before Carl began searching for the frags. It was a slow, tedious process. "Wait until we get one of the Vietnamese with their undigested fishheads and rice," Carl said. "They'll make this job look pleasant."

After he had taken care of the chest wound, he moved into the belly. It was also a mess. There probably wasn't a single organ that hadn't been damaged. Carl moved the intestines out of the belly and onto the sterile drapes to give himself more room to work. We covered them with lap pads that had been moistened in warm sterile saline. As his hands moved through the belly, repairing damage, he began to make some order out of what was formerly a jumbled mess. When he was finished with the other organs, he started on the intestines, visually inspecting them and running his fingers along the underside to carefully check for any hidden frags that might later cause an infection. He ran the bowel four times and had already gotten a dozen frags when he started to put it back in the belly. Then he stopped for a moment. "Call it instinct," he said, "but I'd better run that bowel one more time." Slowly, he felt his way along the bowel again, until he found a final frag near the retro-peritoneum, the inner back lining of the abdominal wall. It was the first time I had seen him rely on his instincts, but it wouldn't be the last. Carl had a knack for sensing problems in areas that other competent surgeons might overlook. I thought he was wonderful.

"The cooks brought some food into the outer office, Van. We ought to eat after this case."

"What time is it, Carl?"

"Breakfast time."

"I'll wait and eat when we're through with our last case."

"Are you kidding? That could be three or four days from now. If you don't eat, you'll collapse."

"I can't eat in the middle of all this."

"Then you'll have to learn."

"I have a stomachache, Carl."

"Try some antacids. It's pretty common."

Even in the worst of cases, Carl never panicked. He could be looking down at a soldier with blood spurting out of a dozen holes and half the insides blown away, and he would assess the situation in a cool, calm manner, starting to make order out of a mess almost immediately. In the middle of the first afternoon, we came up against one case that would have thrown terror into the most proficient of surgeons. The soldier had multiple frag wounds of the chest. The left lung was collapsed, and the right was partially collapsed. A metal fragment had lodged itself in the heart muscle. In a stateside hospital, an operation to remove the frag would have been conducted by a top heart

The Cassandra Within

Undersecretary of State George Ball was one of the earliest critics of America's war in Vietnam. For years he warned Presidents Kennedy and Johnson against commitment, always to no avail: In 1961, when he told Kennedy that his 8,000-man force would grow to 300,000 in five years, Kennedy laughed and said "George, you're crazier than hell." Four years later, as President Johnson sent large combat units to Vietnam, Ball wrote him a pessimistic private memorandum, detailing the disastrous French experience in Vietnam and urging a "trial period" rather than an open-ended commitment.

June 18, 1965
Where We Are Now—
On the Threshold of a New War

In raising our commitment from 50,000 to 100,000 or more men and deploying most of the increment *in combat roles* we are beginning a new war—the United States *directly* against the Viet Cong.

Perhaps the large-scale introduction of American forces with their concentrated fire power will force Hanoi and the Viet Cong to the decision we are seeking. On the other hand, we may *not* be able to fight the war successfully enough—even with 500,000 Americans in South Viet-Nam—to achieve that purpose.

Before we commit an endless flow of forces to South Viet-Nam we must have more evidence than we now have that our troops will not bog down in the jungles and rice paddies—while we slowly blow the country to pieces.

A review of the French experience more than a decade ago may be helpful.

The French fought a war in Viet-Nam, and were finally defeated—after seven years of bloody struggle and when they still had 250,000 combat-hardened veterans in the field, supported by an army of 205,000 South Vietnamese.

To be sure, the French were fighting a colonial war while we are fighting to stop aggression. But when we have put enough Americans on the ground in South Viet-Nam to give the appearance of a white man's war, the distinction as to our ultimate purpose will have less and less practical effect.

Nor is our position in Viet-Nam without its historical ambiguities. From 1948-1954 we identified ourselves with the French *by providing almost $4 billions of United States aid to help the French* in Indochina wage war against the Viet Minh. As soon as our aid contributions began to mount, Ho Chi Minh denounced American "imperialism." . . .

. . . the more forces we deploy in South Viet-Nam—particularly in combat roles—the harder we shall find it to extricate ourselves without unacceptable costs if the war goes badly.

With large forces committed, the failure to turn the tide will generate pressures to escalate.

---

specialist, with the aid of an artificial heart, so the real one could be kept still while surgery was being performed. Unfortunately, we had neither a heart specialist nor a heart machine at the 71st and if the frag wasn't removed, the soldier would die. Carl would have to work on the heart while it was still beating, and move quickly enough so that he would not cause any more damage. It would be like trying to change a tire while a car is moving.

He began by making stitches around the edge of the frag so he could immediately tighten them as soon as the metal was removed, and, hopefully, hold that section of the heart together at least a little bit until he could get the other stitches in. If he made a single mistake, his work would all be in vain. He held a forcep in one hand, ready to grab the frag. In the other was the end of a suture. His movements were swift and sure. Carl told Slim to start pumping blood into all four IVs. We held our breath and I said a quick silent prayer.

In a split second, Carl removed the metal fragment and pulled the suture tight. Immediately, blood came spurting out at least eighteen inches high. Without losing an instant, he dropped the frag into a bucket and tied off the suture. Blood was still escaping at a rapid rate, but Carl continued to stitch the heart as calmly as if he were working in a bloodless field on a less essential organ.

Every few seconds, he'd have me sponge away some of the blood so he could see well enough to tie a knot. He had to be extremely careful to avoid puncturing the other side of the heart with his needle. He timed himself so he sutured in rhythm with the heartbeat.

Finally, that blood stopped flowing. When I looked up at his face, I could see that the tension and lack of sleep had taken its toll. Sweat was rolling down his forehead and along the side of his cheeks. I wiped it away with a sterile 4x4 sponge. His eyes met mine across the table. "You were great," I said.

"No compliments now," he answered. "The job only counts if this kid lives. Let's take a look at his left lung."

"Quick, Van, what's your favorite food?"

"My mother's homemade lasagna. How about yours, Carl?"

"Give me another suture. Mine's lasagna, too. Would you cut right here above the knot? There's this little restaurant in Saint Paul. My wife and I go there at least once a month. The cook makes the best lasagna I've ever tasted. Another clamp, please."

"Mosquito?"

"Yeah."

"You obviously haven't tasted my mother's lasagna if

you think the best is in Minnesota."

"Suture, Van. Ah, but does your mother have the red checkered tablecloth, candlelight, and violin music? Cut it right here."

"Done, Carl! I think I've met a true romantic."

"Bah, humbug. Give me another suture."

During the second night, we did three belly cases, a chest case, and a couple of multiple frag wounds. At one of the other operating tables, a surgical tech had fallen asleep and fell into an open belly while the doctor was repairing a kidney. The tech was carried out of the OR and left to sleep on the floor of the office, but only for an hour. The belly had to be washed out and the whole operating field sterilized again. After a few others fell asleep at the tables near morning, and it looked like the casualties would never end, we all began grabbing some sleep between cases whenever we had the chance. Some people pulled chairs together and slept stretched across them, while others were satisfied with the floor. The OR supervisor's office was comfortable, but the linen closet was quieter. Around midmorning, I found myself a spot in an out-of-the-way corner of the emergency room.

"Van, wake up. The next case is ready."

"Shit! What time is it, Coretta?"

"Eleven. You've had about twenty minutes sleep."

"Any time to grab a bite?"

"Better not right now. You and Carl are assigned to a burn case next. A squad was napalmed by friendly fire. When you smell that OR, you're liable to lose your lunch."

Carl and I went through three burn cases that afternoon, cutting away entire chunks of charred flesh that was so crisp it could be broken in half. The crew in the ER had been unable to remove all the clothes because the soldiers were in such pain. They had to be anesthetized before we could even start prepping them. In some spots, the heat had been so great that the clothes and skin were melted together. Just when we thought we were finished with burns, we got another case, the only survivor of a helicopter crash. In addition to a body that was almost covered with third-degree burns, the soldier had traumatic amputations of both legs. When we removed the pneumatic tourniquets after we had stopped the bleeding at the stumps, we pulled off layers of crispy skin that had stuck to the material. In the middle of the darkest humor, the doctors and nurses would call these patients crispy critters.

"Let's close the peritoneum with O Chromic, Van. You like baseball?"

"I was once the best catcher in the league, Carl. Here—O on a taper."

"Yeah, that should do it. I used to pitch. Cut, please? Had a curve that was good enough—another suture—to get me a tryout with the Yankees in the days when they practically owned the pennant. Scissors, please. Are you a Yankee fan?"

"Nope. Washington Senators."

"Senators? Why bother rooting for a bunch of losers?"

"Loyalty. Harmon Killebrew was my hero."

On the second night, we came under another rocket attack. When the shrapnel hit the surgical-T's metal walls, it sounded as if somebody had taken a handful of gravel and thrown it against the quonset hut. Since there were no windows, I couldn't see the explosions, but I still felt their concussion and jumped each time another rocket hit. "You'll have to steady yourself," Carl said, "or you're going to give this guy an accidental tonsillectomy from the stomach up."

We lowered the table closer to the floor and Carl and I performed the surgery while kneeling. The anesthetist lay on his back, monitoring his gauges from there. In the beginning, my hands shook so badly I could barely hold the instruments. Carl talked quietly and joked with me until I calmed down. After an hour of kneeling, our legs were falling asleep and the pain in the knees was unbearable. We tried raising the table some and operating from a position that was half standing and half squat. That was also painful, this time for the thighs and lower back. Finally, we decided to put the table back to the original position regardless of the V.C. rockets. Besides, by that point, we were so tired we might have even welcomed death. At least then we would be able to get some rest.

"Don't go to sleep on me now, Van."

"Huh? What? Oh, Carl. I wasn't going to sleep."

"I asked for a sponge."

"Right here."

"Clamp that bleeder?"

"Sure thing."

"Why don't you get started on the spleen while I'm down here in the belly?"

"You mean take it out myself?"

"That's right. I've talked you through enough of them. It's time you did one on your own."

"Got a question for you, Van."

"Huh?"

"What day is it, Van?"

"Wednesday. No, Carl, wait. Maybe Thursday."

"Day or night?"

"I think day. Last time I was out in the ER, I thought I saw light through the doors."

"How's the situation out there?"

"Maybe a dozen left, Carl. Mickie says the choppers have stopped bringing new wounded. The rest are all dead."

"Are you sure it's daytime?"

"Not exactly."

"It's probably night, Van. It feels more like night."

"Maybe it does."

Our final case was a pale soldier whose entire belly was blown open. His guts were hanging out and had been held in place by blood-soaked bandages. He was a kid, a boy who didn't look old enough to shave. His face was as smooth as a baby's bottom, and he had a collection of bright red freckles that stood in defiant contrast to his gray white complexion. He had fallen on a V.C. mine. I noticed that his chart said he had been in an area that was classified. I asked Carl about it.

"The kid's unit was over the fence," Carl answered.

"Over the fence?"

"Sure, Cambodia."

"We don't have any soldiers in Cambodia."

"We don't? Who told you that?"

"The government. The newspapers back home."

"Don't believe everything you read and don't believe anything the government tells you."

While I got the soldier prepped and the anesthetist put him under, Carl grabbed a cup of coffee to help him stay awake. When he returned, he looked totally drained. He could barely walk a straight line. I wondered if he would be able to handle another case without sleep. I helped him into a new pair of gloves and he stared blankly at the belly that had been destroyed beyond recognition. "What am I supposed to do with this?" he said dejectedly. After a half minute of hesitation, he started to work in his quick, methodical way, clamping off every bleeder he could locate while I suctioned the blood from the wounded soldier. The boy was losing it as fast as I could suction him out. We had four IVs pumping blood into him. Slowly, the belly started looking better as Carl removed frags and pieced organs back together again. The work that Carl was doing would have been difficult for any surgeon; it was especially tough for one who hadn't slept for at least three days.

It seemed like we were in that belly for hours. As we worked, we could hear the other surgical teams finishing their final cases and leaving the OR one by one, to return to their hooches and a long-awaited sleep. Everyone was so exhausted that the good-byes were barely audible mumbles. Eventually, we were the last ones. We were almost finished when suddenly the soldier went into cardiac arrest. Carl and the anesthetist worked feverishly to resuscitate him. The kid came back for a minute and then arrested again. They pulled him out of it once more. He arrested a third time. Carl frantically tried to put life into this dying boy.

"I've got no readings," the anesthetist said. "Give it up, Carl."

"Fuck off," Carl said. He cut into the chest to do open heart massage. It was a last-ditch effort that rarely was successful.

"Still nothing, Carl. He's had it."

"Shut up and keep working!"

"Carl, he's dead!"

"Then I'll bring the fucker back!"

"Carl!"

He finally stopped trying to resuscitate the soldier, put his hands on the table, leaned forward and shook his head. "I'm tired," Carl said.

He walked out of the OR and back to the office to do the report. After the anesthetist left and a corpsman removed the body, I started to clean the room so it would be ready if another case should come. It was the first time that I had really noticed the mess. Three days' worth of debris was on the floor. Half-empty instrument trays were scattered around the OR. Almost every inch of concrete was covered with blood. Stained sheets lay in one corner. As I was cleaning the operating table, Marcia Coleman, a first lieutenant and the head nurse on nights, came into the room. "You look wiped out, Van," she said. "Go to bed. We have other people who can clean up."

"It's my responsibility. I'll take care of it."

I started wiping blood off the crash cart, but after a few minutes, I told myself it was hopeless. So I went to work cleaning the other equipment. The job seemed overwhelming. Everything was covered with blood. It would take me at least eight hours to do it right. I tried to wash the walls, but I got discouraged there, too. Finally, I just gave up. I walked back to the office. "You were right, Marcia," I said. "I can't do it anymore."

I went into the women's changing room and stripped off my bloody scrubs. My fatigue pants and T-shirt underneath were also covered with blood. There was blood all over my body, but I was too tired to wash it off. I lifted my fatigue shirt from a nail on the wall and put it on, leaving it unbuttoned over my bloody T-shirt. As I walked out of the room, my boots left a trail of blood. Carl was walking out of the men's changing room when I passed it and he was also covered with blood. We walked outside together. It was night.

"You're good help, Lynda," he said. It was one of the highest compliments a surgeon could pay a nurse. As we walked through the darkness toward the hooches I could hear the sound of small arms fire and helicopters in the distance. How much longer would it be before they sent us more broken bodies? An hour? Two? I shuddered at the thought.

Carl put his arm on my shoulder in a gesture of comradeship. "I've thought of little but sleep during the past seventy-two hours," he said. "And now I'm too tired to sleep."

"I know how you feel," I replied.

"You do," he said, looking at me thoughtfully. "Can I buy you a drink?"

"Yeah. I need it."

We went back to his room and he played quiet music on

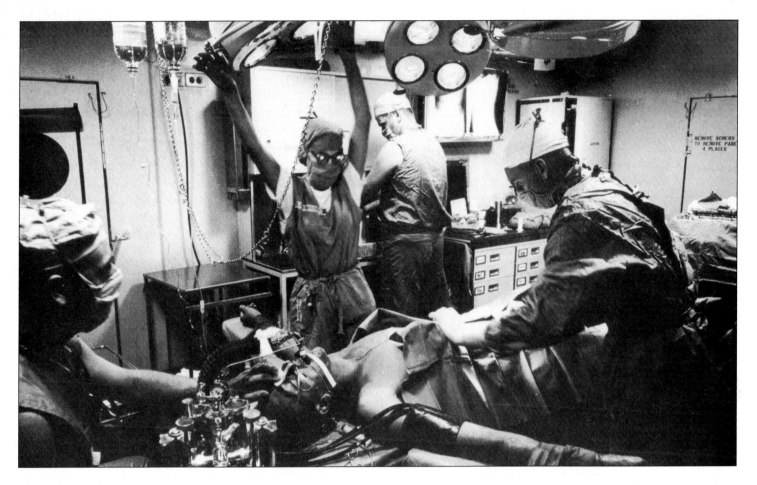

his stereo while we both drank Scotch. We sat cross-legged on the floor, using a packing box as a coffee table. Carl spoke slowly about our war, too tired to reach back in history for his usual colorful quotes. I talked about how I had felt watching the last boy die and how hard it was to put aside the parts of me that wanted to cry for all the dead soldiers.

"You'll learn how," he said. "Or you won't survive this year."

Sometimes we didn't talk with each other as much as we talked at each other, neither of us listening to what the other was saying, each lost in a world of our own. We were both trying to sound philosophical about the death surrounding us, and, for a while, we succeeded. But after too much talking and too much Scotch, I began to shake. In spite of my attempts to hold back the tears, they came. He touched my hand and then moved next to me, wrapping his arms around me and running his fingers through my hair while I sobbed. Finally, his body began to shake and he cried with me.

"Why do they have to die, Carl?"

"Who knows?"

"I don't understand."

"Nobody does," he said.

"But there's got to be a reason."

He grabbed my shoulders and looked into my eyes. "I've had my fill of this war, Van," he said. "I need someone to hold me. It's the only thing that makes any sense."

Surrounded by sophisticated medical machinery, doctors and nurses in Vietnam try to save a wounded soldier.

"I need it, too."

Carl and I didn't make love that night. We slept together in his bed, two bodies covered with the blood of hundreds of young boys, holding tightly to whatever island of sanity we could find. But we also knew we would soon be lovers. And when that time came, it would have nothing to do with his wife and two kids and the house in the country. We were just tired and lonely and sick to death of trying to fix the mutilated bodies of young boys.

Van Devanter also recalled a casualty she treated just before her "hump day":

It was a few days before my hump day, the exact middle of my tour when I would be "over the hump." I was lost in a heavy sleep under my bed when the phone started ringing. The sound was more impossible to ignore than the rockets that had driven me there a couple of hours before. Still half asleep, I listened to the words: "More casualties, Van. We need you in surgery."

By the time I arrived in the operating room, I was alert, with my senses at their peak. I changed immediately to scrub clothes and reported to the head nurse for my assignment. Her short red hair was wild, the front of her scrub dress blood-stained. A mask dangled from her neck.

"There's a bad one in the neuro room," she said. "I need you to pump blood in there."

The neuro room was one of the places I usually tried to avoid. Head wounds were so messy and this one would undoubtedly be bad. But even knowing that, I was totally unprepared for the sight that awaited me when I stepped through the entrance.

Leading to the operating table was the largest trail of blood I had ever seen. I tried to walk quickly through it but slipped. When I regained my balance, my eyes were drawn to the gurney, where several people were transferring the wounded soldier from the green litter to the table. Three intravenous lines ran from bags of blood to his body, one in his jugular vein and one in each arm. The lower portion of his jaw, teeth exposed, dangled from what was left of his face. It dragged along the canvas litter and then swung in the air as he was moved from the gurney to the table. His tongue hung hideously to the side with the rest of the bloody meat and exposed bone. When he was on the table, Mack Shaffner, the facial surgeon, dropped the lower jaw back into place. One of the medics kicked the gurney to the side. It rolled across the room and banged into a wall.

I held my breath to keep from getting sick. For a moment, I was glued to the spot. I had already been through six months of combat casualties, plenty of them gruesome; I thought I had gotten used to it all, but they kept getting worse. I didn't think I could handle this one.

But the shout of the anesthesiologist, Jim Castelano, snapped me out of my trance. "The son of a bitch is drowning in blood," he screamed. "Somebody help me get a fucking airway in him." My training and instincts moved me into action for a tracheotomy. I raced across the room and ripped a prepared instrument pack out of the cabinet, quickly removing the layers of heavy cotton wrap from the tray as I placed it on a Mayo stand and rolled it to him. Scalpels, clamps, sponges, forceps, retractors, scissors, metal trach tube.

A gurgling came from the soldier's throat. Jim's hands were quick. "Don't you dare die, you motherfucker." With two fingers, he felt for the space between the cricoid and thyroid cartilage. "Give me a knife, Van." He made a vertical incision to get through the skin, and a horizontal one between the cartilage. Blood spurted from the neck. Then he pushed the scalpel handle into the space and turned it sideways to open a hole. "Trach tube."

I handed him a crescent-shaped hollow metal tube, which he immediately shoved into the hole. He pulled out the tube guide and more blood shot from the opening. There was an ugly metallic coughing sound as the soldier bucked for breath.

"Suction!"

I brought the suction machine and some clear plastic sterile tubing. Jim forced the suction catheter into the trachea. Immediately, red blood and mucus were sucked through the clear tube. Then it stopped.

"Come on, asshole, cooperate!" Jim pulled the catheter out. A long black string of clotted blood hung from the end. With a sponge he wiped it away before forcing the catheter back into the trachea. More blood and mucus. He retracted the catheter once more. "Breathe, damn you!"

A barely audible metallic sound escaped.

"That's it, soldier, come on." We connected the oxygen line to the trach tube and Jim started using an airbag to regulate the boy's breathing.

I immediately moved into position to help Mack, who was already grabbing instruments from the trach tray to clamp off the largest bleeders in the face and jaw. Meanwhile, the scrub technician set up the sterile field of linens and instruments.

Once the largest bleeders were tied off, Mack put on his gown and gloves and began to repair the damage. Now I fully realized what the head nurse meant when she told me I was needed to pump blood: The soldier was bleeding so fast that three IV lines were not enough.

"No blood pressure," Jim yelled. "Keep that blood pumping and get another IV into him."

I replaced the empty hanging blood bags with new ones and then started a fourth line in his left leg.

"The stethoscope is broken. Van, get me another one."

"Get the crash cart, Van, in case he arrests."

"Who stole my goddamned tape?"

"Van, more towels for his head."

In the middle of the confusion, the neurosurgeon who had replaced Bubba came into the room. He looked at the soldier on the table and shook his head. His face was red. "Who the fuck woke me up for this gork?"

"The brain doesn't look too damaged," Mack answered.

"You're wasting your time."

"We can fix him," Mack insisted. "Just give me a chance."

"Bullshit," the neuro guy answered. "That sucker's going to die and there's not a fucking thing you can do." He stormed out of the room.

Mack yelled after him. "We're going to need your help as soon as we stop the bleeding."

"You call me when you're ready," the neurosurgeon said, "and not a minute before." It was a moment when we all sorely missed Bubba. If he had been here, he would have stayed with us through the night to offer any possible assistance in pulling the soldier through. Unfortunately, not all neurosurgeons were as helpful.

When the circulating nurse arrived, my sole job became pumping blood, while Mack fought against the odds. After a while, I turned it into a routine: Start at the neck, take down the empty bag of blood, slip a new one into the pressure cuff, pump up the cuff, rehang it, and check the temperature in the blood warmer. Then go to the left arm and repeat the process. Next the left leg and finally the right arm. Then start back at the neck and repeat the entire sequence. It took about five minutes to complete the steps at each site, about twenty minutes to make a round of him.

As Mack and the scrub tech clamped and cauterized the blood vessels, little puffs of smoke rose from what was once the soldier's face. The smell of burning flesh filled the room.

Following every second or third time around the soldier, I changed the IV tubing because the blood filters were getting thick with clots. Since we only had two blood warmers, I had to run the other lines through buckets of warm water to raise the temperature. When the buckets started to cool, I changed the water. It was all just another simple job where I could turn off my mind and try to forget that we were working on a person.

But this one was different. The young soldier wasn't about to let me forget.

During one of my circuits around the table, I accidentally kicked his clothes to the side. A snapshot fell from the torn pocket of his fatigue shirt. The picture was of a young couple—him and his girlfriend, I guessed—standing on the lawn in front of a two-story house, perhaps belonging to her parents. Straight, blond, and tall, he wore the tuxedo with a mixture of pride and discomfort, the look of a boy who was going to finish the night with his black tie in his pocket, his shirt open at the neck, and his cummerbund lying on the floor next to the seat. She, too, was tall, and her long brown hair was mostly on top of her head, with a few well-placed curls hanging down in front of her ears. A corsage of gardenias was on her wrist. Her long pastel gown looked like something she had already worn as a bridesmaid in a cousin's wedding, and it fit her in a way that showed she was quickly developing from a girl into a woman. But the thing that made the picture special was how they were looking at each other.

I could see, in their faces, the love he felt for her, and she for him, a first love that had evolved from hours of walking together and talking about dreams, from passing notes to each other in history class, from riding together in his car with her sitting in the middle of the front seat so they could be closer.

On the back of the picture was writing, the ink partly blurred from sweat: "Gene and Katie, May 1968."

I had to fight the tears as I looked from the picture to the helpless boy on the table, now a mass of blood vessels and skin, so macerated that nothing could hold them together. *Gene and Katie, May 1968*. I had always held the notion that, given enough time, anything could be stopped from bleeding. If you kept at it, eventually you would get every last vessel. I was about to learn a hard lesson.

I pumped 120 units of blood into that young man, yet as fast as I pumped it in, he pumped it out. After hours of work, Mack realized that it was futile. The boy had received so much bank blood that it would no longer clot. Now, he was oozing from everywhere. Slowly, Mack wrapped the boy's head in layers of pressure dressings and sent him to post-op ICU to die.

Gene and Katie, May 1968. While I cleaned up the room I kept telling myself that a miracle could happen. He could stop bleeding. He could be all right. Nothing was impossible. *Please, God, help him.* I moved through the room as if in a daze, picking up blood-soaked linens, putting them into a hamper, trying to keep myself busy. Then I saw the photograph again. It was still on top of the torn, bloody fatigue shirt. A few drops of blood were beaded on the edge of the print. I wiped them off and stared.

This wasn't merely another casualty, another piece of meat to throw on the table and try to sew back together again. He had been real. *Gene.* Someone who had gone to the prom in 1968 with his girlfriend, *Katie.* He was a person who could love and think and plan and dream. Now he was lost to himself, to her, and to their future.

When I finished making the room ready for the next head injury—the next young boy—I walked to post-op to see Gene. His bandages had become saturated with blood several times over and the nurses had reinforced them with more rolls of gauze, mostly to cover the mess. Now, his head seemed grotesquely large under the swath of white. The red stains were again seeping through. I held his hand and asked if he was in pain. In answer he squeezed my hand weakly. I asked him if he wanted some pain medication, and he squeezed my hand again. All the ICU patients had morphine ordered for pain, and I asked one of the nurses to give Gene ten milligrams intravenously, knowing that, while it would relieve his pain, it would also make him die faster. I didn't care at that point; I just wanted him to slip away quickly and easily.

The drug went to work immediately. As his respiration slowed and his grip became weaker, I imagined how it would be back in his hometown. Some nameless sergeant would drive an Army-green sedan to the house where Gene's parents lived. The sergeant would stand erect in his dress uniform, with his gold buttons glinting in the morning sun and bright ribbons over his left breast pocket. Perhaps a neighbor would see him walking past a tree in the front yard, one that Gene used to climb before the war; perhaps a little boy would ride his bicycle along the sidewalk and stop near the house to watch the impressive stranger stride confidently up the stairs and to the door. And when the mother and father answered the knock, no one would have to say a word. They would both know what had happened from the look on the sergeant's face.

And Katie? She would probably find out over the phone.

I ran my finger along the edge of the picture before putting it into the envelope with his other possessions. Then I walked outside, sat on the grassy hill next to post-op, and put my head in my hands.

I wouldn't cry, I told myself. I had to be tough.

But I knew a profound change had already come over me. With the death of Gene, and with the deaths of so many others, I had lost an important part of myself. The Lynda I had known before the war was gone forever.

Dr. King's Conscience

Civil rights leader Dr. Martin Luther King, Jr., faced a difficult choice over the war in Vietnam. His personal philosophy of nonviolence and his dismay over the war's drain on domestic poverty and social programs had caused him to speak out against the war as early as 1965. As he did so, however, he faced charges of "Communist sympathizer" from his enemies and worries from other black leaders that he was jeopardizing the civil rights movement. On April 4, 1967, he answered both groups in a sermon delivered at New York's Riverside Church.

Over the past two years, as I have moved to break the betrayal of my own silences and to speak from the burnings of my own heart, as I have called for radical departures from the destruction of Vietnam, many persons have questioned me about the wisdom of my path. At the heart of their concerns this query has often loomed large and loud: Why are *you* speaking about the war, Dr. King? Why are *you* joining the voices of dissent? Peace and civil rights don't mix, they say. Aren't you hurting the cause of your people, they ask. And when I hear them, though I often understand the source of their concern, I am nevertheless greatly saddened, for such questions mean that the inquirers have not really known me, my commitment or my calling. Indeed, their questions suggest that they do not know the world in which they live.

In the light of such tragic misunderstanding, I deem it of signal importance to try to state clearly why I believe that the path from Dexter Avenue Baptist Church—the church in Montgomery, Alabama, where I began my pastorage—leads clearly to this sanctuary tonight.

I come to this platform to make a passionate plea to my beloved nation. This speech is not addressed to Hanoi or to the National Liberation Front. It is not addressed to China or to Russia.

Nor is it an attempt to overlook the ambiguity of the total situation and the need for a collective solution to the tragedy of Vietnam. Neither is it an attempt to make North Vietnam or the National Liberation Front paragons of virtue, nor to overlook the role they can play in a successful resolution of the problem. While they both may have justifiable reasons to be suspicious of the good faith of the United States, life and history give eloquent testimony to the fact that conflicts are never resolved without trustful give and take on both sides.

Tonight, however, I wish not to speak with Hanoi and the NLF, but rather to my fellow Americans who, with me, bear the greatest responsibility in ending a conflict that has exacted a heavy price on both continents.

Since I am a preacher by trade, I suppose it is not surprising that I have seven major reasons for bringing Vietnam into the field of my moral vision. There is at the outset a very obvious and almost facile connection between the war in Vietnam and the struggle I, and others, have been waging in America. A few years ago there was a shining moment in that struggle. It seemed as if there was a real promise of hope for the poor—both black and white—through the Poverty Program. Then came the build-up in Vietnam, and I watched the program broken and eviscerated as if it were some idle political plaything of a society gone mad on war, and I knew that America would never invest the necessary funds or energies in rehabilitation of its poor so long as Vietnam continued to draw men and skills and money like some demonic, destructive suction tube. So I was increasingly compelled to see the war as an enemy of the poor and to attack it as such.

Perhaps the more tragic recognition of reality took place when it became clear to me that the war was doing far more than devastating the hopes of the poor at home. It was sending their sons and their brothers and their husbands to fight and to die in extraordinarily high proportions relative to the rest of the population. We were taking the young black men who had been crippled by our society and sending them 8000 miles away to guarantee liberties in Southeast Asia which they had not found in Southwest Georgia and

East Harlem. So we have been repeatedly faced with the cruel irony of watching Negro and white boys on TV screens as they kill and die together for a nation that has been unable to seat them together in the same schools. So we watch them in brutal solidarity burning the huts of a poor village, but we realize that they would never live on the same block in Detroit. I could not be silent in the face of such cruel manipulation of the poor.

My third reason grows out of my experience in the ghettos of the North over the last three years—especially the last three summers. As I have walked among the desperate, rejected and angry young men, I have told them that Molotov cocktails and rifles would not solve their problems. I have tried to offer them my deepest compassion while maintaining my conviction that social change comes most meaningfully through non-violent action. But, they asked, what about Vietnam? They asked if our own nation wasn't using massive doses of violence to solve its problems, to bring about the changes it wanted. Their questions hit home, and I knew that I could never again raise my voice against the violence of the oppressed in the ghettos without having first spoken clearly to the greatest purveyor of violence in the world today—my own government.

For those who ask the question, "Aren't you a Civil Rights leader?" and thereby mean to exclude me from the movement for peace, I have this further answer. In 1957 when a group of us formed the Southern Christian Leadership Conference, we chose as our motto: "To save the soul of America." We were convinced that we could not limit our vision to certain rights for black people, but instead affirmed the conviction that America would never be free or saved from itself unless the descendants of its slaves were loosed from the shackles they still wear.

Now, it should be incandescently clear that no one who has any concern for the integrity and life of America today can ignore the present war. If America's soul becomes totally poisoned, part of the autopsy must read "Vietnam." It can never be saved so long as it destroys the deepest hopes of men the world over. . . .

And as I ponder the madness of Vietnam, my mind goes constantly to the people of that peninsula. . . . They watch as we poison their water, as we kill a million acres of their crops. They must weep as the bulldozers destroy their precious trees. They wander into the hospitals, with at least 20 casualties from American firepower for each Viet Cong-inflicted injury. So far we may have killed a million of them—mostly children.

What do the peasants think as we ally ourselves with the landlords and as we refuse to put any action into our many words concerning land reform? What do they think as we test out our latest weapons on them, just as the Germans tested out new medicine and new tortures in the concentration camps of Europe? Where are the roots of the independent Vietnam we claim to be building?

Now there is little left to build on—save bitterness. Soon the only solid physical foundations remaining will be found at our military bases and in the concrete of the concentration camps we call "fortified hamlets." The peasants may well wonder if we plan to build our new Vietnam on such grounds as these. Could we blame them for such thoughts? We must speak for them and raise the questions they cannot raise. These too are our brothers. . . .

Somehow this madness must cease. I speak as a child of God and brother to the suffering poor of Vietnam and the poor of America who are paying the double price of smashed hopes at home and death and corruption in Vietnam. I speak as a citizen of the world, for the world as it stands aghast at the path we have taken. I speak as an American to the leaders of my own nation. The great initiative in this war is ours. The initiative to stop must be ours. . . .

We must move past indecision to action. We must find new ways to speak for peace in Vietnam and justice throughout the developing world—a world that borders on our doors. If we do not act we shall surely be dragged down the long, dark and shameful corridors of time reserved for those who possess power without compassion, might without morality, and strength without sight.

Now let us begin. Now let us re-dedicate ourselves to the long and bitter—but beautiful—struggle for a new world. This is the calling of the sons of God, and our brothers wait eagerly for our response. Shall we say the odds are too great? Shall we tell them the struggle is too hard? Will our message be that the forces of American life militate against their arrival as full men, and we send our deepest regrets? Or will there be another message, of longing, of hope, of solidarity with their yearnings, of commitment to their cause, whatever the cost? The choice is ours, and though we might prefer it otherwise we *must* choose in this crucial moment of human history.

I Don't Want to Go Home Alone

from *365 Days*
by Ronald Glasser

Beginning in September 1968 Dr. Ronald Glasser served as a pediatrician in the American military hospital in Zama, Japan. There he collected stories from other doctors and from the young wounded men who poured in from Vietnam. The following story was based on a real incident:

Edwards picked up the stethoscope from his desk. "Look," he said, "you can say what you want about the Army and its problems, but I learned this much from going home: the Army treats you better dead than alive. I know," he added quickly to keep the Captain from talking. "I know, it was my fault. I shouldn't have got involved with taking the body back. But I did."

"It's coming," the corpsman said, stepping away from the window.

Edwards stuffed the stethoscope into his back pocket. "OK. Tell the ward master. How many did they say?"

The Captain put his half-finished cup of coffee on the desk. "One VSI and one SI."

Edwards nodded and then, as if he'd just remembered something, checked his watch against the clock over the door.

"The States are sixteen hours behind us," the Captain offered.

"In time, maybe." Edwards pulled his lab coat off the rack. "Better fill the whirlpools. I'll be down at the landing pad."

In the dimly lit corridor he looked again at his watch. Sixteen hours. It would be eighteen for Nam. What difference did it make, eighteen or a million? He pushed open the double doors to the burn unit.

The huge overhead lights were off, leaving only the night lights to flicker feebly across the shiny tiled floor. He walked quietly down the center aisle of the ward, his footsteps echoing lightly ahead of him. The beds lining the wall were barely visible, the patients no more than lumps against the frames. From the far end of the ward came the faint mechanical hissing of a respirator. He stopped a moment near one of the steel arched Stryker frames to listen. The machine's slow, regular rhythm was almost soothing. How many times he'd heard it before. Someone had said he'd signed more death certificates than any other doctor in Japan. Probably right, he thought, continuing on his way. At Kishine, the respirator was the sound of death, not life; in all his time there, he could not think of one patient who had got off the thing.

"Hi, Doc."

"Oh, Crowley," Edwards said, coming to a halt near the little cubicle at the back of the ward. "Sorry, I didn't see you in the dark."

The side curtain had been partially pulled. Stretched out on the bed, barely lit by the dials of the respirator, was a shadowy form.

"How's he doing, Sergeant?" Edwards asked the ward

master, who was standing at attention by the machine that was slowly, insistently hissing air into and out of the charred body.

"Not too good, sir."

"What's his temperature?"

"Hundred and five. It was a hundred and seven before we put him on the cooling blanket."

"Blood cultures growing out anything?"

"Yes, sir; the lab called back tonight—Pseudomonas pseudomallei. Major Johnson put him on IV chloromycetin and tetracycline."

Edwards bent over to look more closely at the restrained body spread-eagled across the frame. The air smelled sweet, like a dying orchard. "When did he come in?" he asked, peering at the grotesquely crusted body. Even the tips of his toes and fingers were charred and oozing; nothing had been spared.

"Four days after you left. Seventy percent second-degree and 15 percent third. At least Major Johnson thought it was second-degree, but it's beginning to look like it's all third."

Edwards examined the crust about the boy's swollen neck and chest. It had a sick metallic green cast to it. "When did he go sour?"

"He was doing fine until this morning. We had to give him Demerol every time he went into the whirlpool, but he's very hard-core. Nice kid. Then yesterday, he became confused and agitated. On the night shift his temp spiked, and he became unconscious. The surgeons trached him today, and Dr. Johnson put him on the respirator this evening."

Edwards sighed and stepped back from the bed. "How old?"

"What?"

"How old was he?"

Surprised, Crowley reached for the chart.

"Never mind," Edwards said. "Forget it."

"Sir."

"Yes?"

"You're sort of short now, aren't you?"

"Five months."

"That's not long."

"No," Edwards said absently, "no, it's not long."

"The evacs should be in soon."

"Yeah, that's where I'm going. I'll check on him later."

"No need, sir, you'll have your hands full. I'll have you called if anything changes."

As he walked away, Edwards could hear Crowley drawing the curtains closed behind him. The stairwell was empty, and he walked slowly down to the first floor and out onto the concrete walkway.

It was summer outside, and the night was as warm as indoors. He cut across the empty, silent field separating the hospital's squat buildings from the helipad, where the red lights of the landing strip flickered softly in the misty dark. Far away he heard the muffled, dull thudding of the chopper whopping its way through the heavy air, and suddenly he felt alone and desperately tired.

"Gentlemen: You have been assembled here at Yokota Air Base to escort these bodies home to the continental United States. Each body in its casket is to have, at all times, a body escort. Those caskets on the plane that do not at the present time have an escort will have them assigned at Oakland. Whatever the case, no casket will be allowed to leave the Oakland area without a proper escort. Escort duty is a privilege as well as an honor. An effort has been made to find an escort whose personal involvement with the deceased or presence with the family of the deceased will be of comfort and aid. Your mission as a body escort is as follows: to make sure that the body is afforded, at all times, the respect due a fallen soldier of the United States Army. Specifically it is as follows: 1) To check the tags on the caskets at every point of departure. 2) To insist, if the tags indicate the remains as non-viewable, that the relatives not view the body. Remember that non-viewable means exactly that—non-viewable. . . ."

Grimly, with the chopper coming nearer—louder—Edwards walked up a slight rise, past a small, dimly lit sign:

KISHINE BARRACKS
109th UNITED STATES ARMY HOSPITAL
United States Army, Japan
Burn Unit

"Coastal Airlines loads the bodies on an angle. Be sure that if the body you are escorting is being carried by Coastal Airlines that the caskets are loaded head down: this will keep the embalming fluid in the upper body. If the body is loaded incorrectly, namely, feet down, the embalming fluid will accumulate in the feet and the body may, under appropriate atmospheric conditions, begin to decompose."

By the time he reached the evac area, the floodlights were on and the chopper had landed. Coming in from the dark around the back of the evac building Edwards was dazzled by the sudden lights. The Huey, low and glistening, its rotors still whirling, sat like a toy exactly in the middle of the arc lights. Its crew chief and co-pilot were already in the open hatchway unstrapping the litters from their carrying hooks. Edwards watched unseen while the corpsmen hurried out to the chopper to off-load the patients. The choppers usually came in about ten in the morning, but when a bad burn was evac'ed to Japan, they were flown in the same night. Burns are a very special kind of wound, and no physician anywhere wants the responsibility of caring for them, not even for a little while. For openers, burns look bad and the patients die.

"Each of the next of kin as listed in the deceased 201 file

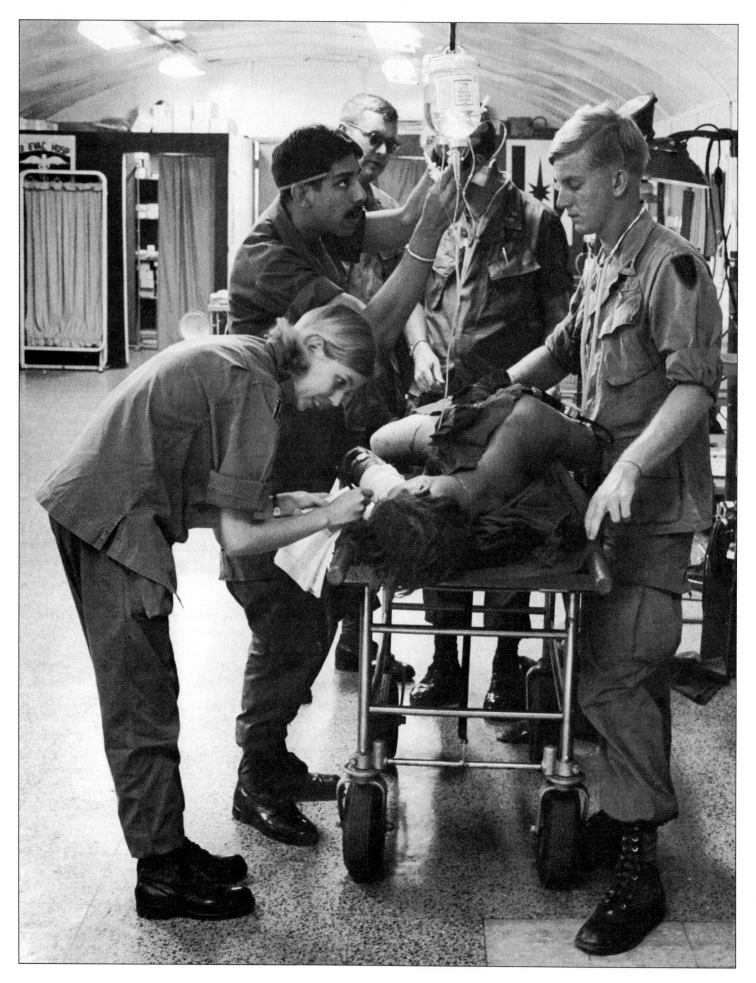

has already been visited by a survivor assistance officer. This was done in person by an officer in uniform from the nearest Army unit. Every effort is made to pick an officer from a similar racial and economic background. These families have already been convinced of the death by either the presentation of personal effects or the relating of an eye-witness report from a member of the deceased's unit. You need not convince the deceased's relatives. The point to remember is that the survivor assistance officer has been there before you and the next of kin have already accepted the death."

He was standing in the reflected glare of the landing lights, with the windy noise of the chopper rushing past him.

"Sir. Sir?" One of the corpsmen was shouting above the whining of the motor. "One of 'em's got a head wound, the other is just burned."

"Call the neurosurgeon," Edwards shouted back. He gave the empty chopper one more look and then followed the medic into the air evac area. By the time he reached the building, the medics had placed the two litters on the movable stretcher racks and one of them, working on the patient nearest the door, was already setting up an IV.

"He's OK, Major," the air-evac Sergeant said. "The head injury's over there."

"One hundred and seventy," the corpsman said as Edwards approached the litter. The wounded soldier, his head wrapped, was lying unconscious on his back, with the blood pressure cuff still wrapped around his arm.

"Expecting trouble, Tom?"

"Well, sir, I figured I'd leave the cuff on. He don't look too good."

"I'll give you that," Edwards said. He began to unwrap the gauze from around the patient's head. The boy was breathing; other than that, he looked dead. Edwards pinched his neck, but there was no response. As he unwound the gauze it became wet and then blood-soaked. Now he was down to the four-by-four surgical pads, and finally to the wound itself. Carefully he lifted up the last pack. Despite himself, he closed his eyes.

"He's 47-percent burned," the Sergeant said, reading the cover sheet of the soldier's medical record. "Took an AK round a little in front of the right eye. Removed the right eye, traversed the left orbit, removing the left eye, and came out near the left temple, apparently blowing out the left side of his head."

"Don't worry. I'll be careful, Bob. Honest, I'll be careful . . ."

"Send him to neurosurgery," Edwards said. "We'll treat his burns up there."

Left. *Staff at the 91st Evacuation Hospital in Chu Lai, South Vietnam, treat a wounded soldier.*

"An IV?"

"No, just send him up."

He walked across to the other wounded trooper. The corpsman had just got the IV started.

"Sorry it took so long, sir," he said. "Hard to find a vein."

The boy was awake, nervously looking at the needle the corpsman had stuck into the back of his hand.

"Hi," Edwards said. "How do you feel?"

The soldier looked up at him apprehensively. The skin on his face had been seared red and all his hair and eyebrows and lashes had been burned away.

"I know you're nervous," Edwards said soothingly. "Just try to relax. I'm the chief of the burn unit. I'll be your doctor for a while until you get better." As he pulled back the blanket the soldier grimaced. "Sorry," he said, lifting the cover more carefully.

The burns, red and raw, ran the whole charred length of the boy's body. Unconsciously Edwards began adding up the percentages of burned area, tallying them in his mind. He suddenly realized what he was doing and, for a moment, as he stood there staring at the burns, he looked stricken. "How did it happen?" he asked gently, carefully dropping back the covers.

"I . . . I was carrying detonators . . ."

"Dear Bob: We are fighting very hard now. I haven't written to Mom and Dad about it. I don't want to worry them. But we are getting hit and badly. I'm the only first lieutenant in the company who hasn't been hit yet. And last week I lost two RTO's. They were standing right next to me. It gets a bit spooky. I know what you said about my flack vest, but you haven't been here and you just don't know how hot it can get. On the move, it's just too damn heavy. You can't carry a 60-pound rucksack in 110-degree heat and an 11-pound flack vest. I make the point wear his, but then someone else carries his gear. It's like your complaint about patients demanding penicillin—sometimes you just can't use it. It's the same with a flack vest. Besides, it wouldn't stop a round, and that's what we've been getting lately. But I'll wear it when I can. By the way, you're beginning to sound like Mom. About what's been happening lately. I'm not complaining, don't get the wrong idea. There is, honestly, something very positive about being over here. I can see it in myself and my men. Not the war itself, God knows that's hopeless enough, but what happens to you because of it. I'll never be the same again. I can feel myself growing. Unfortunately you only see one end of it. That's a bit sad, because there are other endings and even middles. A lot of guys get out of here OK, and despite what they say, they're better for it. I can see it in myself. I'm getting older over here in a way that I could never do at home or maybe anywhere. For the first time in my life, everything seems to count. All the fuzziness is gone, all the foolishness. I can't believe the things that used to bother me, or even that I thought were important.

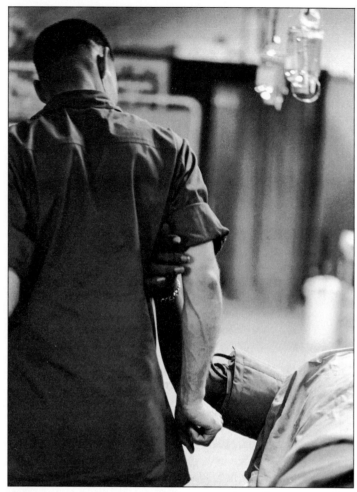

A doctor monitors the blood pressure of an American soldier being treated in Chu Lai.

You really see yourself over here. It works on you, grinds you down, makes you better. Got to go: Thanks for the R and R. Say Hi to all the guys in the burn unit."

"What?" Edwards asked.

"Detonators. I must have taken a round in my rucksack. They just blew up, and then I was on fire. Tried to tear my gear off, but my hands . . . "

"It's all right," Edwards said. The evac Sergeant handed him the patient's medical jacket. Quickly turning the pages, he read: "Eighty percent second-degree and third degree. Debrided under general anesthesia at the 60 evac, Chu Ci. Six liter plasmonate . . . catheterized . . . furacin and sterile dressings . . . Demerol . . . 64-mg. q three hours." He looked at the cover sheet. "David Jensen, MOS B11; 1/30 E-2, 4th Division, 20 years old."

"Twenty years old," he thought, handing back the chart. "Grant's age."

"David," he said wearily.

"Yes, sir?"

"I'm going to have the corpsman take you to the ward."

"Yes, sir."

"The first thing we're going to do is put you in a whirlpool bath to soak off your bandages and remove what

dead skin we can. It's going to hurt."

"Yes, sir," David said, his voice wavering.

"If it hurts, just let us know. Is that understood?"

"Yes, sir."

"You don't have to call me sir."

"Yes, sir; thank you, sir."

"Take him to C-4," Edwards said to the corpsman. "Tell Sergeant Dorsey I'll be right there. And David . . . "

"Yes, sir."

"Burns look and feel a lot worse than they are. You're going to get better."

"Yes, sir."

Edwards watched the corpsman wheel the boy out of the evac area and then left the area himself to go to the neurosurgery ward. It was a long walk. Like all Army hospitals, Kishine is fantastically spread out, its buildings and wards acres apart so that no one shell or bomb can get it all. By the time he got to the ward, the neurosurgeon was already in the treatment room. The patient, partially hidden by the nurse and doctor, was lying naked on the treatment table. There were blood-soaked clothes and bandages all over the floor. Cramer turned his head for a moment, looked at Edwards, and went back to work.

"His frontal lobe is torn up," Cramer said. "I'm going to have to take him up to the operating room and save what I can. What do you think about his burns?"

Looking over Cramer's shoulder Edwards saw that the surgeon's fingers were deep inside the half shell of the boy's skull. "Don't worry about the burns," he said, turning to leave.

"Oh, Edwards," Cramer said as he reached the door. "I know how close you two'd become. I'm sorry."

"Regardless of the branch of service: The emblem of the Infantry, crossed rifles, will be carried on every coffin. The deceased, where the remains are viewable, will be buried in full military uniform. The emblems on his uniform will be that of the service to which he was attached at the time of his death."

He walked down the corridor to the elevator. Leaning wearily against the wall, he pressed the button, and without looking, stepped in even as the door was opening, almost colliding with one of the patients. "Sorry," he said, moving over to the other side of the elevator. The patient, his bathrobe slung over his good shoulder—the other was wrapped in a plaster cast—smiled politely and was about to look away when he saw the doctor's name plate on his uniform.

"Excuse me, sir."

"Yes?"

"Do you have any relatives in Nam?"

"Yes," Edwards said, "I do."

"First Air Cav?"

"Yes."

"Is his name Grant?"

Edwards nodded as the elevator suddenly slowed to a stop.

"Your brother?" The door opened. "I thought so," the trooper said, obviously pleased. "You sort of look like him."

"Come on," Edwards said pleasantly, holding the door.

"I saw him about three weeks ago. There isn't a better platoon leader in the whole cav. But I can tell you this, they were handing him some shit to do, when I saw him. His unit was on their way to getting their ass whipped."

"Are you sure, Grant? Why don't you go into Tokyo? You only have a few days for your R and R. You might as well have a good time."

"But I want to see what you're doing."

"It's not nice."

"And where do you think I've been?"

He had been surprised at how well Grant had handled himself in the burn unit. He had seen more than one visitor walking through the ward trying desperately to be natural, moving stiffly from bed to bed, smiling and talking as if the boys weren't burned at all. When Grant visited, there were two ghastly 90-percent burns stretched out, blistered and dying on their Stryker frames. Grant had stopped to talk to them and stayed with each much longer than he had to. He was very much at ease. He didn't ignore their wounds, or pretend not to see they were so obviously dying. He simply talked to them, interestedly and honestly, with a concern so palpable that no one could doubt his sincerity. He was one of them and, for a moment, watching his brother sitting by their frames, Edwards felt suddenly very much outside it all. He was very proud of his younger brother.

"I've seen worse, Bob. Really . . . a lot worse."

"Sir?"

"Yes, I know," Edwards said gently. "They did get whipped."

When he got back to the burn unit, he found David in the treatment area, already floating full length in one of the whirlpool baths, his head supported on a padded board to keep it above the waterline, the water gently churning about his burnt body. His IV bottle, hanging from a ceiling hook, was still working. A few of the dressings had already soaked off, and the medic was picking them out of the water. Taking an admissions chart off the wall rack, Edwards sat down on a chair next to the huge tub.

"OK?" he asked.

David, clenching his teeth, nodded.

"Just try to relax. I have a few things to ask you." He quickly went over what had happened, the illnesses that David had had, whether he had taken his CP pills, whether he was on any medicines. While he was taking the history, he carefully, in a pre-printed outline of a man

that was drawn on the admissions sheet, sketched in the areas of the burns and their depth, using red for third degrees and blue for second; he kept filling in until almost the whole figure, front and back, was covered.

"David," he said, "we're going to debride you a bit—take off the dead skin. We are going to have to do it every day, a little bit at a time. That way it won't be as painful." David was looking anxiously at him. "Once you know what's going on, it won't be so bad. We're going to put you into the whirlpool every day, and all the skin that is loose, or loosening, is going to be removed. It has to be done." He hesitated a moment and then went on matter-of-factly. "If we don't take it off, it just stays and decays, forming a place for bacteria to grow and divide, and you'll just get infected. That's what we want to avoid, because if the burns get infected no new skin will form. It's going to hurt, and I'll give you something for the pain when I think you need it."

"Yes, sir."

"I've been doing this a long time, David, and I know when it really hurts and when it doesn't. We're going to have to be doing this for some time and we don't want to make an addict out of you, so we're only going to use the pain medicine when we have to. I know you can do it. There have been a lot of troopers, just like you, through here, and I know you're as fine as they are."

David had been staring up at him the whole time. What was left of his lips were clamped tight against the pain of the water churning against his blistered skin. "Yes, sir," he said, his voice trembling.

"OK, John," Edwards said. David looked nervously from him to the corpsman. Pieces of dead skin were already floating free. The corpsman, kneeling down beside the tub, began picking off those pieces that were still attached but had been loosened. "How long have you been in Nam, David?"

"Five . . . five months," David said, watching the corpsman pick a chunk of skin off his chest. He had to tug to get it off. David grimaced, barely suppressing a groan.

"How do you like the Vietnamese women?" the medic asked.

"Don't know," David said, painfully engrossed in watching the corpsman go after another piece of his skin. "Didn't meet any gooks."

"How come?" the medic asked, scooping a piece of skin out of the water.

"We killed 'em all."

Suddenly David let out a scream, and the scream, echoing off the spotless tile walls, pierced Edwards to his heart. His eyes clenched tight, the boy was fighting valiantly for control. Blood began oozing from the new patch of raw skin on his chest, and Edwards could see the tears rolling down his burned cheeks.

"Where you from, Doc?" the cab driver asked.

"Japan."

"Oh," the cabbie said, pulling away from the curb. *"Thought so, saw the Fuji patch on your sleeve. Nice place, huh?"*

"No," Edwards said.

"I heard that Japan was paradise."

"I work in a burn unit."

"Oh, get many burns over there?"

"There's a war on. Remember?"

"You mean, you get those guys in Japan?"

"Yeah," Edwards said. *"We get those guys . . . "*

"Major, Major?"

Edwards opened his eyes. It was the ward master.

"Excuse me, sir. Those flights back from the States are tough. I'm sure you haven't caught up with the time change. Why don't you take a sleeping pill and get some rest?"

"Think I'll take your advice," Edwards said, closing his clipboard. He wrote a Demerol order for David and then went to his room. As tired as he was, though, he couldn't sleep. Every time he drifted off, he'd see Grant's tag: "Remains, non-viewable." And all that time in the States he thought he could handle it.

He woke up in the morning exhausted, put on his wrinkled uniform, and went to the ward.

Johnson was already in the office. "Hi," he said, turning around from his desk. "You know you didn't have to work today—or yesterday, for that matter."

"I know." Edwards hung up his jacket. "There's really not much else to do."

Both he and Johnson had shared the same office for almost a year now. Johnson had been the plastic surgeon working with the burn unit at Duke University. He had been drafted and assigned to Kishine.

"You want to go on rounds?" Edwards asked.

Johnson pressed the button on the intercom. "Julian, we're gonna start rounds." He pushed himself away from the desk. "Let's go."

"How's the fellow on the respirator?"

"He died this morning," Johnson said, picking up his notes. "I told the corpsman to leave you alone."

They walked down the ward, stopping at each bed. Fifty-percent burns, 80-percent burns, hand burns, half-burned, arm burned, 70-percent burned, third-degree, first-degree, second-degree, Pseudomonas infections, staphylococci infections, split thickness grafts, full thickness grafts, swing flaps, corneal burns, esophageal burns, tracheal burns, contractures, isolated tendon repairs, urinary tract infections, open wounds, closed wounds, furacin dressings; sulfamyelon, penicillin, chloromycetin, actinomycin D, renal failure, congestive heart failure, gram negative shock, steroids, isoprel, epinephrine, full diet, soft diet, liquid diet, hyperalimentation, normal saline, plasmonate, albumin, blood-type A, type O; unmatched,

matched, cross-matched. . . .

"Your grafts are holding up nicely, Harold."

"Sergeant, increase Dermitt's Demerol to q three hours, prn."

"Let me see Denton's temp sheet."

"How's Leon's titers?"

"Robinson, you're doing fine."

"Jergons, I want you to do more P.T. with that hand."

They moved on down the ward. On each bed or posted on the wall above the frames were the patches of the units each patient belonged to: the yellow and black of the 1st Air Cav; the red and blue eagle of the 101st Airborne; the 25th Division, the 9th, the big red one of the 1st and the Americal—even the unconscious patients had their service identification. There was a 1st Air Cav patch over David's frame.

"You worked him up?" Johnson asked, taking David's chart out of the rack.

"Yeah," Edwards said, looking at the Ranger patch that someone had placed below the Cav emblem. "Eighty-percent second or third." Johnson put down the chart, and they moved on.

After rounds, Edwards had the ward master take down all the unit patches. "Sergeant, I don't care what you think about morale. They're out of the war now, and I want those damn playthings off the walls. That's an order. Off the walls."

He went down to the bacteriology lab and then to his office. Johnson had gone to X ray to check on a few films. He sat down at his desk and looked at the two weeks' accumulation of correspondence that had been piled neatly at the corner of his desk. He was reaching for the first letter when the phone rang.

"Major Edwards, this is Captain Eden. There are two generals who will be visiting Kishine today. The Colonel wanted me to make sure you'll be free to take them around."

"What time?" Edwards asked, balancing the phone on his shoulder while he read a letter.

"We're not sure."

"I'm afraid I'll be busy this afternoon. You'd better tell the Commander to take them through Kishine's pride and joy himself." Without waiting for an answer, he hung up.

The intercom was buzzing. "Major, Jensen's in the whirlpool."

"OK, be right there; thanks."

David was already in the tub, being debrided. Edwards knelt down by the side of the tub and checked the burns. At some places, on the thighs and chest, he could see down to the muscle fibers crisscrossing under the burned fat. "David, I'm going to stop your IV," he said, straightening up. "You're going to have to start eating. The ward master told me you didn't touch your breakfast. Hurt?"

Chewing on what remained of his lips, David winced.

"Jessie, why don't you give him twenty-five of Demerol."

"Yes, sir," the corpsman said.

"Why didn't you eat?"

"No one was there to feed me," David said, watching the corpsman open the medicine cabinet and fill the syringe.

"We don't feed you here," Edwards said. "You feed yourself. You've got to start using your hands sometime." He waited while the medic searched for a place to give the injection. "In his arm," he said.

The corpsman found a small, unburnt area near the elbow and plunged the needle into the skin. David, watching him, visibly relaxed. He turned his head on the board and looked at Edwards.

"We can help you grow new skin, stop your infections, graft you—if it comes to that. But it will all be for nothing if you leave here with all your joints tied down by scar tissue. If you don't exercise and keep the scar tissue and new skin over your joints loose and flexible it will tie 'em down like iron. All that new skin and scar that will be forming has a tendency to contract with time. If you don't keep it loose, you'll leave here as much a cripple as if someone had shot off your arms and legs. Your hands aren't that bad, David. We'll start today with them."

"But I can't hold a form."

"We'll put wooden blocks on them, and as you get used to handling one size, we'll make the blocks smaller. Understood?"

"Yes, sir."

"You married, David?" Edwards asked.

"No."

The corpsman, pulling off a piece of skin, left an area red and oozing. David, stretched out and relaxed in the water, his head bobbing a bit, didn't even notice.

"Engaged?"

"Yes, sir."

"Would you like me to write her for you?"

David closed his eyes. "No, sir, I don't think so."

"All right. I'll check on you later."

When he got back to the office he found Johnson working at his desk.

"Coffee?" Johnson asked.

"No, thanks."

"We're getting three more today. Colonel Volpe called. Apparently you said you'd be too busy to take two VIP's around."

"That's right, I'm no goddam press agent. You show 'em around."

That evening, despite the fact that Johnson was on call, Edwards went back to the ward. All the patients had been settled in for the night. The ward master was in the treatment room, cutting adhesive tape into twelve-inch strips.

"What's new, White?"

"Nothing, Doc, really. Same old thing."

"How's Jensen doing?"

White put his scissors back into his pocket. "He's doing all right. We drew two blood cultures on him this evening and sent a titer off for moniliasis. He had some difficulty using the blocks, but he got a few bites down; seems as if the sulfamyelon is bothering him—stinging him. You never know who it's going to bother."

"And the three new ones?"

"They're OK," White said. "Hardly burned at all. Don't even know why they came here."

"It's the Army's idea," Edwards said, and giving him a parting pat, walked out into the unit. David was on a Stryker frame halfway down the ward, lying on his stomach. White sulfamyelon cream was smeared all over his burned back, buttocks, and legs.

"How's it going?"

"Fine, sir."

"The ward master told me that you did all right at supper."

"Yes, sir."

Later that evening, one of David's blood cultures began to grow out Pseudomonas arinosa. The bacteriology lab called the ward, and the ward master called Edwards. He told the ward master to restart David's IV and put him on 200 mg of polymyxin every four hours.

The next morning, after rounds, Johnson got him alone. "About Jensen's polymyxin," he said. "Do you think his kidneys are good enough to handle that big dose?"

"What would you suggest?" Edwards asked.

"You could destroy his kidneys with that much polymyxin."

"I could save him too."

"If he's going to die," Johnson said, "he's going to die. He's 80-percent burned, and his blood culture is already growing out Pseudomonas."

"I know. That's the great thing I learned from my trip back to America. His death is expected. It is expected since there are 80 percent burns, and it is expected that 80 percent will become septic. The whole thing is expected. You're supposed to get burned in Nam; you're supposed to get your legs blown off; you're supposed to get your chopper shot down; you're supposed to get killed. It's just not something that happens. It's expected."

When Edwards came back to the ward, he found David lying on his back, and the corpsman was smearing on the last of the sulfamyelon, spreading it over David's charred stomach as if it were butter.

"This stuff stings, honest, Doc," David said. "It just keeps stinging."

"I know," Edwards said. "It does that sometimes, but it will get better with time. You sort of build up a tolerance to it. The point is that you need it now. It keeps your skin from getting infected and gives the new skin a chance to grow. Believe it or not, sulfamyelon is one of the major breakthroughs in the treatment of burns."

"Can't I have something for the stinging?"

"No, David, I'm sorry."

That evening, down in the hospital bacteriology lab, his second blood culture started growing out another patch of pure Pseudomonas.

When Edwards came to work up the new admissions the next day, he stopped by to see David. Unable to lift his head, he was fitted with prismatic lenses so he could see around him without having to lift his head. Someone had hooked a book rack onto the frame, but there was nothing on it. He was just lying there with the glasses on, staring at the ceiling.

"I asked the therapist for a mirror today," he said before Edwards had a chance to say hello.

"What did she say?"

"She didn't say anything."

"This is not the time for mirrors," Edwards said. "When things start healing up, I'll get you one. Don't worry, David, we've had guys here a lot worse off than you. They all healed. It took a while, but they did."

That afternoon they got in two more burns from Nam. One was from Laos. At least that's what the soldier said; his records read Vietnam.

In the evening, Edwards brought David a book. He found him on his stomach again, and he put the book on the night table next to the frame.

"How does the skin grow back?" David asked, speaking to the floor. The day before he had mentioned that there were sixteen different colors in the floor tiles. "I mean, where's it gonna come from?"

"From you."

"Yeah?" David said. "How?"

Edwards pulled up a chair. "You have enough, you don't really need very much," he explained. "The skin grows back from the areas around the hair follicles; the follicles go down pretty deep, down into the area below the skin. Below the burns the new skin grows out from the lining of these follicles, like grass out of a valley. These linings are like nature's reserves. The new skin just keeps growing out from them, creeping over the burned area, until all these little growing areas come together."

"Why am I going to have to be grafted then?" David asked sullenly.

Edwards sensed the despair in his question. "Sometimes," he said, trying to sound reasonable, "if the burns are too deep, deep enough to destroy the follicles, then there is no skin to grow back, so we have to graft."

"Where are you going to get the skin for that?"

"From your friends, David," Edwards said gently, "from your friends."

The morning culture again grew out Pseudomonas. That afternoon they took David to the operating room and covered his legs and part of his stomach with cadaver skin. When Edwards visited him again that evening, he complained that his head hurt and that the sulfamyelon was stinging even more.

"What will you do when you get home?" Edwards asked. David was sullen. "School, I guess."

"You've got to be more positive than that," Edwards said coaxingly.

"I was positive before I got burned."

"I'm telling you, you're going to be OK."

"I didn't even see it," David said reproachfully. "I was just walking. I wasn't even point. I swear to God, I didn't even hear it. Can you believe that?" he said loudly. "I couldn't even goddamn hear it."

Within three days the cadaver grafts failed, refused to take, and Edwards had to order it pulled off, like the rest of the dying skin. David, lying in the water, saw him as soon as he walked into the treatment room.

"I'm handling it, dammit," he said belligerently. "Just leave me alone, will you? Just goddamn leave me alone."

That evening David ignored his presence.

"I saw you with some letters this afternoon," Edwards said, noting that the whitish scar tissue under David's chin had a pale greenish cast to it. "Nice handwriting. Your girl?"

"No, my family."

"What did they say?"

"It's in the drawer."

Edwards opened the drawer of the nightstand next to the frame. It was a rather bright letter, careful, measuredly written, filled with support and concern. There was a section about Carol, how much she loved David and how happy she was that he was finally out of the fighting.

"Did you answer?" Edwards asked.

"I didn't know how."

"They know you're burned," Edwards refolded the letter. "It seems to me they're holding up quite well. The least you could do is help them out."

David slowly turned his head. His eyes, hollow holes, stared coldly and defiantly at Edwards. "I've been throwing up all day. I can't keep anything down."

"Yes," Edwards said calmly, putting the letter back in the drawer. "I know."

"I'm not going to make it, am I? No, no, don't interrupt. I know I'm not. That stuff you keep putting into my IV bottle—the only other guys who get it are the ones on respirators. I know," he said, almost triumphantly. "I've checked on the way to the whirlpool. I know." It was all there in his eyes—the pain, the suffering, the loss of belief.

It caught Edwards off guard. "I told you about the pain, didn't I?" he said angrily. "Have I bull-shitted you yet? Look, if you were going to die, I'd let you know. Right? I'd give you the chance to tie things up, understand?" A certain distance entered David's stare, a vague confusion that was more pathetic than his glaring hopelessness.

Edwards got up. "Now, dammit," he said, "I want you to think of an answer to that letter. I'll be back in the morning and I want an answer. Is that clear?"

Depressed and angry, he left the ward. Outside he

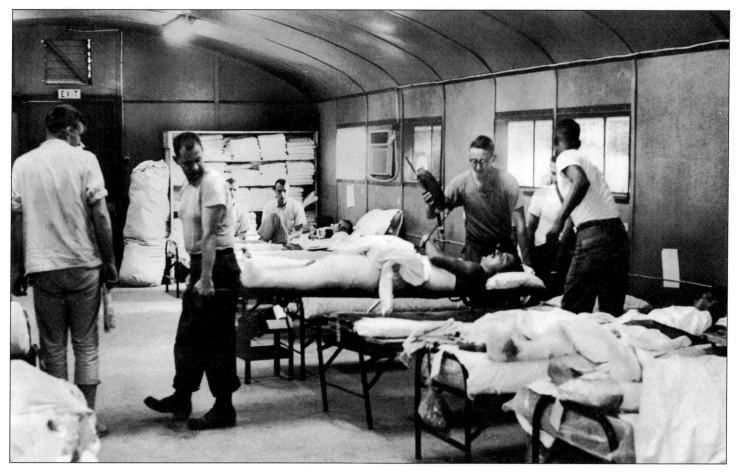

Litter bearers bring a patient into a recovery ward at the 93d Evacuation Hospital in Long Bien.

passed groups of patients from the other wards, some standing around talking, others doing nothing, or being pushed around in wheelchairs by their buddies. Johnson was right, he thought. David would die. He was probably, all things considered, dead the moment the round hit the rucksack.

Edwards went back to his room and sat there on the edge of his bed. There was really nothing left to do. Almost unconsciously he got up and walked wearily over to his desk, pulled open a drawer, and took out a folder that contained a passage he had once read. It had struck him so forcibly at the time he had made a Xerox copy of it.

. . . the dying experience is extremely traumatic to the young adult, to his family and the treating staff. The meaning of dying is appreciated by the young adult, but the reality of personal death is not accepted. He lusts for life, he now has the full emotional capability to sense the personal depth of meaning in death. As he strives for self-sufficiency and for independence, he can appreciate clearly the total passivity and the absolute dependency of the dying experience. In the solitude of death, the young child or the mature adult can turn to another for comfort without feeling childish or dependent. The newly emancipated, self-sufficient young adult may have too much personal pride to allow himself to accept the support and the understanding he so desperately needs as he moves toward death. The specific emotional reaction of the newly mature young man to the prospect of personal death is RAGE. He feels that life is completely within his grasp so that death

above all else is the great ravisher and destroyer. These mature young men who have worked, trained and striven to reach self-confidence and self-sufficiency now appreciate what they can do and what they can enjoy and that suddenly it will all end. They are so ready to live, to them death is a brutal, personal attack, an unforgivable insult, a totally unacceptable event. The intensity of his natural understandable rage at this process of dying may cause an accentuation of physical pain. Normal bitterness may be expressed by lack of cooperation or even by open antagonism. The dying young adult may alienate himself from his family. If the physician and the treatment staff can understand this natural rage that they see in the young adult about to die, they may be able to help him cope with his emotional reaction in a fashion that does not disrupt the necessary treatment. The young physician himself responds with the normal rage reaction of the young dying adult. He sees death as a destroyer that must be fought with every means possible. This normal, youthful rage may lead the physician to assault the dying patient with all kinds of treatment procedures in an attempt to keep death away. The task of the physician is not to comprehend the incomprehensible, but to make the natural work of death and the mourning the most meaningful and most productive for the people with which he deals.

The phone woke him a little past three in the morning.
 "Major!"

Letters Home

One of the soldier's connections to the home he left behind are the letters he writes and receives. They express the raw emotions of young men exposed to unfamiliar, sometimes inhumane and inhuman, conditions. Their immediacy shows perhaps more than any other kind of writing what it felt like to be in Vietnam.

William Broyles, Jr., wrote in his introduction to Dear America, *a collection of correspondence to and from soldiers in Vietnam edited by Bernard Edelman for The New York Vietnam Veterans Memorial Commission: "Usually we wrote our letters late in the afternoon, after we had made our way to a new position and dug our foxholes, in that violet hour before the patrols went out and the night became the enemy." The following are but two of the dozens of letters reprinted in that volume.*

Hi Vern,   13 March [1968]

The shit has been hitting the fan, but I've managed to miss the spray.

One guy was shooting at my ambush last night. I reported it as heavy contact and got eight barrels of artillery to shoot white phosphorus and high explosives in the wood line. We found a body this morning so the colonel was happy. . . .

You'd be surprised how similar killing is to hunting. I know I'm after souls, but I get all excited when I see a VC, just like when I see a deer. I go ape firing at him. It isn't that I'm so crazy. I think a man who freezes killing a man would freeze killing a deer. I'm not perverted, crazy, or anything else. Civilians think such thinking is crazy, but it's no big deal. He runs, you fire. You hunt so I think you'd feel the same way. It isn't all that horrifying.

When you see a man laughing about it, remember he talks the same about killing a deer. Of course, revenge has a part in wanting him just like you want a deer for a trophy and meat. I know I'm not nuts. If I killed a man in the U.S., everyone would stare. Last night I killed and everyone has been patting me on the back, including the battalion commander. What do you think?

A friend got killed on an ambush last week. [The colonel] told him to move in the middle of the night. As he drew in all his claymores, Charlie hit. Last night they told me to move twice. It'll be a cold day in hell when I move. Thirty minutes later I reported "Moved." The colonel isn't about to come out to see where I am. I'm chicken but not stupid!

It isn't all that horrifying. It's rough living in the field, but big deal. They sell mohair tailored sports coats for $35 here and sharkskin suits for $60. I'll buy a few before I leave. What a deal! . . .

1Lt. James Simmen, from Danville, California, was a platoon leader with the 5th Battalion, 60th Infantry (Mechanized), 9th Infantry Division in the area south of Saigon during 1968. His battalion later transferred to the 1st Infantry Division, operating in the Parrot's Beak near the Cambodian border. He now works as a carpenter in Alaska and has written three unpublished novels. This letter was written to his brother, assistant pastor at St. Catherine's parish in Martinez, California.

My Darling Claudia,   6 July [1967]

It's raining outside. A damp smell in the air and the raindrops slamming onto the plasterboard roof. Sound of cricket and frog, and the rumble of distant bomb explosions shake the earth here many miles away. Lightning flashes bare the heavens for a brief glimpse at a troubled sky watching over a war-torn land. The area is flooded, and mud clings to boots with a slurp-sucking sound. Soaked uniform hanging on chair to dry and shriveling up into a wrinkled mass. A chilling air is coddled by two ceiling fans and swirled through my body. I miss you, my darling. The night is cold, and you are warm and loving and soft.

At times like this, my darling, I feel as if I would do anything if I could just be back again with you. Sometimes you have to pretend you're not really lonely or else you'd find yourself going out of your mind. But when the day is done, and you're lying alone with your thoughts, then there's no more fooling and that's when it really hurts. The days seem to go by quickly, but the weeks seem forever. Today I have been in Vietnam 73 days, 10-1/2 weeks, a little over 2-1/2 months. The guys who are over here now tell me, looking back, that the time flew by. But right now it seems so very long until you're in my arms again.

Darling, it's midnight, so please forgive the short letter but I'm very tired now. Be careful Dia.

I love you,
Michael

1Lt. Robert Michael Murray, who served with Company A, 5th Special Forces Group, based at Bien Hoa, from April 1967 to April 1968, wrote this to Claudia Johnston. They married in May 1968, two weeks after he returned from Vietnam. He is now an attorney, practicing in White Plains, New York.

"Yeah." Edwards fumbled across the night table for the lamp switch.

"This is Sergeant Cramer. Jensen's temperature just spiked to 105."

"OK," Edwards said, switching on the light and sitting up. He cleared his throat. "I'll be right over." Even as he was hanging up, he was reaching under the bed for his shoes.

The ward master met him at the entrance to the unit and followed him hurriedly down the ward.

"He's becoming disoriented."

"What about the cultures?" Edwards asked quickly. "Still Pseudomonas?"

"No, this morning's grew out Klebsiella."

David was lying on the frame. All the covers were off, and he was trembling.

"106," the medic said, reading the stool-smeared thermometer.

"Better add some kanamycin and Keflin to the chloromycetin. How's the blood pressure?"

"Stable."

"How much kanamycin and Keflin?" Cramer asked.

"A lot, a lot. Just get it!"

Cramer looked at him and quickly left to get the antibiotics.

"David, David," Edwards leaned over the frame. "David!"

Slowly he opened his eyes, but there was no light in them, no gleam.

"Listen," Edwards said, lowering his voice. "I'm going to have to put you on a cooling blanket; it's not going to be comfortable, but your temperature . . . "

"I can't think of anything," David said, closing his eyes again.

"He's been confused for the last hour," the medic said.

A moment later, the ward master came back with the antibiotics already drawn up into two syringes. While he shot the drugs directly into the IV bottle, Edwards said, "We'd better put in a central venous pressure. How's his urine output?"

"Down 60cc in the last two hours."

"Does he have any blood cross-matched?"

"Four units."

"Respirator?"

"There's one down in central supply. We can get it any time."

"What about his moniliasis titers?"

"Still normal."

"White count?"

"The lab technicians are doing it now."

"Let's see his electrolytes."

"Doc."

Surprised, Edwards turned around. David had stopped shivering.

"Doc!"

Edwards hurriedly bent over the frame.

David stared up at him, his eyes strangely clear and deep. "You didn't have to come, not all the time."

"I wanted to," Edwards said.

"They told me about your brother and your taking him home." David was about to go on when, gasping, he suddenly bolted upright and, struggling against the restraints, vomited up a great flood of bright red blood.

Dying in the burn unit is not normally that dramatic. There is usually very little blood; burns die inside out, down at the cellular level, where the billions of struggling cells just simply give up. It is for the most part a kind of gentle going; breathing becomes labored and distant, circulation falls apart, hearts dilate, livers and spleens grow to twice their size, lungs gradually fill with fluid, and there is always a certain period of confusion. But after it, a comfortable time of unconsciousness, where nothing is done and everything—even the last breath—is a rather leisurely giving up.

Suddenly, with the blood still welling out of his lipless mouth, David went rigid and, arching backwards, collapsed against the frame. Edwards grabbed the suction off the wall and, pulling open David's jaw, began sucking out his mouth, trying to clear the blood and vomit out of his airway. The gasping stopped and there was the more comfortable sound of air moving in and out.

"Get the blood," Edwards ordered, reaching for the oxygen mask. He was turning up the oxygen flow just as Cramer came running back with the blood.

"Call Johnson. Set up a cut-down tray and get a tracheotomy set."

The ward master unhooked the IV from its bottles. "The blood is still ice cold," he said.

"Just hang it," Edwards ordered, holding open David's jaw, trying to get out more of the blood. "Just goddamn hang it. And call the general surgeon . . . David! David!" He pressed the oxygen mask over the boy's mouth and he could feel the new skin slipping away under the pressure of the mask's rubber edges. "David! David! Can you hear me? OK, listen, you have a stress ulcer. We might have to operate tonight. You have a lot of blood and stuff in your lungs. I'm going to have to put you on a respirator. It will help you breathe, so I'll have to make a little hole in your windpipe. It won't hurt." He looked up, checking the blood running down into the IV tubing. "It's just to help you breathe. Honest. Just to breathe."

The corpsman had set up the tracheotomy, and Edwards held the oxygen mask in place while the ward master quickly cleaned David's neck as best he could. The noise coming from inside the lungs was getting louder again. Even with the oxygen David was having to fight to breathe.

"I'm going to make the hole now," Edwards said, removing the mask. Little bits of skin came away with it.

"Doc," David gasped. "Take me home, too . . . please, Doc . . . I don't want to go home alone."

Vietnam on Film

After its end in 1975, the Vietnam War became the subject of an increasing number of films as Hollywood came to realize the war had potentially great box-office appeal. And, although there are exceptions, each new film seemed to attract critical attention greater than that usually afforded new releases, largely because they treated such a controversial subject.

Before the postwar watershed, Vietnam had been portrayed on film sparingly and somewhat uniformly. John Wayne's jingoistic *The Green Berets* was the first feature-length film to cover combat in Vietnam; after its release in 1968 Hollywood seemed to lose interest in Vietnam, except to occasionally turn out thrillers or horror movies with Vietnam veterans as psychotic villains. Yet in 1978, Hollywood began to take a more mature look at the war. That year marked the release of the Academy Award–winning film, *The Deer Hunter*, as well as *Coming Home* and several lesser-known films: *Go Tell the Spartans*; *Who'll Stop the Rain*, based on Robert Stone's *Dog Soldiers*; and *The Boys in Company C*. The next year the controversial *Apocalypse Now* was released, followed in the 1980s by a plethora of Vietnam-related movies, including *Cutter's Way* (1981), *First Blood* (1982), *Uncommon Valor* (1983), *Platoon* (1986), *Hanoi Hilton* (1987), and *Hamburger Hill* (1987), to name several. The following pages provide a sampling of Hollywood's vision of Vietnam.

A helicopter comes in for a landing as the camera rolls on the set of Apocalypse Now, *which was made in the Philippines.*

Platoon's scar-faced Sergeant Barnes (Tom Berenger).

The good sergeant, Elias (Willem Dafoe), is restrained by his men during a fistfight with his nemesis, Barnes.

Platoon

Platoon (1986) is one of the most graphically compelling films ever made about Vietnam. Director Oliver Stone, a veteran himself, carefully reconstructed the physical world of the combat infantryman in Vietnam. The result was technically awe-inspiring, accurate down to the last shoelace, and it gave the viewer a horrifically realistic sense of the war. Much more than earlier works, *Platoon* showed what the war on the ground in Vietnam was really like.

The plot centers around Chris Taylor (Charlie Sheen), a young soldier who joins a combat platoon near the Cambo-dian border. The unit is led by two sergeants, Elias (Willem Dafoe) and Barnes (Tom Berenger). Elias is the good leader, a fighter who cares for his men and has a great heart. Barnes personifies evil; he is a killing machine so efficient that his actions seem to exist in a moral vacuum.

Vietnam, however, was not a moral vacuum, and the struggle between the good and evil sergeants takes on larger meaning as the film progresses. Throughout *Platoon*, though, it is the director's physical precision that compels the viewer. Stone recreates Vietnam with an artist's accuracy: the terrible heat and climatic conditions, the overwhelming American technology versus the primitive—yet intractable—enemy, the violence and exhaustion of combat, and the breakdown of human values in an inhuman situation are all given voice in the film.

Above. *Charlie Sheen portrays the twenty-one-year-old Chris Taylor.*

Full Metal Jacket

Full Metal Jacket (1987) is a two-part look at the process and results of getting men ready to fight in Vietnam. To make the film, director Stanley Kubrick adapted Gustav Hasford's *The Short-Timers* to the screen. The result is as chilling and graphic as Hasford's profoundly disturbing tale.

The film opens at Parris Island, the Marine Corps's training center, where raw recruits are terrorized by an archetypal drill sergeant (played by retired Marine DI Lee Ermey). The sergeant's extraordinary profanity and brutal methods strip these young Americans of their humanity, turning them into hyperefficient and soulless killing machines. Among his charges are young men nicknamed Private Joker (Matthew Modine) and Private Gomer Pyle (Vincent D'Onofrio). The latter, overweight and hapless, becomes a victim of the sergeant's sadistic training. Lingering over boot camp, Kubrick concludes the film's first half with a shocking scene of violence that demonstrates just how efficient the drill sergeant's methods were.

Full Metal Jacket then follows Private Joker to Vietnam, where he is assigned to

Full Metal Jacket's brutal DI, Gunnery Sergeant Hartman (Lee Ermey).

be a good-news reporter for a military newspaper ("We run two types of stories here," his editor tells him. "Grunts who give half their salary to buy gooks toothbrushes and deodorants, winning hearts and minds. And combat actions that result in a kill, winning the war."). Joining a friend from boot camp, Joker ends up in Hue City during the 1968 Tet offensive. Fighting has turned the city into an eerie landscape of blasted rubble, where dan-

ger lurks behind every corner. In Hue, the film's climactic scene draws together all the dehumanizing aspects of war, seen through the eyes of a soldier already thoroughly dehumanized by his Marine training and his earlier experiences in Vietnam.

Released within months of *Platoon*, *Full Metal Jacket* was considered far less accessible, almost too recondite for average audiences. However, its brutally ac-

curate rendition of boot camp, as well as its uncompromising rendition of personal combat in Hue City, caused many critics to praise the film as an unorthodox, yet compelling, vision of the Vietnam War's dehumanizing effects.

Private Eightball (Dorian Harewood) goes down during the battle of Hue.

The Deer Hunter

Michael Cimino's powerful tale, *The Deer Hunter*, stirred controversy from the moment it was released in 1978. Although popular with American audiences (and with the American Academy of Motion Picture Arts, which awarded it five Oscars), many domestic and foreign critics decried the film's avoidance of political issues and its two-dimensional (some said racist) depiction of Vietnam and the Vietnamese.

Yet *The Deer Hunter*'s purpose is not to solve the "problem" of Vietnam. It is instead the story of how war—any war—affects the warriors. Vietnam is little more than the background to Cimino's more general tale of how men are either strengthened or destroyed by the terrors of armed conflict.

The hero, Michael (Robert De Niro), survives war because he embodies the enduring values of the mythical American frontiersman: strength, self-reliance, courage, and a certain warrior-hunter's code of honor. His friends, Nick (Christopher Walken) and Steven (John Savage), are less fortunate. War robs them of their spirits, leaving Steven embittered by a crippling wound, Nick destroyed morally by torture and drugs.

In the end, *The Deer Hunter* is also a peculiarly American tale. Most of the film takes place in a small Pennsylvania hometown, where timeless rituals—a family wedding, a hunters' outing, a funeral wake—forge binding ties between men and their families and between men themselves. The film's closing scene—family and friends singing "God Bless America" while mourning a casualty of war—underscores *The Deer Hunter*'s affirmation of traditional American values.

Robert DeNiro's Michael (left) and John Savage's Steven are held captive by the Vietcong.

Apocalypse Now

When *Apocalypse Now* was finally released in 1979, some critics likened its production to the Vietnam War itself: wildly out of control, unsure of its purpose, and doomed to failure. The comparison was apt in some respects. At the very least, the film's $31-million price tag (original budget: $12-14 million), overly long production schedule, indecisive conclusion (two endings were filmed), and failure at the box office gave detractors plenty of ammunition.

But Francis Ford Coppola's first Vietnam film was nonetheless a landmark in cinematic treatment of the war. The film's sheer physical ambition—its bloody helicopter gunship attack, garishly all-American USO show and cast-of-thousands jungle fortress—exceeded all earlier presentations of Vietnam. *Apocalypse Now* also tried to address some of the war's moral and spiritual dimensions at a time when Americans themselves were just beginning to re-examine their painful involvement in Southeast Asia.

The plot is essentially a Vietnam-based rewrite of Joseph Conrad's *Heart of Darkness*. Captain Willard (Martin Sheen) has been ordered to travel up the river into Cambodia to assassinate an "insane" Green Beret colonel named Kurtz (played by Marlon Brando). Willard and his men descend into madness and death as their journey becomes a nightmare of unseen enemies and surreal violence. When Willard and Kurtz finally meet, they symbolize a conflict of extremes: Willard as the good soldier who follows orders in the face of darkest evil; Kurtz as the guerrilla, a warrior-philosopher to whom the ends justify all means. Ironically (and just like the American effort in Vietnam) the good soldier wins the battle but loses the war.

Above: Cyndi Wood performs in a surrealistic USO show during Willard's voyage upriver in Apocalypse Now.

Following pages. The scene greeting Willard as he arrives at Kurtz's Cambodian lair.

Rambo

Some films about Vietnam do not philosophize about the complex and intractable nature of the war. *Rambo: First Blood Part II* (1985) is one of these films. The brain child of Sylvester Stallone, its politics are profoundly simple: The hero, a misunderstood Vietnam veteran, rescues American POWs held illegally by beastly Vietnamese captors after the war has ended. Along the way Rambo takes on traitorous American bureaucrats, sadistic Slavs, and of course hordes of easily slain Vietnamese soldiers. As the camera lingers on Stallone's bulging muscles and exotic weapons, the hero systematically wipes out everyone and everything that stands between him and the completion of his mission.

The movie was a big hit. Part of its popularity stemmed from Stallone's well-known formula of constant action, suffering heroics, and elaborate violence. But another reason for *Rambo*'s success was Stallone's ability to capture the nearly wistful American longing for an uncomplicated Vietnam story. No guilt, no politics, just evil Asian Communists getting their comeuppance from an all-American hero. That "blow-'em-all-away" simplicity appealed to Americans fed up with terrorism, guerrilla wars, and other messy real-life problems.

Sylvester Stallone portrays the muscular, monosyllabic Rambo.

Uncommon Valor

Like *Rambo*, *Uncommon Valor* (1983) addresses the question of POWs and MIAs supposedly remaining in Vietnam after the war is over. And like Stallone, director Ted Kotcheff tries to keep it simple, showing aging-yet-spirited heroes battling both the Communists and the "system" that has propagated a conspiracy of silence about the war Americans want to forget. The result is an action-adventure film that avoids most of the complications of the Vietnam experience.

In *Uncommon Valor* a former colonel (Gene Hackman) assembles a group of Vietnam veterans for a surreptitious raid into Laos in order to rescue the colonel's son, still held by Pathet Lao and Vietnamese forces in a special prison camp. Their resentment against the U.S. government for "failing" them both then and now is palpable, and it helps the colonel justify their "outlaw" raid. First they train for their mission in Texas. Then, after a series of adventures and complications, the team finally makes it to Laos and pulls off a daring rescue.

What sets the movie apart from the more overtly jingoistic *Rambo* is its fine performances and portrayal of the Vietnam veteran's pain and sense of failure. In *Uncommon Valor* the raiders sense that their rescue mission will help them recover the pride they—and America—lost in Southeast Asia the first time around.

The rescue. Gene Hackman, playing the retired colonel hired to lead the raid, is at far left.

Gardens of Stone

Francis Ford Coppola's *Gardens of Stone* (1987) presents the inner torment of the Army during the war in Vietnam. Built around the lives of two career sergeants, it shows how soldiers who loved the Army hated a war they knew could not be won.

Sergeants Clell Hazard (James Caan) and "Goody" Nelson (James Earl Jones) are members of the Army's elite Old Guard, whose duties include burying men who have been killed in Vietnam at Arlington National Cemetery. Hazard hates the war but wants to prepare young men for survival in that frustrating conflict. His struggle comes to represent the confused state of America during the war: unsure of purpose, yet patriotic and idealistic.

Coming Home

Coming Home (1978) focused on the pain of veterans returning to "The World" and the families that awaited them. It is the story of an Army wife (Jane Fonda) who falls in love with a crippled, antiwar veteran (Jon Voight) while her gung-ho husband (Bruce Dern) is fighting in Vietnam. Fonda's liberation and tender affair with Voight contrast with her marriage, which is destroyed when her husband returns from Vietnam crippled in spirit and soul.

Above. *James Caan and Anjelica Huston portray a sergeant assigned to the Army's ceremonial unit at Fort Myer , Virginia, and his Washington Post-reporter girlfriend in Gardens of Stone, set in 1968 and 1969.*

Right. *John Voight as the paraplegic Vietnam veteran, Luke Martin, and Jane Fonda as Sally Hyde, the Marine captain's wife who falls for Luke.*

For every American fighting in Vietnam there were five soldiers who supported him. These men did hundreds of odd jobs. They drove trucks, cooked meals, painted fences, or fixed jeep engines. Some counted artillery shells, or flak jackets, or casualties. The vast majority of Americans in Vietnam spent their tours in these pursuits, fulfilling the mechanical and bureaucratic demands of a modern war machine.

Whether combat soldier or rear-echelon troop, every soldier enjoyed some kind of time off after the job was done. How a soldier spent leisure time depended on where he was: At a firebase it might be a boring routine of no place to go, nothing to do unless the USO show came through. Elsewhere it was better: in-country breaks in Saigon or a military rest area, or—best of all—a week-long R&R vacation in some Asian paradise far from the war.

Preceding page. *A soldier on leave in downtown Da Nang, spring 1965.*

The Officer in Charge of the Dead

from *A Rumor of War*
by Philip Caputo

*Philip Caputo landed in Da Nang, South Vietnam, on March 8, 1965, as a young second lieutenant of the 9th Marine Combat Brigade—the first U.S. combat unit in Vietnam. After several weeks in the field he was assigned to a staff position in the rear, a job he describes in his 1977 memoir, **A Rumor of War,** one of the early books about Vietnam.*

As fighting increased, the additional duty of casualty reporting officer kept me busiest. It was also a job that gave me a lot of bad dreams, though it had the beneficial effect of cauterizing whatever silly, abstract, romantic ideas I still had about war.

My job was simply to report on casualties, enemy as well as our own; casualties due to hostile action and those due to nonhostile causes—the accidents that inevitably occur where there are large numbers of young men armed with lethal weapons or at the controls of complicated machinery. Artillery shells sometimes fell on friendly troops, tanks ran over people, helicopters crashed, marines shot other marines by mistake.

It was not the simple task it seemed. The military has elaborate procedures for everything, and keeping records of the dead and wounded is no exception. The reports were written on mimeographed forms, one for KIAs, one for WIAs, and a third for nonhostile casualties. Each form had spaces for the victim's name, age, rank, serial number,

and organization (his unit), and for the date, the description of his injuries, and the circumstances under which they occurred. If he had been killed, the circumstances were almost always described in the same way, and the words could have served as an epitaph for thousands of men: "killed in action while on patrol vicinity of Danang, RVN."

The KIA reports were long and complicated. Much information was required about the dead: their religion, the name and address of their next of kin, beneficiaries of their servicemen's life insurance policies, and whether the money was to be paid in a lump sum or in installments. All reports had to be written in that clinical, euphemistic language the military prefers to simple English. If, say, a marine had been shot through the guts, I could not write "shot through the guts" or "shot through the stomach"; no, I had to say "GSW" (gunshot wound) "through and through, abdomen." Shrapnel wounds were called "multiple fragment lacerations," and the phrase for dismemberment, one of my very favorite phrases, was "traumatic amputation." I had to use it a lot when the Viet Cong began to employ high-explosive weapons and booby traps. A device they used frequently was the command-detonated mine, which was set off electrically from ambush. The mines were similar to our Claymore, packed with hundreds of steel pellets and a few pounds of an explosive called C-4. If I recall correctly, the gas-expansion rate of C-4 is 26,000 feet per second. That terrific force, and the hundreds of steel pellets propelled by it, made the explosion of a command-detonated mine equivalent to the simultaneous firing of seventy twelve-gauge shotguns loaded with double-0 buckshot. Naturally, anyone hit by such a weapon was likely to suffer the "traumatic amputation" of something—an arm, a leg, his head—and many did. After I saw some of the victims, I began to question the accuracy of the phrase. *Traumatic* was precise, for losing a limb is definitely traumatic, but *amputation*, it seemed to me, suggested a surgical operation. I observed, however, that the human body does not break apart cleanly in an explosion. It tends to shatter into irregular and often unrecognizable pieces, so "traumatic fragmentation" would have been a more accurate term and would have preserved the euphemistic tone the military favored.

The shattering or fragmenting effect of high explosive occasionally caused semantic difficulties in reporting injuries of men who had undergone extreme mutilation. It was a rare phenomenon, but some marines had been so badly mangled there seemed to be no words to describe what had happened to them. Sometime that year, Lieutenant Colonel Meyers, one of the regiment's battalion commanders, stepped on a booby-trapped 155-mm shell. They did not find enough of him to fill a willy-peter bag, a waterproof sack a little larger than a shopping bag. In effect, Colonel Meyers had been disintegrated, but the official report read something like "traumatic amputation, both feet; traumatic amputation, both legs and arms; multiple lacerations to abdomen; through and through fragment wounds, head and chest." Then came the notation "killed in action."

The battalion adjutants phoned in reports of their units' casualties, and I relayed them to the division combat casualty reporting center. That done, I filed copies of the reports in their respective folders, one labeled CASUALTIES: HOSTILE ACTION and the other CASUALTIES: NON HOSTILE. I believe the two were kept separate because men killed or wounded by enemy fire were automatically awarded Purple Hearts, while those hit by friendly fire were not. That was the only real difference. A man killed by friendly fire (another misleading term, because fire is never friendly if it hits you) was just as dead as one killed by the enemy. And there was often an accidental quality even about battle casualties. Stepping on a mine or stumbling over the trip wire of a booby trap is a mishap, really, not unlike walking in front of a car while crossing a busy street.

Once the reports were filed, I brought Colonel Wheeler's scoreboard up to date. Covered with acetate and divided into vertical and horizontal columns, the board hung behind the executive officer's desk, in the wood-framed tent where he and the colonel made their headquarters. The vertical columns were headed, from left to right, KIA, WIA, DOW (died of wounds), NON-HOST, VC-KIA, VC-WIA, and VC-POW. The horizontal columns were labeled with the numerical des-

ignations of the units belonging to, or attached to, the regiment: 1/3 for 1st Battalion, 3d Marines, 2/3 for 2d Battalion, and so forth. In the first four vertical columns were written the number of casualties a particular unit had suffered, in the last three the number it had inflicted on the enemy. After an action, I went into the colonel's quarters, erased the old figures and wrote in the new with a grease pencil. The colonel, an easygoing man in most instances, was adamant about maintaining an accurate scoreboard: high-ranking visitors from Danang and Saigon often dropped in unannounced to see how the regiment was performing. And the measures of a unit's performance in Vietnam were not the distances it had advanced or the number of victories it had won, but the number of enemy soldiers it had killed (the body count) and the proportion between that number and the number of its own dead (the kill ratio). The scoreboard thus allowed the colonel to keep track of the battalions and companies under his command and, quickly and crisply, to rattle off impressive figures to visiting dignitaries. My unsung task in that statistical war was to do the arithmetic. If I had been an agent of death as a platoon leader, as a staff officer I was death's bookkeeper.

Sometimes I had to verify the body counts. Field commanders occasionally gave in to the temptation to exaggerate the number of Viet Cong their units had killed. So the bodies were brought to headquarters whenever possible, and I counted them to make sure there were as many as had been reported. That was always pleasant because the corpses had begun to decompose by the time they reached headquarters. Decomposition sets in quickly in that climate. Most pleasant of all was the job of identifying our own dead. The battalion adjutants usually did that, but whenever there was confusion about the names of the dead or when the descriptions of their wounds were incorrectly reported to regiment, I had to do it. The dead were kept in a fly tent adjacent to the division hospital. They were laid out on canvas stretchers, covered with ponchos or with rubber body-bags, yellow casualty tags tied to their boots—or to their shirts, if their legs had been blown off. One of the simplest ways to identify a dead man was to match his face against his photograph in a service record book. Some of them did not have faces, in which case we used dental records, since teeth are almost as reliable a means of identification as fingerprints. The latter were used only when the casualty had been decapitated or his jaw shattered to bits.

The interesting thing was how the dead looked so much alike. Black men, white men, yellow men, they all looked remarkably the same. Their skin had a tallowlike texture, making them appear like wax dummies of themselves; the mouths were opened wide, as if death had caught them in the middle of a scream.

They smelled the same, too. The stench of death is unique, probably the most offensive on earth, and once you have smelled it, you can never again believe with conviction that man is the highest being in earthly creation. The corpses I have had to smell as a soldier and war correspondent smelled much worse than all the fish, birds, and deer I have scaled, skinned, or gutted as a sportsman. Because the odor of death is so strong, you can never get used to it, as you can get used to the sight of death. And the odor is always the same. It might vary in intensity, depending on the state of decomposition, but if two people have been dead for the same length of time and under the same conditions, there will be no difference in the way they smell. I first made that observation in Vietnam in 1965, when I noticed that the stench of a dead American made me just as sick as that of a dead Vietnamese. Since then, I have made it again and again in other wars in other places, on the Golan Heights and in the Sinai Desert, in Cyprus and Lebanon, and, coming full circle back to Vietnam, in the streets of Xuan Loc, a city much fought over during the North Vietnamese offensive in 1975. All those dead people, Americans, North and South Vietnamese, Arabs and Israelis, Turks and Greeks, Moslems and Christians, men, women, and children, officer and enlisted, smelled equally bad.

My first day on the job as a casualty reporting officer was June 21, 1965. Early that morning, a patrol from 2d Battalion fought a small action with the VC near Iron Bridge Ridge. Around noon, my field phone buzzed; it was the 2d Battalion's adjutant reporting four friendly casualties, one dead, three wounded. I put some hostile-action forms on my desk and said, "Okay, go ahead." One by one, beginning with the KIA, he gave me their names and service numbers and the descriptions of their wounds. There was a lot of static on the line, and he had to spell the names phonetically: "Atherton. Alpha Tango Hotel Echo Romeo Tango Oscar November. First name John. Middle initial double-u, as in Whiskey . . . gunshot wound upper body . . . killed in action while on patrol vicinity of Danang . . ." His voice had the rote, practiced sound of a radio announcer reading the stock market results.

I wrote quickly. It was extremely hot in the tent. Sweat dribbled off the tip of my nose and onto the forms, smudging the print. The forms stuck like flypaper to the forearm of my writing hand. One of the reports became badly smeared, and I asked the adjutant to read the information back to me. He was halfway through when the switchboard operator broke in. "Crowd One Alpha"—that was my new code-name—"this is Crowd Operator breaking . . . breaking . . . breaking." That meant he was going to cut me off to clear the line. "Crowd Operator, this is One Alpha working working," I said, meaning I had not yet completed my call. "One Alpha this is Crowd Operator. Cannot hear

Right. *South Vietnamese troops ride past the bodies of four of their comrades killed in an earlier ambush.*

you. Breaking." There was a click. "You dumb son of a bitch," I yelled into the dead phone. Sweating heavily, I cranked the handle of the EE-8. After ten or fifteen minutes, the operator answered and reconnected me to 2d Battalion. Their adjutant came back on the line and picked up where he had left off. ". . . Multiple fragment wounds, lower half of both legs. WIA, evacuated . . ."

When the reports were called into division and filed, I went over to operations to find out how many enemy casualties there had been. Webb Harrisson, one of the assistant operations officers, leafed through a small pile of messages. "Here it is," he said. "Four Charlies, all KIA." I walked into the colonel's tent and made the proper changes on the scoreboard with my grease pencil. The Ex-O, Lieutenant Colonel Brooks, looked at the figures. He was a bald, stocky man whom the troops had nicknamed Elmer Fudd because he resembled the comic-book character.

"Keeping the old board up to date, are you, lieutenant?" he asked.

"Yes, sir," I said, thinking, What the hell does it look like I'm doing?

"How recent are those figures?"

"As of this morning, sir."

"Very good. Colonel Wheeler is giving a briefing for General Thompson this afternoon and he'll want the latest casualty statistics."

"Yes, sir. Who is General Thompson?"

"He's from MACV." Military Assistance Command Vietnam, Westmoreland's headquarters.

Sometime later, a jeep drove into headquarters carrying the dead Viet Cong and two civilians who had been injured in the fire-fight. The civilians, both women, rode in the back of the jeep. One was old and frail-looking, and had minor scratches on her arms. The other, in her early or mid-thirties, lay on her stomach in the back seat. Pieces of shrapnel had lodged in her buttocks. The bodies were on a trailer hitched to the jeep.

The driver parked behind the adjutant's tent and unhitched the trailer. It tipped forward, the hitch clanging against the ground and the bodies tumbling over on top of each other. A half-severed arm, with a piece of bone protruding whitely through the flesh, flopped over the side of the trailer, then flopped back in again. Stretcher-bearers came up and carried the young woman to the regimental aid station. The old woman shuffled along behind, spitting blackish-red betel-nut juice into the dust.

I checked to make sure there were four bodies. There appeared to be. It was difficult to tell. Tossed around in the trailer, they had become entangled, one barely distinguishable from another. Three of them were entangled, anyway. The fourth did not have arms below the elbow, and his legs had been shot or blown off completely. The others had been mangled in other places. One had been hit in the head, his brains and the white cartilage that had

moored them to his skull spilling onto the bottom of the trailer. Another, hit in the midsection, had been turned inside out, the slick, blue and greenish brown mass of his intestines bulging out of him. There was a deep, dark red pool of blood at the low end of the trailer. I turned away from the sight and told the driver to get the bodies out of there.

"Sorry, sir," he said, starting up his jeep. "I was told to leave the bodies here. I've got to get back to the motor pool."

"Who the hell told you to leave the bodies here?"

The driver shrugged. "Some officer told me, lieutenant. I've got to get back to the motor pool."

"All right, shove off."

The marine drove away. I went into the tent and told Kazmarack to take the corpses to the cemetery where the enemy dead were buried. Kazmarack called it the body dump, and it was more that than a proper cemetery.

Captain Anderson said, "Leave the bodies here, Mister Caputo."

"Sir, they're going to smell pretty bad in another few hours."

"The colonel wants the bodies here."

"What the hell for?"

"He wants the clerks around here to look at them. There isn't much action around here, so I guess he wants them to get used to the sight of blood."

"You're kidding, captain."

"No, I'm not."

"Well, I don't think much of that idea. Christ, let's just bury the poor bastards."

"Lieutenant, I think what you think doesn't make much difference. The Old Man wants these people to get used to the sight of blood, and that's what they're going to do."

"Well, there's plenty of blood in there, but I'm not sure they're going to get used to it. Plenty of other stuff, too, guts and brains."

"I'll tell you when to get rid of the bodies."

"Yes, sir."

So the corpses were left lying in the sun. As the colonel had ordered, the headquarters troops were marched past the trailer to look at the dead Viet Cong. They filed by like visitors passing before an exhibit in a museum. The sun burned down, and the bodies began to smell in the heat. The odor, at first faint because the VC had been dead only a short time, was like cooking gas escaping from an oven burner. One by one, the marines walked up to the trailer, looked into it, made some desperate jokes when they saw what was inside or said nothing at all, then walked back to their desks and typewriters. The sun burned hotter in the empty sky; the smell grew stronger. It blew into the adjutant's tent on a puff of breeze, the cooking-gas odor and a stench that reminded me of hydrogen sulfide used in high-school chemistry classes. Well, that was all the corpses were, masses of chemicals and decaying matter.

The personal effects of Specialist 4 Raymond Ford, killed in action in South Vietnam, February 20, 1966.

Looking outside, I was pleased to see that the show was almost over; the marines at the end of the line were filing past the trailer. Because of the smell, they kept their distance. The smell was not unbearable; several hours would pass before it got that bad. It was, however, strong enough to prevent these men at the end of the line from lingering, as those at the front of the line had done, thus depriving them of the chance to look at the corpses long enough to become accustomed to the sight of blood. They just gave the bodies a brief glance, then moved quickly from the trailer and the growing stench.

The procession ended. Kazmarack and another clerk, Corporal Stasek, hitched up the trailer and drove off toward Danang. Anderson left for a staff conference that had been called in preparation for General Thompson's visit. Ten minutes later, he came lumbering back into the tent, his red, jowly face pouring sweat.

"Mister Caputo, we've got to get those bodies back here."

I looked at him incredulously.

"The Old Man wants the bodies back here so he can show them to the general when he briefs him," Anderson said.

"Stasek and Kazmarack are gone, sir. They're probably in Danang by now."

"I know they're gone. I want you to find somebody who can handle a jeep. Tell him to catch up with those two and have them bring those bodies back here ASAP."

"Captain, I don't really believe we're doing this."

"Just get moving." He turned and walked on with quick, jerky little steps.

I managed to find a driver who knew the route and told him what to do. I returned to the tent, where, in the spirit of the madness in which I was taking part, I made up a new title for myself. I wrote it on a piece of cardboard and tacked the cardboard to my desk. It read:

2LT. P.J. CAPUTO. OFFICER IN CHARGE OF THE DEAD.

The Donut Dollies

from *F.N.G.*
by Donald Bodey

Life at an American firebase in Vietnam was often a monotonous stream of privation, disease, bad food, and nerve-wracking combat patrols. To raise troop morale, female Red Cross volunteers visited firebases, bringing music, goodies, and most of all themselves. In Donald Bodey's war novel F.N.G., the protagonist, Private Gabriel "Chieu Hoi" Sauers (chieu hoi is a Vietnamese term for surrender), his buddy Callmeblack, and others at their firebase are treated to a visit from these "donut dollies:"

The morale of the troops on the LZ is past its low point. For the next few days it usually rains about half the time instead of all day long, and there is plenty of sun. We keep after our rot and mine starts to clear up a little, which is enough to make me feel better. The sores turn to scabs and the salve keeps the scabs soft. It's hard to keep from picking at the scabs, but the skin underneath where they come off is very pink, even on Omar. The instructions on the cans of salve say to keep applying it after the scabs come off in order to avoid scars, but there isn't enough salve for everybody to do this. Beside, it doesn't all disappear. There are sores where I keep salving but it keeps spreading, only not as fast. The medicine dries white, and

every time the sun is out guys are sunning themselves with white shit all over. It makes me think of some memory from a long time ago, something to do with a kid's birthday party, I think, but I can never quite remember it exactly.

Callme's R&R is up but I don't expect him to get back for another three or four days. It's a standard procedure for transients to sham as long as they can in base camp.

One morning, just when we think we've got it beat, this cold rain comes down and puts out the fires of hope we've all been having that the 'soons are over. The three of us are sitting around inside the deep hooch, bitching because the roof has a new leak and we don't even feel like going outside to try to fix it. Omar is stretched out with his back against the wall and his feet up on the pallet that I'm sitting on. Murphy is sitting on the top bunk on Omar's side, hunched over with his elbows on his knees, swinging his feet back and forth. I'm in a kind of daze. I'm depressed by the rain, which seems different this morning. It is the middle of the day and it hasn't quit. All the time it's been raining I've never heard thunder and never seen lightning. It rains without thunder and lightning, and I'm curious about how much rain has fallen during the season. I know an inch has fallen in the night and during the morning, because I left my canteen cup outside. Another inch falls the next night and day, and another one falls before Callme comes back on the first bird that comes in when it is clear the day after that. He looks different.

"Hey, man," I say, "did you get a tan while you were over there, or what? You look different."

"I *am* different, dude. I had me a ton of fun. I mean, dig it, I fucked for three straight days. Bought me a whore as soon as I got there, traded her in after a day, then traded that one in the next day. Then I got a cute l'il thing that wanted more dick than I had left in me."

"Didja leave me any holes I won't fall in if I go to Bangkok on my R and R?" Omar says.

"Homes, they might move the whole fuckin' country by the time you get yours."

He has a Polaroid and takes my picture, then one of all of us together. Then Smith takes one of me and Callme-black. At first I can't believe what the picture shows because I haven't seen myself from head to toe in over nine months, and I am skinny. I've never been skinnier than I am now. I knew I was losing weight because I'm never hungry, but it shocks me a little to see a picture of myself. Callme also has a stack of pictures that he took in Bangkok, and we smoke some dope and go through the stack one at a time while he tells us about each one. Most of them are pictures of his whores: small girls who are probably not more than sixteen years old. They look a lot different than the Vietnamese. They wear dresses and heels and extra-heavy makeup around their eyes, which makes the eyes look bigger but still not round. Their teeth are all even and white and I can feel the latest hardon slip from one side of my barndoor buttons to the other while Callme is telling us about his week in Thailand, then his four-day sham in the Rear, where he fucked a laundry girl and thinks he might have gotten the clap from her. If he had discovered the clap before he left the Rear he might have gotten to stay back there another couple days, but he just started dripping today. He digs into his ruck. It's a different ruck than the one he had been carrying but it isn't new, just cleaner. He gives us each a small pipe made from bamboo and some kind of a shell shaped like an acorn.

"And, Chieu Hoi," he says, "I brought you these so you'll rattle more out there in the Bush." It is a beautiful set of beads, black and white beads carved in random shapes. Callme said the Thai who sold them to him explained that each shape had a different meaning, but Callme couldn't remember any of them except the shape that is sort of like a pitcher or a long-necked bird. There are five of that kind on the string and they are all very very close in shape. That bead is for good luck.

"Say, brother, I got me five more pieces of good luck now. That oughta get me outa here safe and sound." I put the beads on over the string that Ass gave me so long ago now and I like the feeling I get, but it is not a feeling that fits into words. I slap Callme five and say thanks. We blow another bowl and go through the pictures by ourselves. I keep staring at the picture of me and Callme. Callme looks great and I look like shit, except for the smile on my face. Callme is clean and I am still filthy, and that bothers me too. For all the time I've been over here I've been wishing I had a camera, and I still don't have one. Callme brought a bottle of whiskey back with him, and we debate whether to save it for later or not. The debate lasts about a minute. He draws a line on the label and says that is how much of it we'll drink this time, and we start in, sipping from C-rat tins. We keep the bottle down in the hooch and go outside to sit on top. We're drunk when the Z begins to buzz.

It starts down by the pad. Guys are hollering and slapping high fives all around. We don't know what it is all about, but whatever it is will soon get to us because we can see it travel up the hill as one guy passes it on to another, then little groups scatter into every direction and the hollering keeps going. A fairly fat guy from Artillery who has on pure black sunglasses yells "Donut Holes!" He

A USO entertainer tries to teach a few dance steps to a youthful American soldier in South Vietnam.

Posing for snapshot souvenirs, a USO performer makes the day for a group of GIs.

makes a circle with two fingers and finger-fucks it. The thumb on his right hand is missing.

A rush goes through me: excitement. The Red Cross has volunteers, women who go everywhere the military goes. In the Rear, they man USO clubs, and I saw some of them walking around base camp when we were shipping out. They were dressed in light blue dresses and none of them seemed very good-looking. But that was then. I haven't seen a round-eyed woman for over nine months.

"Say, fuckin' hey," Omar shouts. "I gotta get my black ass tight." He disappears into the other hooch. Chas is sitting on the wall, and he straightens up and begins a Charles Atlas routine.

"Tell me," he says, "do I look like I'm a war hero them girls are gonna want a piece of?"

"You look like Popeye the sailor man, man."

Chas almost spits the pipe out of his mouth and starts laughing.

"I'm gonna get a controlled buzz on," Callme says.

"Want another can of booze before I hide it?"

"Hell, yes." I pump what's left in my tin and hand it to him. The whole Z is alive with action. About every hooch has at least a couple guys shaving out of their helmets, and there is music coming from everywhere. I wonder what the girls are going to do and how long they're going to stay. They've got to have their share of courage to come out here; even though it's safe to us, I'd think they would be scared.

Callme comes back to the top without his shirt on. His rot is not as bad as it was before he left on R&R but there are scabs as big as pocket watches on both sides of his chest. I wonder if rot is contagious, and since it is so wicked-looking I wonder what his whores thought of it. I wonder what mine will think, and what my mother will say.

A few minutes later we see the birds coming, still far away, over the muddy river. There are three helicopters, and the way one circles above the other two it must be a gunship. So the Army guards its goodies with its best weapons. I wonder how many Donut Holes have been killed over here. The birds stay in that same fluttering formation—the Cobra flying circles around the Slicks—and as they come closer it makes me think of how a little bird will chase a big, slow buzzard. When they get closer to the pad, the Cobra becomes the buzzard and circles slowly very high. The two Slicks come bobbling onto the pad, which is surrounded by a couple dozen guys. Some of them have on white tee shirts. The lifers sent word around that we were all supposed to get into our flak jackets, but almost nobody has one on.

By now there is a general cheer coming from all over the Z, like the beginning of a ball game. About everybody is standing on hooch roofs, in pairs or in groups as big as squads. A few hooches away there is a guy who hits each of his armpits with half-minute doses of an aerosol deodorant. I had forgotten deodorant even came like that, and he begins spraying under the arms of all his buddies too, with plenty of flair.

When the first bird lands, the cheer from the pad is almost as loud as the sound of the bird's rotors. One guy takes off his white tee shirt and lays it on the sandbags where the first leg steps. It is surely the first leg that isn't rot-infested to step there, ever. It is definitely a woman's. Omar has a set of field glasses and Callme says he's going to pull rank if Omar doesn't give them up soon enough. Smith passes them to Callme, then I get them and zero in on the leg, the girl, the Donut Hole. She is definitely American. There are four of them and they have on the blue outfits. The dresses—ah, dresses—are pretty short, so there's a lot of leg that shows through the parade. The parade is made up of the four girls walking up the hill from the pad. The dude who dropped his white tee is escorting the first one, and as they come up the hill he gets outdone by a big black dude who stretches himself across some mud. The guy with the chick on his arm barely hesitates. He walks right across the guy's back and reaches back to get the girl's hand. She hesitates, though, so the guy reaches back with both hands, and the first girl walks across the dude's back. He lies there until all four of them have walked across him, then stands up and bows to the cheers he gets. The mud that covers him from face to feet looks almost orange against his black belly.

The second bird comes down when the pad is clear and it has supplies in it, stuff that the girls brought. There's never been an easier detail to summon than the detail that carries those boxloads of shit up the hill. One more bird comes in after the second Slick leaves, and it's got F.N.G.s on it. It's the same every time F.N.G.s get here: they get out of the bird and stand and everybody knows they're new because of their clothes but nobody does anything for

them. It's a sort of initiation. We got dropped into a hole the squad had to cut out of the Bush for us because it was still a rough Z. Even then, even though there wasn't the organization there is here, it was as though us F.N.G.s were invisible for a while. There are six of them standing down on the pad now, not getting any attention and not knowing what the hell to do. What they really don't know is that this isn't an ordinary day.

The girls walk right by the dike that separates our hooch from Artillery's parapets, and by now they have mud splattered on the blue dresses. One is a blonde with short hair and glasses the shade of her salmon fingernails. There are two black chicks. One is short and heavy and the other one is tall and good-looking, sexy, with teeth like tiny white toilets. Callme moans when she goes by, and I try to give him a look that says he doesn't have any soul claim. Then I moan as the redhead comes, last, with legs showing to the thighs, legs that need pantyhose as much as I need a rubber. My dick unfolds. Maybe we're downwind, if there's a wind; maybe they've overdone it; maybe I'm sniffing more than my share of air, but I smell perfume and it is the sweetest thing I've ever smelled in my life. I can actually feel my mouth water when they go by, and as though I am isolated I can pick out the tones of their voices from the noise of the GIs like I'm doing a documentary and they are wearing microphones. Maybe the whiskey and that little bit of pot has *me* wired, but for an uncountable minute I am completely gone from here, yet here too. All the maddening reality recedes and all I am aware of is these chicks setting their boxes all around the biggest parapet, and I feel like I'm at a movie or a play and that I'll be able to leave when it's over.

GIs come up the hill from every direction and they're all carrying something and they all give me the impression they're as mesmerized as I am, and everybody is trying to look a little different than he did an hour ago. A lot of the dudes sitting across the parapet from us look almost clean and I've never noticed how many tattoos there are. A couple guys have cigars.

They are unpacking the boxes, and the redhead stands up on an empty one and waits while the whistles and shouts die down. I'm close enough to see that she has freckles.

"As most of you know, we are Red Cross volunteers. And the Red Cross designates us as Red Cross Donut Dollies. And, as we all know, you guys don't call us dollies, you call us Donut Holes. It's not what you call us that we care about. It is how you like our being here that counts." There's plenty of applause, and it is strangely polite, like we'd just as soon listen to her and the rest of them as hoot and holler. The others are done unpacking now and they've all moved out from the center. The lucky guys with cameras are burning up film. I'd take a few of the girls, but I'd take some of the dudes because I like seeing everybody looking happy. Callme is dashing back with two C-tins of whiskey. His face looks like the guy in his R&R pictures, but his fatigues are dirty already. He doesn't have a shirt on but he found a flak jacket somewhere and he's wearing that, open down the front with grenade rings woven into the zipper. He's got one part of a pair of sunglasses woven through the grenade rings. When he hands me my whiskey either the flak jacket or his armpits smell like fish worms.

The girls have a tape deck and a small amp. They brought three speakers, and a guy from the other side of the parapet digs up a speaker from somewhere, so within a few minutes, while the dude from Commo is hooking all the shit into Artillery's generator, a chant begins. It starts around a few guys from Three Squad who are all wearing hats they made out of sandbags and vines. They all have sunglasses on and get up on top of the parapet wall and form a chorus line. All four of them start clapping, then leaning toward the rest of us as if this were all rehearsed, like they are part of the show, and quick as hell everybody around the parapet is clapping his hands. The clapping starts out slowly at first, everybody starting to clap every time the chorus-line dudes kick their legs. Then the music comes on.

"God damn the pusher man . . ."

I hope that somewhere on the nearest hill there's a dink with a good set of binoculars. They're only used to Psy-Ops helicopters passing over with propaganda messages blaring into the jungle, but right now there is a speaker aimed in every direction and there are a hundred GIs singing along. *Charlie, this is the enemy, these black and white guys singing "Goddamn, ol' Uncle Sam."* And these girls have done this before; they have their routine down pat. After a couple minutes of us clapping for ourselves and whistling, some guys waving their hats in the air, the chorus line doing too many bows, the girls huddled near the tape deck looking in every direction and clapping along with us, they start the music up again without saying anything. It is a song I don't know, something funky, and the fat black chick takes over. She bumps and grinds and flows with the steady *boom-boom-boom* of the beat. She soon has fifty dancing partners standing on the parapet. I'm not one of them, but Callme and Chas are up there. Part of the time they're dancing with the Donut Holes and part of the time they get their own twosome going. *Jesus, for a camera.* Six-foot-plus Callme, with his flak jacket on, probably mostly to cover his rot, over a pair of shoulders like a roll of cold tar, and squatty Chas, as Irish-looking as a leprechaun, doing a boogie with each other.

The girls are digging back into their boxes and dragging out some stuff while the music switches to some instrumental, something jazzy. When Callme and Murphy jump down off the wall, I hand Callme his whiskey back.

"You niggers sure got rhythm," I say.

"You honky muthafuckers sure know how to get high."

He's probably saying that because Murphy comes up with a bowl and we duck down below the parapet long enough to blow about half of it. Omar comes back from wherever he's been and takes the bowl to finish it. He's got blue shades on, a tee shirt that was yellow once, and a shit-eating grin on his face. So here's Two Squad, *may we all make it.*

The Donut Holes hook the amp into a mike and turn the volume way down. Then a resupply Slick comes in and we all give the pilots the finger and a hearty boo, and the chicks turn the volume back up. The bird is hovering over the landing pad and we can't hear what the chick is saying. She stands there with the mike in her hand and her hand on her hip. *Goddammit, I'd have a picture of that too, show how war is hell.* I keep flashing on how the spirit has changed so much. Round-eyed women, amplified jams; it's American, *more American than a covey of lifers sitting around a peace table in Paris,* and a spirit like this could do a lot for the war effort if it could be made to go beyond when the chicks leave. A guy vaults over the parapet. He's got his helmet liner on and is probably wearing six sets of beads. His whole chest is covered with beads, and the beads swing ahead of him constantly because he jives along the inside of the parapet wall with his head way forward. He is walking around with his fist in the air and shouting something to the dudes he goes past, but I can't hear him. He goes about halfway around before he takes a shortcut to the middle where the blonde and the black beauty are shouting into each other's ears. They have put the microphone down on a stack of sandbags between them because nobody can hear anything until the Slick takes off. The dude with all the beads picks the microphone up and the dude working the amp turns up the amp. Like he is Jesus with a shitload of fish, this guys starts in on the amp with a harmonica, and little by little we can hear it better and better. He blows some quick blues.

"Hey," he shouts, "let's sing that fuckin' helicopter an old Army Hymn."

"Yeah," we shout all at once, like a chorus.

Then with the mike and the amp and about a hundred GIs singing, we almost drown out the sound of the bird with the hymn—

> Him
> Him
> Fuck him

—and we do it again and all point at the pad. The girls evidently haven't heard the Army Hymn and they laugh through the first verse and help with the second time through. The ringleading dude is between the redhead and the big black chick, and they and probably all of us point at the bird and sing it once more—

HIM, HIM, F-U-U-U-CK HIM

—and the bird, that has never come closer than ten feet to

the ground, does something I've never seen one do before: it climbs mostly straight up but a little backwards too. It keeps on climbing and climbing until it is higher than Slicks usually fly, and it swings way up there like the pair of girls' underpants that Prophet tied to the end of his kite when he came back from R&R.

Then the girls divide us into two teams and two girls lead each team in a game of charades that lasts about half an hour. Then they set up ten sandbags in the parapet and choose ten guys to play musical chairs. It seems pretty ridiculous at first, but it gets interesting because it has to be the roughest game of musical chairs ever. When there are only four sandbags left, the five dudes in the circle fight like hell for a seat and one guy gets knocked cold. The Donut Dollies think he is faking it at first but pretty soon a medic turns him over and she gasps. Like this is some kind of school play, when the chick gasps the guy starts coming to and finally gets some applause when he gets back to his feet. The medic is escorting him out, but when he comes to the only puddle in the parapet he scoops up two handfuls of mud and slings it at the dudes sitting on the sandbags. When there is only one sandbag left and two guys walking around it the chicks let the music go on a long time. These

Red Cross volunteers Barbara McDaniels (right) and Tee Johnson quiz GIs on sports trivia near Bien Hoa, 1969.

two guys are stalking around the sandbag like two kittens. They swat at each other and try to shove each other away. When the music stops the little guy dives head first onto the bag and the other guy tries once to get him off but can't. The winner gets a pair of boxer shorts, still in the package. He tears the package open and pulls them on over the cutoffs he's wearing.

The last song on the tape is by the Animals, "We Gotta Get Out of This Place." It's always been a popular song, but it has never been sung by as many guys at once. The Donut Holes blow us kisses good-bye after they pass out Red Cross packs and give pocket Bibles to anybody who wants one. When the group goes by us this time, I get the feeling the chicks are tired and that their smiles are almost used up. I'm tired too and I focus on the redhead's neck, covered with freckles.

A White House Meeting

by James C. Thomson, Jr.

*"Minutes of a White House Meeting, Summer, 1967" enjoyed an underground circulation in government circles where its author, James C. Thomson, Jr., was a bright young Far Eastern specialist in the State Department, and on the National Security Council staff, during 1961-67. An earlier Thomson satire in the same vein was reproduced anonymously in Arthur Schlesinger, Jr.'s, A Thousand Days. But by the time this one ran in the **Atlantic Monthly** of May 1967, for all the scarcity of things to laugh about in Washington that year, it rasped on short nerve ends. One of the real-life characters in the satire phoned a mutual friend at Harvard, where Thomson was now an assistant professor of history, and angrily allowed that Thomson should abandon any thought of ever returning to a government job. The **Atlantic's** editors were told that President Johnson was also unamused, and had remarked that "Minutes" sounded to him "like something that kid Moyers would write." The irritation is understandable: Thomson's spoof of the jargon, the pretensions, and the foibles of high-level government bureaucrats is so close to the real thing it stings.*

SCENE: Situation Room

CAST: National Security Council Staff

Hon. Herman Melville Breslau, Special Assistant to the President for National Security Affairs

Hon. Charles Homer, Special Assistant to the President for Peaceful Reconstruction in Vietnam

Hon. Frederick Ulan, Deputy Special Assistant to the President for European and International Economic Affairs

Hon. Charles Rentner, Special Assistant to the President for Public Image Affairs

Mr. Brown (South Asia)
Colonel Black (Pentagon)
Mr. Blue (Latin America)
Mr. White (Africa)
Mr. Gray (Miscellany)
Mr. Rose (Far East)
Mr. Gold (China Watcher)
Mr. Green (White House Fellow)

Mr. Breslau opened the meeting with a commentary on the latest reports from Vietnam. In general, he felt, the events of the previous day were a wholesome and not unexpected phase in South Vietnam's growth toward political maturity and economic viability. The fall of Saigon to the Viet Cong meant that the enemy was now confronted with a challenge of unprecedented proportions for which it was totally unprepared: the administration of a major city. If we could dump rice and airlift pigs at Hue and Danang, he was pretty sure that the other side would soon cave. He cautioned, however, that this was merely a hunch. "It is not the kind of smell you can hang your hat on."

Mr. Homer said that Mr. Breslau was full of crap; Mr. Breslau had never understood Vietnam and should stop trying. Things were very, very bad, but they would get infinitely worse if we dumped rice and pigs.

Mr. Breslau suggested that we move around the table rapidly so that we could all get back to work. Did Mr. Ulan have business to raise?

(The white telephone rang, and Mr. Breslau answered it. It was a test ring.)

Mr. Ulan said that he had spent the previous day with the German financial mission, and of course could not go into detail, but might shorthand some of the considerations which involved, on the one hand, a reading of what the electoral situation would be after Braunschweig (which was itself quite sticky), and on the other hand, a close calculation of the odds if we didn't (or, conversely, if they didn't), and on the third hand, a pretty shrewd look at the long-term consequences of any action at all when you factor out the balance of payments curve.

Mr. Breslau commented that the Germans were a fascinating bunch. He hoped that Mr. Ulan had taken a good hard look at the real numbers involved. He had always felt that numbers were important. Mr. Ulan said yes.

Mr. Rentner hoped that Mr. Breslau wouldn't mind his reporting to the staff the President's deep pleasure and pride in Mr. Breslau's performance the previous Sunday on the *What's My Line?* show. The President's regard for Mr. Breslau and the entire staff had never been higher. The President was also very pleased with the new Harris poll, due out on Monday, which indicated that 86 percent of the people approved his recently announced decision to make foreign policy decisions on the basis of Harris poll findings.

Mr. Brown said that the reports of imminent mass starvation in India were more serious than we had expected; a presidential decision might be required this week.

Mr. Rentner said that it would take a good three weeks to set up and test-run a Harris poll on that kind of question.

Mr. Breslau said he hoped the Indians would take a good hard look at the development of chemical fertilizers. He asked Mr. Brown to ride herd on this one.

Mr. Homer noted that neither Mr. Breslau nor Mr. Brown knew a goddamn thing about Indian agriculture.

Colonel Black explained the previous night's raids on North Vietnam. We had knocked out 78 percent of North Vietnam's petroleum reserves; since we had knocked out 86 percent three days ago, and 92 percent last week, we were doing exceptionally well.

Mr. Breslau asked about the weather over North Vietnam. His Air Force experience in World War II had taught him, he said, the importance of weather.

Colonel Black said that it didn't look good for the next few days.

Mr. Breslau said this was too bad since some people might think we were having a pause.

Mr. Ulan wondered if maybe it wasn't time for another pause.

Mr. Breslau said that a pause was clearly out of the question now that the 12,000 student leaders and 3 million housewives had once again called for a pause. The President did not like to be crowded, especially now that Hanoi was hurting.

Mr. Ulan wondered if Hanoi was really hurting.

Mr. Breslau suggested that we move along since he had another meeting coming up.

Mr. Blue reported the execution by the new Brazilian government of all the nation's university rectors.

Mr. Breslau commented that the new government had, nonetheless, really done its homework in the economic field; the overall curve was very promising.

Mr. White reported that the Rhodesia thing might come unstuck over the weekend. The Zambians were wobbly and could use some massaging. The President might call in their ambassador and pump up his tires.

Mr. Breslau said we should probably lie low on this until the new task force report on Africa was completed. In any event, the President didn't like to be crowded by foreigners. Perhaps the Potomac River *Sequoia* cruise for black African ambassadors would take care of the problem.

Mr. Homer said that if the African *Sequoia* trip was anything like the Middle Eastern one, we were due to lose another thirty countries and 200 million people. The Turkish ambassador had had to sit through the film *A President's Country* seven times now and was requesting transfer to another post.

Mr. Rentner expressed doubt that such reactions were widespread. The President was very fond of that film. Furthermore, USIA audience surveys in Korea, Taiwan, and South Vietnam had shown overwhelmingly favorable response to it.

Mr. Gray said that the interagency nuclear desalinization package was moving forward and might go for a decision this week if we could get the AEC, the ICC, the IFC, AID, State, DOD, BOB, and NASA aboard. Agriculture, he added, was playing it cool and might need a needle.

Mr. Breslau asked Mr. Gray to ride herd on this one. He hoped that they would take a good hard look at the real numbers involved.

Mr. Breslau announced that the ban on having NSC staff members talk to the press was causing some serious prob-

lems since the press had decided that the staff was no longer significant. The President would now like all staff members to talk to the press as much as possible, stressing the significance of the staff. They must be careful, however, to avoid talking substance to the press.

Mr. Rentner agreed that this was a good move and the staff should increase its visibility. He added that staff members should scrupulously avoid contacts, however, with Joseph Kraft, Joseph Alsop, Walter Lippmann, Max Frankel, Douglas Kiker, the New York *Times* people, and the Washington *Post* people. These contacts would be handled by Mr. Breslau and himself.

Mr. Rose said that he was quite worried about the public relations aspect of the fall of Saigon.

Mr. Breslau said he thought we could live with that one. He was very much reminded, he added, of one of his favorite scenes from *Hellzapoppin'*. What fascinated him more than Saigon was the reported purge of the assistant managing editor of the *Hankow People's Daily*; in writing his book on Communist China in 1953, he had concluded that the assistant managing editors of riverport newspapers were often the key indicators of policy shifts. Did Mr. Gold have a comment?

Mr. Gold said he would certainly look into this.

Mr. Breslau said that he had received Mr. Green's long study of the Vatican's relations with San Marino; he only wished the entire staff could read it. Mr. Green said thank you.

Mr. Homer noted that neither Mr. Breslau nor Mr. Green knew a goddamn thing about Italian politics.

(The white telephone rang, and Mr. Breslau answered it. It was Mrs. Breslau. The meeting was adjourned.)

China Beach

from *Vietnam-Perkasie: A Combat Marine Memoir*
by W. D. Ehrhart

Bill Ehrhart grew up in the small town of Perkasie, Penn-sylvania, joined the Marines in 1966, and served in Viet-nam from February 1967 to February 1968. He was eighteen years old when he arrived, nineteen when he left; his account captures the youthfulness of those who fought America's Indochina war.

"You been sayin' you wanna go swimming in the South China Sea since the day I met you," said Gerry. "There it is, sucker; go to it."

"Yahoo!" I shouted, tossing my towel aside and racing full tilt across the beach. "Last one in's a rotten egg!" I high-stepped in to my knees, plunged headfirst, glided underwater, surfaced like a breaching whale, and began stroking strongly away from shore. The water was warm, the surface flat and calm, and my body hadn't felt so buoyant and free in months—years, it seemed. I did a flip turn, pushed off an imaginary wall, came out on my back, and started slowly sculling, squirting water out of my mouth like a fireboat on the Fourth of July. Gerry paddled up beside me, and we both began to tread water.

"Salty," he said, spitting out a mouthful.

"Fuckin'-A!" I shouted, "Just like me. I'm salty! Halfway there, chump. It's all fuckin' downhill from here."

The In-Country Rest & Recuperation Center at China Beach, Danang, wasn't exactly Hong Kong or Singapore,

but it gave Marines a chance to escape the war for a day or two. The facility included a snack bar where you could buy beer and soda, hamburgers and hot dogs, and listen to the juke box, an outdoor theater for movies, a small barracks for Marines spending the night, and a long stretch of wide, clean beach. Lieutenant Kaiser had given me two days off to celebrate the halfway point in my tour of duty, and Gerry and I had hopped a truck for the beach that morning. We didn't have to be back till the next evening.

Gerry and I paddled around awhile, letting the water massage our bodies and soak the dirt from armpits and toes and fingernails. We played a game of submarine, and stood on the bottom on our hands.

"I wish there were some waves," I said. "I'd like to do a little body surfing. Let's get out awhile." We stretched our towels out on the sand and lay down in the hot sun. The beach was lined with Marines in camouflage shorts and cut-off utility trousers. At either end of the beach were lifeguard towers, each with two lifeguards and a fully dressed armed Marine.

"Boy, this is weird," I said.

"What?"

"This beach. No girls; just guys."

"Whadja expect? Joey Heatherton?"

"'Course not. But the beach, you know, there's supposed to be girls. Back in New Jersey, Christ, you should see

Ocean City on Memorial Day. Fuckin' fur-pie everywhere. Wall-to-wall beavers. Two piece bikinis with little hairs stickin' out around the crotch. Tits hangin' out. Legs right up to the asshole."

"Hey, shut up, will you? Jesus, you wanna blow a fuse?" I piped down, and we both lay there for awhile with our eyes closed.

"Gerry?"

"Yeh?"

"I haven't gotten a letter from Jenny in three weeks."

"Last week it was two weeks. Don't worry about it, will you? She probably went on vacation or something."

"She'd have told me about that. Anyway, she could write on vacation. It's startin' to worry me, you know? What if she's been in a car wreck or something? Jesus, I'd go nuts."

"If somethin' happened to her, somebody would've written to you."

"I don't know. When I was in boot camp, a high school friend of mine got killed in a car wreck. Suzie Brenner. We weren't boyfriend and girlfriend or nothin', but we were pretty tight. My parents didn't tell me till I got home on leave."

"You're gonna go Section Eight, you keep thinkin' like that, pal. Look, she's okay. It's probably just the mail. Talbot says mail gets sent the wrong fuckin' place all the time. Just be patient, will ya? Take it easy. I'm thirsty. Salt water's got my mouth all parched. Let's go get a beer."

"You can't go in the slop-chute in your bathing suit. Gotta get dressed."

"You wanna go in the water anymore?"

"Nah, I guess not. Nothin' to do without any waves. Beach is too protected here. They got great waves down by Phuoc Trac."

"Yeh, they got beau coup VC, too," said Gerry. "They even got the fish trained, I bet. Fuckin' flounder swim right up to you, blow up right in your face."

"Look, Rocky; fan mail from some flounder," I said.

"What's it say, Bullwinkle?" said Gerry.

"Just listen. Ka-boom!!!"

We got dressed and walked up to the snack bar. The juke box was playing loudly.

"That asshole Haller'd have a field day around here," I said. "Listen to that shit. They don't even sing anymore. Just get loaded up on drugs and scream and throw up into the microphone. What the hell's goin' on back there in The World?"

"Aw, Haller's okay," said Gerry. "You ever talk to him?"

"Only when I have to." I downed two beers and two cheeseburgers in two minutes. "More beer! More cheeseburgers!" I hollered, thumping the empty can on the table. A young Vietnamese woman came over to the table with another round. "Ah, sweet cheeseburger queen, the girl of my dreams," I beamed. A guy at the table next to us patted her on the backside.

"You're gonna shit your fuckin' brains out tonight, sucker," Gerry warned. "You better go easy on that pogey-bait. Your stomach ain't used to it anymore."

"I don't care, I don't give a fuck; I ain't had a cheeseburger in eight months. This is hog holiday!" I roared, piling on pickles, onions, relish, catsup and mustard. "Bury me with a beer in each hand."

"Okay, buddy, just remember you asked for it," said Gerry. "Come to think of it, so did I." He grabbed another cheeseburger for himself. "When's Lieutenant Kaiser leaving?"

"Couple of weeks, maybe three. Sometime in early September."

"What're you goin' to do about Gunny Johnson?"

"Oh, I got him pretty well under control. I did everything he said when he got here; soon as he went back to sleep, I changed it all back the way it was. He never even noticed; he's just a lifer, man; he don't really care. Long as he thinks you think he's the boss. That fuckin' crap down on the river slowed him up a bit, too. Don't talk so loud anymore."

"What's happening with Sergeant Wilson, you heard?"

"Lieutenant said they were shipping him back to the States. That's the last I heard. They're gonna give Seagrave another stripe and make him chief scout."

"Yeh? I thought they'd give it to Walters or Newcome."

"Naw. Wally and Mogerty are good, all right, but they're too crazy. Gravey's real steady. Don't get rattled and don't cut loose. He ain't Sergeant Wilson, but you just don't find many around like him. That guy's so smart—never finished tenth grade and taught himself Vietnamese. Learned Arabic when he was on embassy duty. All kinds of stuff—and a really good guy, too. I'm gonna miss him. Anyway, Gravey's a good choice; he'll take it real seriously. We're birthday buddies, 'dja know that? September thirtieth. He's exactly one year older than me."

"Geez," said Gerry, "nineteen and he's a sergeant already."

"You watch, pal; I'll be a sergeant before I turn twenty. Be eligible in December, and I ain't even nineteen yet. They're losin' bodies left and right around here. Gotta promote somebody, and Lieutenant Kaiser's been givin' me 4.9s and 5.0s on my pro & con marks. That oughta make up for the points I lose on time in service."

"Jesus, Ehrhart, how do you rate? I'm almost twenty-one and I ain't even a corporal yet."

"That might change pretty quick."

"You know somethin' I don't know?"

"I might."

"Well. Fork over. What is it?"

"Well, listen, don't buy the champagne yet, but I think you're on the list this time."

"How do you know?" said Gerry, poking his head up from behind a fourth cheeseburger.

"Lieutenant Kaiser looked. Amagasu's on it, and he said you are, too."

In-country R&R, Da Nang.

"Hot damn! It's about fuckin' time."

"What the hell, man, you don't do nothin' but sit around twirlin' your tumblers all day. Big deal. Janitor could do that."

"Fuck you."

"I can't eat any more."

"Me neither. Wanna go swimming again?"

"I'm too drunk. And too full. Sharkbait." I burped loudly.

"Come on," said Gerry. "We could swim back to The World. We could swim to Sweden! Let's go. Only take us a couple of months. Straight out there to Hawaii, then southeast to the Panama Canal and over to Africa; turn left, up to Europe, through the English Channel and we're home free! How about it? We can be there by October. Think of it: blondes everywhere! Free love! Ingrid Bergman!"

"We can use our cocks for masts!" I shouted. "Tie our jungle jackets to 'em. Here come the Vikings! Arf, arf!

Shiver me timbers, Brunhilde; I'm Beowulf, and this here's my sidekick, Tonto. We're lookin' for mead an' ale. Which way's the bedroom?"

"Wanna see the Hammer of Thor, Brunhilde? I've slain thousands with it."

"Look at 'em all lyin' there smiling. Line forms to the rear; no pushing! You're next, blondie."

"What're we waitin' for? Let's start stroking."

We both sat there for awhile, looking out to sea.

"Whaddaya wanna do?" asked Gerry.

"I don't know. Whadda you wanna do?"

"My stomach's feelin' a little shaky."

"So's mine. What time is it?"

"1430."

"Movie don't start till after dark."

"You wanna stay tonight?"

"I don't know. Do you?"

"Probably be the only time we get to come up here. I hate to waste it."

"Me, too."

"Well?"

"I don't know."

We both sat there for awhile.

"Let's hitch a ride back to Battalion," said Gerry.

"Okay."

We had a wonderful four-holed outhouse at Battalion that was truly one of the engineering masterpieces of the Navy SeaBees. It was really a small walk-up hooch made of plywood, with a screen door and screened-in windows all around the upper half of the walls. The bench-type seat was sanded smooth to prevent splinters in tender places, and toilet paper hung on pegs within easy reach. The outhouse was built on high stilts to allow 55-gallon drums to be placed beneath each hole; these were removed daily, doused with gasoline and burned, a process known as "burning the shitters."

Though it was well after dark, Gerry and I had hardly left the outhouse since we'd gotten back from China Beach. After a number of trips back and forth between Gerry's hooch and the outhouse, we'd both given up and decided to remain seated, saving us both a lot of time and trouble.

"I almost didn't make it that last time," said Gerry.

"Jesus, I feel awful," I said. "Whadda they put in those cheeseburgers, anyway? Drano?"

"Water bo burgers," said Gerry, "imported from Hanoi." Suddenly gunfire erupted off to the south. It rapidly built to a steady sustained pitch, punctuated by explosions that sounded like grenades, mortars and light artillery.

"What the hell's goin' on?" I said, craning my neck back over my shoulder. "Jesus, look at that. You can see right over the berm from up here. I never noticed that before."

"Looks like Hoi An," Gerry said. At that moment, a general alert sounded through the compound, the great wailing sirens like fire whistles shattering the darkness.

Marines began to pile out of hooches, hotfooting it helter-skelter for the berm. "Shit," said Gerry.

"Forget it," I said. "They'll never miss us. I ain't goin' anywhere. My asshole's so sore, I can't move."

"They're really gettin' hit down there. Better lace up your boots, just in case we gotta move in a hurry."

"This is amazing. You can see right over the berm from up here. Wonder why Charlie's never taken a shot at somebody takin' a crap."

"Even the gooks got some sense of decency. Jesus, somebody's *really* takin' a shellacking."

"Looks like two different places," I said. "That one on the right's Hoi An, probably the MACV compound. That other place on the left must be the national police headquarters at Hieu Nhon."

"Yo! Get outta there. Ya fuckin' deaf? General alert," someone hollered from the bottom of the steps. It sounded like the sergeant of the guard.

"We can't," I hollered back. "We're sick." The door opened.

"You two?!" said Sergeant Barron.

"Hi, Sarge," said Gerry. "We're sick. Can't move, doctor's orders."

"We went to China Beach today," I added. "They put Drano in our cheeseburgers. We been sittin' here since 1800. Honest."

"Somebody's gotta guard the crapper," said Gerry. "If they overrun us, we'll hold out to the last roll of ass-wipe."

"Did you know you can see right over the top of the berm from up here?" I pointed out. "We'll let you know if we see 'em comin'."

"You guys are gonna get your heads blown off," said Barron. "Serve you right, too. Why'd they ever let you in my Marine Corps?"

"That's what I'd like to know," said Gerry.

"We're volunteers of America," I said. "What's goin' on down there, anyway?"

"The prison in Hoi An and the national police headquarters at Hieu Nhon are both under attack. Looks like they're probably trying to spring the prisoners. MACV says they've got recoilless rifles and B-40s."

"Well, I was close. MACV takin' anything?" I asked.

"Just enough to keep 'em pinned inside their compound. Said the gooks are all over the city. Platoon from Delta tried to get through to Hieu Nhon, and stepped right into the shit. Colonel told 'em to forget it and pull back. Listen, you can stay in here if you want to—but be damned well ready to move. They just might try to hit here."

"Sure, Sarge. Thanks."

The fighting continued without slackening. From where we were, four miles away, it sounded like a continuous dull roar. You could see the soft flash of individual explosions and a wild criss-crossing of tracer rounds, some of them spinning up toward the stars before dying out like Roman candles. The whole thing looked like one of those animated representations of an atom, distorted and flattened into half a globe, the horizon hiding the other half. We could see half a dozen secondary fires.

"I wonder where Co Chi is tonight," I said.

"Who?"

"Miss Chi. You know, the secretary at Hieu Nhon I told you about. The really pretty one. Long hair. Always wears a white ao dai."

"Oh, yeh. The one Trinh said wanted your picture."

"Yeh."

"You think she's there tonight?"

"I don't know. Don't know where she lives. Never said anything to her but hello. Doesn't speak English—and she's real shy."

"She wouldn't live there."

"I don't know. I hope not."

"Jesus."

"Yeh."

A tremendous explosion erupted, sending fire and burning debris high into the air; two more explosions followed.

"Wanna bet the VC just blew into the prison?" I said.

"No bet," said Gerry. "Who do they got in there?"

"Who'd they have in there. Everybody. VC, detainees, suspects, murderers, robbers. Like a political prison and county jail all in one. Couple thousand inmates, maybe. Charlie just got a whole new division."

We lapsed into silence for awhile.

"This is unreal," said Gerry.

"What?"

"Watching this. Like the movies or somethin'."

Neither of us said anything else for a long time. Almost imperceptibly at first, the fire began to slacken; then it dropped off noticeably until there was only sporadic gunfire. Long periods of silence were briefly interrupted by bursts of machinegun and automatic rifle fire, an explosion here and there, all of it happening far away, almost on another planet. Half an hour passed. There was no shooting at all now.

"Jesus," said Gerry. Another fifteen minutes passed.

"That coulda been us," I said. Dark forms began withdrawing from the berm. Screen doors on hooches banged softly.

"How do you feel?" Gerry asked.

"Like I just had an enema of battery acid. How 'bout you?"

"Nothin' left inside of me. I've shit everything out—stomach, heart, liver, brain, the whole nine yards."

"Wanna try to sleep?"

"I guess so," said Gerry. "But I'm takin' one of these with me." He pulled up his trousers and stuck a roll of toilet paper in one of the big thigh pockets. I did, too.

Tet: Three Views

The Tet offensive, an audacious series of Communist assaults against South Vietnam that began during the Tet (Lunar New Year) holiday of January 30-31, 1968, changed forever American attitudes toward the war. For years military and administration figures had assured the American public that the war was gradually being won. Those claims stood in stark contrast to the images now before the nation: Vietcong infiltrators inside the American embassy compound in Saigon, heavy fighting in virtually every South Vietnamese city and major town, U.S. military strong points under siege, the beautiful city of Hue reduced to rubble. The sheer scale and ferocity of the Communist attacks shook American confidence, and fueled a growing chorus of doubt and protest against the war.

Following are three perspectives on the meaning of the Tet offensive. Columnist William S. White echoed a theme popular among the "hawks" at the time; Walter Cronkite, anchorman for "The CBS Evening News," delivered a rare personal editorial perspective at the conclusion of a special report; and Art Buchwald's analysis was widely noted for its biting satire of the military's optimism in the wake of Tet.

Red Gains in Viet Cities Like Last Nazi Spasm at The Bulge
by William S. White
(the *Washington Post*, February 12, 1968)

In the Vietnam War the position now may be summed up in a somber sentence. The phase of agony—for those who must fight it, for those in authority here and in Saigon who must conduct it, and for those private men who in duty and in conscience must support it—has ended. Opening now is the phase of anguish, and conceivably also of the last real crisis.

For whatever may be said of the enemy spasms of recent weeks, and however debated may be which side won and which lost, one stark reality now towers above all else. The Communist assailants are farther away than ever before from any intention to listen to any honest overture and are accordingly putting all their chips into the pot, to win all or to lose all.

To grope as best one can through the miasma of Washington today—a miasma surely not exampled since Lincoln's ordeals of the Civil War a century and more ago—the weight of all the evidence suggests certain other clear realities.

The Communists—the Vietcong Fifth Column and the now heavily committed regular troops of North Vietnam—scored undeniable propaganda and morale successes in their suicide guerrilla assaults upon the cities and civilians of South Vietnam. They did, however, suffer enormously wasteful casualties; and in naked objectivity their operation, apart from propaganda terms, is likely in the end to turn out to have been self-defeating—with one immense and poignant qualification. . . .

Granted some tolerance for the undoubted weaknesses—and some compassion for the ghastly burdens—of the Saigon regime this brutal eruption will at last sink into the category of an ugly episode rather than as a victory.

For the real name of the game militarily is still the major battle shaping up at Khe Sanh, an action capable of dwarfing in meaning and violence all that has gone before. The highest American military authorities—and there is really no reason, except among peaceniks lost in rage and terror, to suppose that these devoted professionals are liars or fools—believe that we can take the enemy's measure here and possibly fatally blunt his main cutting edge.

One of the ablest military heroes known to this columnist, a man totally unconcerned with hissing political argumentation, sees this climactic test at arms as holding a potential parallel to the Battle of the Bulge of the Second World War. There the Germans undertook a suicide spasm of their own. There the Germans won a giant propaganda windfall. But in the harsh ultimate logic of warfare they lost there. For the commitment was in truth a commitment not of wisdom but of desperation and could only have paid off given a disruption of Allied morale that never came.

This is not to say that any man should refrain from "dissent" or criticism for a moment. But rational dissent and criticism do not mean pillorying a general in the field like Westmoreland; do not mean attempts by a tiny Senate minority to destroy a Secretary of State [McNamara] for remaining faithful to an American commitment of honor; do not mean trying to expose the last details of American intelligence operations before hostile eyes. And they do not mean conscious and determined defeatism.

From CBS television, the concluding minutes of *"Who, What, When, Where, Why: Report from Vietnam by Walter Cronkite,"* aired February 27, 1968.

Tonight, back in more familiar surroundings in New York, we'd like to sum up our findings in Vietnam, an analysis that must be speculative, personal, subjective. Who won and who lost in the great Tet offensive against the cities? I'm not sure. The Vietcong did not win by a knockout, but neither did we. The referees of history may make it a draw. Another stand-off may be coming in the big battles expected south of the Demilitarized Zone. Khe Sanh could well fall, with a terrible loss in American lives, prestige, and morale, and this is a tragedy of our stubbornness there; but the bastion no longer is a key to the rest of the northern regions, and it is doubtful that the American forces can be defeated across the breadth of the DMZ with any substantial loss of ground. Another stand-off. On the political front, past performance gives no confidence that the Vietnamese government can cope with its problems, now compounded by the attack on the cities. It may not fall, it may hold on, but it probably won't show the dynamic qualities demanded of this young nation. Another stand-off.

We have been too often disappointed by the optimism of the American leaders, both in Vietnam and Washington, to have faith any longer in the silver linings they find in the darkest clouds. They may be right, that Hanoi's winter-spring offensive has been forced by the communist realization that they could not win the longer war of attrition, and that the communists hope that any success in the offensive will improve their position for eventual negotiations. It would improve their position, and it would also require our realization, that we should have had all along, that any negotiations must be that—negotiations, not the dictation of peace terms. For it seems now more certain than ever that the bloody experience of Vietnam is to end in a stalemate. This summer's almost certain stand-off will either end in real give-and-take negotiations or terrible escalation; and for every means we have to escalate, the enemy can match us, and that applies to invasion of the North, the use of nuclear weapons, or the mere commitment of 100-, or 200-, or 300,000 more American troops to the battle. And with each escalation, the world comes closer to the brink of cosmic disaster.

To say that we are closer to victory today is to believe, in the face of the evidence, the optimists who have been wrong in the past. To suggest we are on the edge of defeat is to yield to unreasonable pessimism. To say that we are mired in stalemate seems the only realistic, yet unsatisfactory, conclusion. On the off chance that military and political analysts are right, in the next few months we must test the enemy's intentions, in case this is indeed his last gasp before negoti-

ations. But it is increasingly clear to this reporter that the only rational way out then will be to negotiate, not as victors, but as an honorable people who lived up to their pledge to defend democracy, and did the best they could.

This is Walter Cronkite. Good night.

"We have the enemy on the run" says General Custer at Big Horn
by Art Buchwald
(the *Washington Post*, February 6, 1968)

LITTLE BIG HORN, DAKOTA, June 27, 1876.—

Gen. George Armstrong Custer said today in an exclusive interview with this correspondent that the battle of Little Big Horn had just turned the corner and he could now see the light at the end of the tunnel.

"We have the Sioux on the run," Gen. Custer told me. "Of course, we still have some cleaning up to do, but the Redskins are hurting badly and it will only be a matter of time before they give in."

"That's good news, General. Of course, there are people who are skeptical about the military briefings on this war and they question if we're getting the entire truth as to what is really happening here."

"I just would like to refer you to these latest body counts. The Sioux lost 5000 men to our 100. They can't hope to keep up this attrition much longer. We know for a fact Sioux morale is low, and they are ready to throw in the towel."

"Well, if they're hurting so badly, Gen. Custer, how do you explain this massive attack?"

"It's a desperation move on the part of Sitting Bull and his last death rattle. I have here captured documents which show that this is Phase II of Sitting Bull's plan to wrest the Black Hills from the Americans. All he's going for is a psychological victory, but the truth is that we expected this all the time and we're not surprised by it."

"What about the fact that 19 Indians managed to penetrate your headquarters? Doesn't that look bad?"

"We knew all along they planned to penetrate my headquarters at the Indian

lunar new year. The fact that we repulsed them after they held on for only six hours is another example of how badly the Sioux are fighting. Besides, they never did get into the sleeping quarters of my tent, so I don't really think they should be credited with penetrating my headquarters."

"You seem to be surrounded at the moment, General."

"Obviously the enemy plans have gone afoul," Gen. Custer said. "The Sioux are hoping to win a big victory so they'll be able to have something to talk about at the conference table. Look at this latest body count. We've just killed 3000 more Indians and lost 50 of our men."

"Then, according to my figuring, General, you have only 50 men left."

"Exactly. They can't keep up this pressure much longer. The truth of the matter is that their hit-and-run guerrilla tactics haven't worked, so they're now resorting to mass attacks against our positions. Thanks to our interdiction of their supply lines, they are not only short of bows and arrows, but gunpowder as well."

An aide came in and handed Gen. Custer a sheet of paper. "I knew it," the General said. "The latest body count shows they've lost 2000 more injuns in the last hour. They should be suing for peace at any time."

"How many did we lose, General?"

"Our losses were light. We only lost 45 men."

"But general, that means you have only five men left, including yourself."

"Look, we have to lose some men, but we're taking all precautions to keep our losses to a minimum. Besides, we can always count on the friendly Indians in these hills to turn against the Sioux for starting hostilities during the Indian lunar new year."

The aide staggered back in, an arrow in his chest. He handed Gen. Custer the slip of paper and then dropped at his feet.

"Well, they just lost 500 more. And we only lost four. It looks as if they've had it."

"But, General, that means you're the only one left."

"Boy," said the General, "would I hate to be in Sioux shoes right now."

Encounter on Tu Do Street

from *Dog Soldiers*
by Robert Stone

Robert Stone's **Dog Soldiers,** *which won the National Book Award, is a complex tale of greed and violence set in Vietnam and America. In this opening scene Converse, a journalist about to become involved in heroin trafficking, meets his spiritual opposite on a bench in Saigon.*

There was only one bench in the shade and Converse went for it, although it was already occupied. He inspected the stone surface for unpleasant substances, found none, and sat down. Beside him he placed the oversized briefcase he had been carrying; its handle shone with the sweat of his palm. He sat facing Tu Do Street, resting one hand across the case and raising the other to his forehead to check the progress of his fever. It was Converse's nature to worry about his health.

The other occupant of the bench was an American lady of middling age.

It was siesta hour and there was no one else in the park. The children who usually played soccer on the lawns were across the street, sleeping in the shade of their mothers' street stalls. The Tu Do hustlers had withdrawn into the arcade of Eden Passage where they lounged sleepy-eyed, rousing themselves now and then to hiss after the passing of a sweating American. It was three o'clock and the sky was almost cloudless. The rain was late. There was no

wind, and the palm crowns and poinciana blossoms of the park trees hung motionless.

Converse glanced secretly at the lady beside him. She was wearing a green print dress and a canvas hat with a sun visor. She had offered him a weary smile upon his sitting down; he wondered if there would be compatrial conversation. Her face was as smooth as a young girl's but gray and colorless so that it was difficult to tell whether she was youthfully preserved or prematurely aged. Her waxen coloring was like an opium smoker's but she did not seem at all the sort. She was reading *The Citadel* by A. J. Cronin.

The lady looked up suddenly from her book, surprising Converse in mid-appraisal. She was certainly not an opium smoker. Her eyes were clear and warm brown. Converse, whose tastes were eccentric, found her attractive.

"Well," he said in his hearty, imitation-Army accent, "we'll have some weather pretty soon."

Out of politeness, she looked at the sky.

"It's certainly going to rain," she assured him. "But not for a while."

"Guess not," Converse said thoughtfully. When he looked away, she returned to her book.

Converse had come to the park to catch the cool breeze

that always came before the rain and to read his mail. He was killing time before his appointment, trying to steady his nerve. He did not wish to appear on the *terrasse* of the Continental at such an early hour.

He took a small stack of letters from his case and looked them over. There was one from a Dutch underground paper which published in English, asking him for a Saigon piece. There were two checks, one from his father-in-law and one from a newspaper in Ireland. There was also a letter from his wife in Berkeley. He took a handkerchief from his shirt pocket, wiped the sweat from his eyes, and began to read.

"Well, I went to New York after all," his wife had written, "spent nineteen days there. Took Janey with me and she wasn't really much trouble. I'm back at the theater now in time for a brand new beaver special which is the most depressing flick this place has put on yet. Everybody here says hello and take care of yourself.

"New York was pretty scary. Forty-second Street is incredible now. It makes Three Street feel nice and homely. You'll find it a lot less pleasant the next time you go buy a hot dog at that place on Broadway you used to go to. I went there out of spite anyway—shit like that doesn't bother me as much as it does you. Also I rode on the subway which I bet you wouldn't do.

"Took Janey up to Croton for a visit with Uncle Jay and his Hudson River Bolsheviks. We went to a National Guardian party and that really took me back, with all the folk singers and the tame spades. We ate somebody's idea of Mex food and there were mariachis from the Puerto Rican Alps and people telling stories about how Sequeiros was their buddy. No spicy stories for you this time because I didn't make it with anybody. If Gallagher was there I might have made it with him but he wasn't. Everybody's pissed at him up there."

Looking up, Converse saw a street photographer in a Hawaiian shirt advancing toward his bench. He put up his hand in a gesture of refusal and the man turned back toward Eden Passage. The Tu Do Street cowboys had come out from wherever they spent their siestas and were revving up their Hondas. There was still no breeze.

Converse read on:

"The heaviest thing that happened while we were in New York was we went to a parade which was for the War. Three of us—me, looking relatively straight, and Don and Cathy looking modified freaky. We weren't too well received. You had to see that action to believe it. There were eight million flags and round little Polish priests goose-stepping around with their Boy Bugle Corps, Ukrainians with sabers and fur hats, German Veterans of the Warsaw Ghetto Battle, the Brotherhood of Former Concentration Camp Guards, the Sons of Mussolini, the Baboons Union. Incredible. My flash was that these people are freakier than we ever could be. One tends to think of them as straight but when you see them they're unreal. I had this

snoutface meatyard accost me—'The rats are coming out of their holes,' he said. I told him, 'Listen mother, my husband is in Vietnam.' "

Converse looked up from the letter again and found himself staring vacantly at the lady beside him.

The lady smiled.

"Letter from home?"

"Yes," Converse said.

"When I was up in Croton, Jay asked me if I knew what was going on. With *everything*. He said he didn't understand anything that was going on at all. He said maybe he should take drugs. Sarcastically. I told him he was damn right he should. He said that drugs condition the intellect to fascism and came on about C. Manson and said he would rather die than surrender his intellect. He also said he didn't need dope which is a laugh because if there was ever one man who needed it *bad* it's him. I told him that if he'd turned on he'd never have been a Stalinist. He brings out the sadist in me. Which is weird because he's really such a nice man. Our argument reminded me of when I was a kid me and Dodie were walking with him when we passed an integrated black and white couple. Jay dug the shit out of that naturally because it was so progressive, and he wants to show us kids. 'Isn't that nice?' he says. Dodie, who couldn't have been more than ten, says 'I think it's disgusting.' Dodie could always play him like a pinball machine."

Converse folded the letter and looked at his watch. The lady beside him had set down her A. J. Cronin.

"Everything fine with your folks?"

"Oh yes," Converse said, "fine. Family visits and things."

"It's easier for you fellas to do your jobs when you know everything's all right back home."

"I find that's true," Converse said.

"You're not with AID, are you?"

"No." He sought for a word. "Bao chi."

Bao chi was what the Vietnamese call journalists. Converse was a journalist of sorts.

"Oh yes," the lady said. "Been here long?"

"Eighteen months. And you. Have you been here long?"

"Fourteen years."

Converse was unable to conceal his horror.

There were faded freckles in the gray skin under the lady's eyes. She seemed to be laughing at him.

"Don't you like this country?"

"Yes," Converse answered truthfully. "I do."

"Where I make my home," she told Converse, "it's not nearly so hot as it is here. We've got pine trees. People say it's like northern California, but I've never been there."

"That must be up around Kontum."

"South of there. Ngoc Linh Province."

Converse had never been to Ngoc Linh Province; he knew very few people who had. He had flown over it, and from the air it looked thoroughly frightening, a deep green maze of iron-spine mountains. The clouds were full of rocks. No one went there, not even to bomb it, since the Green Berets had left.

"We call it God's country," the lady said. "It's sort of a joke."

"Aha." Converse wondered if all the flesh of her body were the same dingy gray as the skin of her face and if there were any more faded freckles in it. "What do you do up there?"

"Well," the lady said, "there are five different languages spoken by tribespeople up around us. We've been doing language studies."

Converse looked into her mild eyes.

Of course.

"You're a missionary."

"We don't call ourselves that way. I suppose some people would."

He nodded in sympathy. They never like the term. It suggested imperialism and being eaten.

"It must be . . ." Converse tried to think of what it must be . . . "very satisfying."

"We're never satisfied," the lady said gaily. "We always want to do more. I think our work's been blessed though we've certainly had our trials."

"That's part of it, isn't it?"

"Yes," the lady said, "it's all part of it."

"I've been to northern California," Converse told her, "but I've never been to Ngoc Linh."

"Some people don't like it there. We always loved it. I've only been away for a day and I'm already missing it so."

"Going to the States?"

"Yes," she said. "For only three weeks. It'll be my first time back."

Her smile was mild but resolute.

"My husband was back last year, just before he was taken from us. He said it was all so odd. He said people wore wide colorful neckties."

"A lot of people do," Converse said. Taken? "Especially in the big cities."

He had begun to sense a formidable strength in the lady's bearing. She was quite literally keeping her chin up. Softness in the eyes, but what depths? What prairie fires?

"In what sense," he asked, "was your husband taken?"

"In the sense that he's dead." Clear-voiced, clear-eyed. "They'd left us pretty much alone. One night they came into our village and took Bill and a fine young fella named Jim Hatley and just tied their hands and took them away and killed them."

"God. I'm sorry."

Converse recalled a story he had been told about Ngoc Linh Province. They had come into a montagnard hootch one night and taken a missionary out and tied him up in a mountain shelter. To his head they fixed a cage in which a rat had been imprisoned. As the rat starved, it began to eat its way into the missionary's brains.

"He was a happy man all his life. No matter how great your loss is, you have to accept God's will with adoration."

"God in the whirlwind," Converse said.

She looked at him blankly for a moment, puzzled. Then her eyes came alight.

"Land, yes," she said. "God in the whirlwind. Job Thirty-seven. You know your Bible."

"Not really," Converse said.

"Time's short." The languor was leaving her voice and manner, but for all the rising animation no color came into her face. "We're in the last days now. If you do know your Bible, you'll realize that all the signs in Revelations have been fulfilled. The rise of Communism, the return of Israel . . ."

"I guess it looks like that sometimes." He felt eager to please her.

"It's now or never," she said. "That's why I hate to give up three weeks, even to Bill's parents. God's promised us deliverance from evil if we believe in His gospel. He wants us all to know His word."

Converse discovered that he had moved toward her on the bench. A small rush of admiration, desire, and apocalyptic religion was subverting his common sense. He felt at the point of inviting her . . . inviting her for what? A gin and tonic? A joint? It must be partly the fever too, he thought, raising a hand to his forehead.

"Deliverance from evil would be nice."

It seemed to Converse that she was leaning toward him.

"Yes," she said smiling, "it certainly would. And we have God's promise."

Converse took his handkerchief out and cleared his eyes again.

"What sort of religion do they have up in Ngoc Linh? The tribespeople, I mean."

She seemed angry.

"It's not a religion," she said. "They worship Satan."

Converse smiled and shook his head.

"You don't believe in Satan?" She did not seem surprised.

Converse, still eager to please, thought about it.

"No."

"It's always surprised me," she said softly, "things being what they are and all, that people find it so difficult to believe in Satan."

"I suppose," Converse said, "that people would rather not. I mean it's so awful. It's too spooky for people."

"People are in for an unpleasant surprise." She said it without spite as though she were really sorry.

A breeze came from the river carrying the smell of rain, stirring the fronds and blossoms and the dead air. Converse and the lady beside him relaxed and received the wind like a cooling drink. Monsoon clouds closed off the sky. Converse looked at his watch and stood up.

"I've enjoyed talking to you," he said. "I've got to move on now."

Senator Aiken's Solution

On October 19, 1966, George Aiken, a long-time Republican senator from Vermont, proposed a novel solution to the crisis in Vietnam. Aiken's proposal, described by some as "declare-victory-and-get-out," characterized the frustration felt by many—especially conservatives like Aiken—at the uncertain mission of the United States in Vietnam. These are excerpts from Senator Aiken's speech, as reported in the **Congressional Record.**

Passing over the early years of our Vietnam involvement, the record of which is already abundantly clear, I would like to present the situation as it existed in February 1965, when the total of American combat troops in South Vietnam was less than 20,000.

In spite of confident reports by our highest military authorities at that time, there actually existed a clear and present danger of military defeat for the American forces.

In the face of this imminent danger, a detachment of marines was dispatched to Da Nang, and a program of building up military forces in Vietnam was launched. . . .

Insofar as our commitment to Vietnam represented an effort to sustain the credibility and integrity of the U.S. Armed Forces, the act of escalation cannot brook any serious dissent.

In February of 1965 and for some months thereafter, such a situation persisted.

However, at the present time it is not possible to sustain a clear and present danger of military defeat facing U.S. Armed Forces.

The enemy has apparently dismissed any idea of engaging in major formal combat with superior U.S. forces, and has resorted to a war of harassment and surprise guerrilla tactics.

Faced with the harassment of the Vietcong and the North Vietnamese military forces, casualties to American forces in Vietnam are inevitable. . . . But these casualties in no way sustain the prospect of a military defeat. . . .

The U.S. Government has asserted frequently and emphatically that there is no military "solution" or objective in this war. . . .

Considering the fact that as every day goes by, the integrity and invincibility of the U.S. Armed Forces is further placed in question because there is no military objective, the United States faces only two choices: Either we can attempt to escape our predicament by escalating the war into a new dimension, where a new so-called aggressor is brought into play or we can deescalate the war on the ground that the clear and present danger of a military defeat no longer exists and therefore deescalation is necessary in order to avoid any danger of placing U.S. Armed Forces in a position of compromise.

Faced with these alternatives, the United States could well declare unilaterally that this stage of the Vietnam war is over—that we have "won" in the sense that our Armed Forces are in control of most of the field and no potential enemy is in a position to establish its authority over South Vietnam. . . .

This suggested strategy is not designed to solve the political problem of Vietnam.

It is simply designed to remove the credibility of U.S. military power—or more loosely the question of "face"—as the factor which precludes a political solution.

The lady looked up at him, holding him with her will.

"God has told us," she said evenly, "that if we believe in Him we can have life eternal."

He felt himself shiver. His fever was a bit alarming. He was also aware of a throbbing under his right rib. There was a lot of hepatitis around. Several of his friends had come down with it.

"I wonder," he said, clearing his throat, "if you'll be in town tomorrow would you care to join me for dinner?"

Her astonishment was a bit unsettling. It would have been better, he considered, if she had blushed. Probably she couldn't blush. Circulation.

"It's tonight I'm leaving. And I really don't think I'd be the sort of company you'd enjoy. I suppose you must be very lonely. But I think I'm really a lot older than you are."

Converse blinked. A spark from the Wrath.

"It would be interesting, don't you think?"

"We don't need interesting things," the lady said. "That's not what we need."

"Nice trip," Converse said, and turned toward the street. Two moneychangers came out of Eden Passage and moved toward him. The lady was standing up. He saw her gesture with her hand toward the moneychangers and the arcade and the terrasse of the Continental Hotel. It was a Vietnamese gesture.

"Satan," she called to him, "is very powerful here."

"Yes," Converse said. "He would be."

Liberty in Penang

from *. . . And a Hard Rain Fell*
by John Ketwig

John Ketwig was drafted into the Army and arrived in Vietnam on September 5, 1967. This is his recollection of R&R on a resort island off the Malaysian coast. Many soldiers fighting the war enjoyed, however briefly, this dream come true: time off in a tropical paradise.

At long last, I boarded a C-130 to Cam Ranh Bay, where I would catch a jet to Penang. The R-and-R center was little more than a wooden barracks and a few offices, but it was the essence of civilization compared to our hootch in Pleiku. I stared at the facilities in Cam Ranh Bay for a long while. These guys had window air-conditioners! We would board the plane the next morning, so I took a bus to the beach. Like a Florida resort, the white sand reflected the sun in waves. The bay was blue, palm trees swayed gently in the breeze, and sunbathers stretched on multicolored beach towels. As the bus approached, the driver pointed out a two-story building to our left. This, he said, was a hospital, and during the Tet offensive the Cong had come ashore in rubber rafts, set up automatic weapons at both doors, and rolled a grenade inside. The grenade exploded, and the survivors, despite their wounds, rushed out the doors, to be mowed down. The bodies fell in bloody stacks. I waded up to my ankles, but I could not bring myself to swim in the bay after that story. Even in this bastion of civilization, death lurked too near.

Early the next morning a bus took us to a civilian jetliner. As we settled into our seats, wearing civilian clothes, the stewardesses offered cold washcloths and drinks. Soon we were airborne, headed away from Vietnam.

By the time I had devoured a steak, the plane was lowering onto the Malay peninsula. We landed on the mainland, at a former British airfield called Georgetown, then took a ferry to the island of Penang. In the golden sun, the cluster of buildings and the turmoil of Chinese junks reminded me of Hong Kong harbor. Tiny fishing boats hovered around large freighters like honeybees around a fragrant bloom. We docked and were herded into a smoke-filled room for orientation. We would be on our own for five days. The ferry would leave at 8:00 A.M. on the dot; we had best be there. It is a small island; deserters would be rounded up easily. They suggested hotels and reassured us that violence and crime were virtually unknown on Penang. As we converted our savings to Malaysian currency and emerged into a throng of taxicabs, I searched the hotel pamphlets. I chose the Hotel International. It was the most Americanized, and there would be nightly dancing and refreshments on the roof for R-and-R guests.

The splendor of the lobby made me pause. Wall-to-wall carpet, framed pictures, and soft lighting were luxuries I had not seen in months. I hadn't really missed them until now, but standing in the midst of a room devoted solely to comfort and convenience made me painfully aware how primitive my last few months had been. Safely inside my room I turned the lamps off and on again and again, flushed the toilet, took an hour shower, and searched the television dial for an American show. The two languages of Malaysia, Chinese and Malay, sounded the same to me, and the high-pitched voices superimposed over familiar American TV shows made me laugh. From the window I watched multicolored cars jolt their way through midcity traffic, listened to horns honking and tires squealing. A rainbow assortment of neon signs jiggled and blinked in a fascinating display. In the distance, the ships bustled about the harbor. To my left, a large green mountain loomed up over the red tile roofs of the city as if shielding them from ocean storms.

After I had become familiar with the room and all its wonders, I went off in search of a lady. Well, if not a lady, at least a female. I hoped she wouldn't be a lady.

I walked across the sedate lobby, through the doors into a maelstrom of activity. Street merchants with overladen carts vied with a bustling sea of humanity, most dressed in neat Western clothes. There were plenty of peasants, but they were clean and courteous. There were a large group of taxi drivers, all trying to be heard over the others. "Hey, man! Pretty girls! You want a girlfriend? Want to buy suit? Many pretty girls! I get you good steak and french fries! Ice cream, Joe? I take you to ice cream! I show you good girls, all kinds. Malay. Chinese. Indian. Make love very good, Joe. You want girlfriend?" The average American confronted by this scene might think it barbaric or primitive, but it was refreshing. In the Nam the language was vulgar: "I take you Mama-san. Number one suck dick, boom-boom, you fuck ass, you fuck cherry girl, number one cocksucker!" Here, the language was civilized, to the point but not vulgar; and the references to food and clothes seemed to reinforce humanity. I wasn't an animal, and the crudeness in Vietnam, even though GIs had taught the people those words, had always turned me off. I was a human being. I had human needs, but here the hawkers respected me enough to talk about them with decency. I was aching for sexual relief, but not bestiality. The offers spoke to that need in a way I had not heard for months. In no time I was in a taxi, careening through the narrow streets toward an assignation that would have been considered filthy and degrading in America but was respectable and benevolent in this scenario.

We squealed to a stop on a sidestreet. Stucco two-story buildings towered over the narrow sidewalk. There was no garbage, no one carried weapons. We had been told that Penang was 100 percent safe, and this quiet residential neighborhood reminded me of home. I was ushered into a large room, with a Buddhist shrine in one corner and a jukebox to the side. I sank onto an overstuffed couch, sipping a Scotch and water. A group of girls entered, giggling and laughing in some unknown language. Unlike the whores in Vietnam, their actions were demure, virginal. Most were Oriental, Chinese, but there were dark-skinned Malays and Indians, and even a plain and formless Caucasian girl with glasses. Quietly, respectfully, they asked questions. "Where are you from?"

"Pleiku."

They giggled. "Where are you from in America?"

"Rochester, New York."

"Aaah. Upstate. You live near Niagara Falls?"

I must have shown my surprise. "About two hours away. I live near the Finger Lakes, in a small farming village."

"Do you have cows? A horse?"

"No. But there are cattle farms nearby. Sometimes the cows get loose and walk in our garden. Mostly it is a fruit area. Apple trees. Cherries. Corn and wheat."

"How long have you stayed in Vietnam?"

I sighed deeply. I didn't want to think about it. It seemed like a lifetime. "Eight months."

"Oh. Velly good. You short-timer. You like dance?"

I hadn't thought about participating in music, really enjoying music, in a long time. My thoughts raced, and a quick daydream caused a delay. "I don't dance much. I play drums in a band, and I never learned to dance much. I would rather play. It is more fun to make music, especially when you don't know how to dance well." The words, propelled by a torrent of thoughts too long repressed, tumbled out. Hearing myself speaking too loudly, too excitedly, I stopped abruptly.

"We have many bands here. They will let you play. You tell us when you want to play, if you like the band, and we can arrange it for you. You are here to enjoy yourself, to have a good time and forget everything. Just tell us what you like, and we'll find it for you."

I was dumbfounded. No one had given a rat's ass for my feelings, my likes and dislikes, in so long. "Does the army help you do that?" It was a dumb question, blurted out.

"The army?" Everyone giggled. "No. The American army? They don't come here. We have seen many soldiers, talked to so many very sad men. They tell us about America, about the war. It is our job to make five short days as pleasurable as possible, to show you a good time. We try very hard. It is important that we be good to you. You tell us what you like, and we will try hard to make your holiday enjoyable. We are very good. You will see!"

My stupid question had embarrassed me, and the fact that I was relaxing in the company of eight beautiful women, small-talking in a whorehouse, about to negotiate a deal to procure a girl and fuck my brains out for five days also made me uneasy. My experience with whores had been in the Nam, and these girls were a totally different breed. Neatly dressed in American-style dresses, but with hints of silken lingerie; hair clean and shiny and, in some cases, carefully styled; restrained, modest, coherent, they were ladies. Again, in this environment, female compan-

Two Americans entertain themselves in the company of a prostitute from Saigon's Venus bar.

ionship was necessary and natural. The warm smiles and sparkling eyes were kind, inviting. Life had not been kind for a long, long time. It took me a few minutes to adjust to basic human decency, and I squirmed nervously. My underarms dripped. I was out of my element. These people were so very comfortable with the idea of baring their hearts and bodies for my pleasure, and for months I had thought only of fucking like a barnyard animal! My eyes darted from one to another, focused on a full breast, a shapely calf, a hint of black lace. Another Scotch was eroding the tension, if not the discomfort. Mama-san entered, looking for all the world like a Currier and Ives Chinese grandmother. Her white hair was swept back into a tight bun. A print apron was tied around her waist, bringing an image of homebaked apple pie to my racing mind. Most of all, her smile was soft and warm and motherly.

We exchanged pleasantries. She asked if I was married. No. Was I virgin? It was a matter-of-fact question, important to her. No. I grinned, and the girls twittered. Mama-san was the businesswoman, and she came directly to the point. "Would you like to vacation with one of my girls? Or more! You may have more than one! They are very beautiful, no?"

"Yes. Very beautiful, and very kind. I cannot believe they are familiar with Niagara Falls!"

"These are very good girls, very kind. We have no mean girls here. No VD. My girls are checked every week. Would you like to hire one of my girls? Price is forty dollars American for one night, one hundred and fifty dollars American for five days and nights. The girl you choose will be your companion all day and all night, and can show you Penang, help you find bargains. Would you like one of my girls?"

I was enjoying myself immensely, but it was obvious this lady wanted to get down to business. I had been here an hour, casually drinking her Scotch and eyeing her employees. It was time to get serious. Unsure of myself, wondering how one chose a prostitute in this civilized atmosphere, I muttered "Yes."

There was a long, nervous pause. Everyone was looking at me. Feeling very nervous, very unpolished, I blurted out my frustration. "I can't choose. They're all too nice!"

Mama-san smiled warmly. "Let me introduce you." She proceeded from left to right, lifting each girl to her feet, having her turn. The girls strutted a bit, smiling suggestively, as their talents and qualifications were described. Again, it was so tasteful there was no hint of vulgarity. "This is Mei-Ling. Mei-Ling is twenty, Malaysian Chinese, has a year of college. She has a beautiful body and uses it well. Mei-Ling is a swimmer and has wonderful muscle control. She is very quiet and thoughtful, but a very popular girl.

"Chao-Da is Indian, twenty-four, and an accomplished seamstress. She makes many clothes for all the girls and sells her wares in the market. Chao-Da loves to dance and is familiar with many positions of lovemaking.

"Ellen is mixed English and Chinese ancestry, although she looks more English. She is educated and very popular. Ellen is a favorite with the GIs because of her round eyes and natural blonde hair, and also because she enjoys making love to a man with her mouth.

"Lin was a secretary but came to us to earn more money. Her father is dead, and she supports her mother and her family. She is eighteen, Cantonese-Malay, and a wonderful cook. The boys tell me she is very adventurous and unpredictable." The dark-eyed girl was beautiful, perhaps a little fuller than the others, but surely this was a body made to provide pleasure for her man. Her eyes seemed alive, mischievous, sensual. More important, this was the girl who had mentioned making arrangements for me to play drums. I interrupted Mama-san. "Lin is very beautiful. I would like to spend some time with her." I was not satisfied with the choice of words, but Mama-san did not seem to mind. We made financial arrangements while Lin retreated upstairs. In a few moments she was back, carrying a suitcase. Her smile was warm, friendly, reassuring. In Chinese, she ordered another Scotch. "I have to attend to Buddha for a few moments, if you don't mind." I settled on the couch, very aware of the cold wetness under my arms. I watched her body as she knelt before the shrine, holding smoking joss sticks and chanting to the golden image. God, she was so feminine, so soft and rounded. She rose and turned to me, smiling.

"I hope you don't feel afraid of me," I whispered.

"Afraid? No. Why do you say that?"

"Well, you felt you had to pray before going off with me. I don't want to take you to something you find unpleasant."

She moved closer, took my hand. Her eyes reassured me as she spoke. "John, I am Buddhist. I must make an offering to Buddha each evening. I want very much to go with you. I know you will be kind. I enjoy my work, and I want very much to make you feel good." She patted my sex gently, suggestively. "I have known many men from Vietnam. I know the hurt and the frustration you hold inside. I know you want to make love to me. I want to make love to you too, I really do, and to pleasure you. Together, we will work it out. All I ask is that you be honest with me, tell me what you want, and allow me to do my job. We'll have to see if we can do something about that!" Her eyes dropped to my throbbing organ, then darted back up to form a caricature of a wink that pulled her whole face out of shape. "C'mon, let's have a good time!" She took my hand and tugged me toward the door. I grabbed the suitcase and hurried after her, feeling more comfortable all the time. I looked for the taxi. He was gone, but Lin summoned

a bicycle-powered rickshaw. "I know you miss cars," she grinned, "but this is Penang, and the rickshaws are so much cheaper. We'll take taxis when we need to, but you will see more this way." She spoke to the wrinkled, bearded driver, and we settled into the narrow seat. Perched behind us, the old man sang softly as we pedaled through the placid streets. I put my arm around her shoulders, mostly because the seat was so small, and Lin cuddled against me. I was in Paradise! The sun had started to fall, and its fiery light brought a feeling of warmth and contentment. We wound through narrow streets, past stuccoed walls with wrought iron gates and carefully manicured lawns. Exotic plants and flowers, always neatly and carefully arranged, burst from every available nook and cranny. Antique gaslights gave a Victorian, nostalgic atmosphere, as if I had been transported back in time and the horrors of the war hadn't ravaged my mind yet. The cars were mostly British, the quaint Austins and Morrises that had been in the background of so many pictures in *Road & Track.* I smelled a meal cooking, heard birds singing. An Englishwoman in a tweed suit walked up the sidewalk carrying a briefcase, waved, and called out a cheery hello! We rattled over the cobblestone streets, Lin allowing me to retreat into my thoughts and cope with this foreign world. I *must* be in Paradise! The softly swaying palms reminded me of the Deep South, and the courteous and genteel people had been as comforting as the legendary "southern hospitality" of long ago. We were approaching the business center and fell into the flow of traffic, snaking in and out through cars and motorbikes and neat pedestrians. When we got to the hotel I paid the old man, and Lin tugged me into a store.

When we emerged, we had a collection of Japanese beauty products. There were translucent honey-based soaps, bath oil, body oil, and powders. Not particularly comfortable in a cosmetics store, I had stared at the bright lights and plate-glass displays while Lin shopped. There were elaborate pastel formations on turntables, bold silver-foil proclamations highlighted by pink and red spotlights. I was fascinated by the glitz and glitter, childish in my delight. Lin tore me away, I paid for the shopping bag full of exotica, and wondered why such a beautiful woman would need such an expensive assortment of beauty products. We bustled through the hotel lobby, into an elevator, and into my room. Safely inside, I had to try all my toys again, and I flushed and tuned and switched the gadgets while Lin busied herself in the bathroom. It was dark, and I stood at the window, spellbound at the sight of a city at night. Neon signs of red and blue turned and flashed overhead as the peculiar golden glow of a thousand headlights blended into a stream of light. On the banks of the stream the crowd bustled in a multicolored chaos. I watched as they patiently obeyed the "Don't Walk" sign, then dutifully moved as one when the light changed. There was a pattern, a purpose, an order underlying what appeared to be confusion. Chaos controlled. Civilization. All of the sinister sides of the human psyche I had known for months seemed nonexistent. I marveled at these people, so unconcerned while horror and death lurked so near. It was all very real to me, so much a part of everyday life; and yet these people hurried on as if it were insignificant.

Lin's touch on my shoulder brought relief from the dilemma my thoughts had created. She drew me away from the window and closed the drapes. "We have to get you ready for dinner," she said softly. "Relax. I'll take care of everything." Again, she patted my groin and it responded. Slowly, sensuously, she unbuttoned and unclasped my clothes, and I felt them fall to a heap on the floor. She caressed me, she poked and probed and stroked me; then she led me to the bath. The air was heavy with steam as she knelt and slid my underwear down. I was excited. I slipped into the water at her urging, recoiling from the heat, but Lin insisted, and I was in her power. Fragrant bubbles parted to receive me, and I tried to settle back in spite of the fear my flesh was being cooked off my bones. Lin guided me into a reclining position, adjusting a large sponge at my neck, bending a knee. Adjusting to the temperature, I allowed myself to be guided. Soft music filtered in from the bedroom. Lin lit a small scented candle and doused the harsh incandescent light. Slowly, carefully, she removed her dress, then her slip. In the golden candlelight, she gathered her long black hair and pinned it into a pile on top of her head. I watched her move, so seductive, so feminine in lacy maroon underwear. She knelt beside me, leaned close. "Let it heal you, John," she whispered. "The heat will draw the hurt out. Just relax and let me make you feel better." She reached behind her back, and the soft bra slid to the floor as she leaned her breasts against the tub and reached beneath the bubbles. Rubbing the fragrant soap into my skin, she traced tiny circles from my forehead to my toes, then back. I leaned forward to give her access to my back, sweat beading on my forehead. Suddenly, I heard the water receding down the drain. I was puzzled. When it was gone, and I felt a chill, she rinsed me with splashes from a plastic bowl. I blushed, stretched out naked in front of her, as she deftly kept her naked breasts from my view behind the rim of porcelain. I was aching. "Stand up and turn around, please." I did. I felt her hands on my buttocks, sliding the soft soap in tiny circles, closer and closer to my thighs. She dipped more hot water, and the circles moved lower. More water. One hand slipped between my legs, began stroking. I exploded against the tile, my knees near collapse. A splash of hot water accompanied the final spasm. Suddenly I felt weak and cold.

She knelt and toweled me, silently, carefully. She led me to the ready bed, shimmering in the glow of another scented candle. Cool oil cascaded over my shoulders and back, and strong but gentle hands caressed it into my skin.

She moved to my feet, worked up my legs to my buttocks, slipping one hand under my belly. I rolled over, and she knelt between my legs as she pushed the oil into my chest, then lower. She took the pins down from her hair, and swayed her head to let the silken cascade move over me. I was throbbing again, when I felt her kiss. Then, spent, I rolled over and felt the soft talcum being caressed into tired shoulders. Her touch was soft, delicate, and yet insistent. When I was ready again, she stood, turned her back, and slid the maroon bikini to her ankles. She looked over her shoulder and whispered, "Are you ready?" then turned without waiting for an answer and raised her arms to push the mound of hair up on her head. I reached for her and drew her down close to me, feeling her warmth for the first time.

After a shower together, we dressed for dinner, I in my jeans and shirt, Lin in fresh lingerie and skirt and blouse. We collapsed into a rickshaw for a chaotic ride to a fine new hotel, where the doorman in a white coat with bronze buttons bowed as we entered. In the restaurant I was dazzled by the formal place settings, forks and spoons and cone-shaped napkins neatly aligned to enhance the shimmering crystal and china. We had steaks and French wine, and Lin spoke of upstate New York with knowledge and a trace of awe. We talked of her family, her background. She was, as Mama-san had said, supporting her family, and she showed me pictures and spoke of her young sister's grades. Why, I asked, was she a prostitute? What's a girl like you . . . ? Matter-of-factly, she gestured at the ornate room. "I enjoy living well," she whispered. "I have money, clothes. I enjoy the nicer things. But there is more. I like GIs. They are so hurt, so vulnerable. I feel I am like a doctor. One guy said I should be a shrink. I do not know this 'shrink,' but I know I am doing something very important. I know how sad it is, to try to live your life in five days. I cannot do so much if I am a nurse in a white dress." She looked down. I reached for her hand, and she looked at me with her eyes pleading, filling with tears. "Last month I met a guy. He showed me pictures of his wife in America. He was very kind, and it was no big thing, you know? He did not go to Hawaii, and I asked why. You know what he said? He said he could not make love to his wife anymore because he felt dirty!" She spit out the last word, and a tear started down her cheek. "He wanted her so much, but he could not face her. He drank too much, but he was so kind, and he cried. He cried all the time. Finally, I told him to write to her and tell her everything. If she loves him, it will be okay, you know? So he writes to me and says everything is okay, and thank you so much, and then I get a letter from one of his friends, and he's dead! That never happened before, but I have to think, How many of my boys are dead? I try very hard to be kind, because everyone tells me about Vietnam, and I know a few days away are very special. I do not feel ashamed. Do you understand? I try to do something very nice for very hurt people."

We left the hotel, and Lin spoke Chinese to the rickshaw boy. We went to the old Victorian British palace, walked hand in hand across the broad parade field to the waterfront. Beneath towering trees a sidewalk lined with gaslights edged the harbor. We sat on the stone wall, watching faint outlines of ships and junks gliding silently into place for the morning's business. Ribbons of multicolored light wrinkled on the swells, weaving a tapestry of color and motion. We walked slowly, discussing movies, music, the meaning of life, war, and peace. In the tranquillity I told her things I had never told another human being, and she accepted the burdens willingly. A full, crystalline moon danced upon the water as I sobbed, dredging up the horrors of Dak To and the girl at the firebase. We sat on a park bench and talked about cornfields and the Finger Lakes, lilies of the valley in spring, a Rolling Stones concert in Buffalo, and baseball. By the time we returned to the hotel it was 4:00 A.M., and we were dear friends.

Time, the great enemy in The Nam, became more of an enemy on R and R. Time had suddenly accelerated to a dizzying blur. We ate and danced. We toured temples and a park where monkeys begged for bananas. I played drums, poorly. I shopped for a suit, a guitar, records. I ate ice cream with a passion. We rode an inclined railway to a majestic view of the island. Like a kid at Disneyland, I absorbed the multicolored clothes and the orderly chaos of city life. Like Alice, I gloried in a Wonderland of freedom and mystery. For seventeen months I had lived in a perpetual nightmare, and this brief reprieve was so totally different it overwhelmed me. For five days, there was no rank. The maid cleaned my hotel room. The fresh white sheets were not infested with rats or snakes or insects. There was no threat, no artillery, no death. No one barked orders. There was only pleasure, and pleasure proved addictive.

I resisted the urge to sleep. The stimuli that assailed all my senses excited each nerve ending till sleep was unnecessary. When exhaustion intervened, Lin stroked and comforted me. Mostly, as we wandered the island hand in hand, we talked. As I drew her views out, I found them remarkably similar to my own. By the end of the fifth day, we were talking about the future. I promised to return, and to take her home with me. I had found what I wanted, what I needed in life. All of the past would be forgotten. A few days before, I had measured my future in seconds. Now I dreamed of children and the excitement Lin would experience as I showed her America. We wept openly as I boarded the ferry that would take me to the plane. The day before, we had gone to the market, and Lin had made a feast of giant shrimp, fresh vegetables, and wine. My laundry was immaculate. My hair was neatly trimmed. My mind was blown, and my heart was no longer my own.

An American flirts with a Vietnamese woman, Saigon.

R & R

The U.S. military's Rest and Recuperation (R&R) program was a highlight of every serviceman's tour of duty in Vietnam. Technically, a soldier was eligible for R&R after ninety days in-country, but the military encouraged him to wait at least six months before he took his five days off.

When a soldier went on R&R, the military issued him a new uniform, exchanged his military scrip for cash, lectured him on venereal disease and good manners, then flew him to one of many Asian cities: Tokyo, Taipei, Singapore, Manila, Penang, Kuala Lumpur, Hong Kong, Sidney, even Honolulu—a popular spot for reunions with stateside wives and sweethearts. (In addition to their R&R, troops would receive passes for short stays at such South Vietnamese beach resorts as Vung Tau and China Beach.) Arriving at his destination, the soldier endured more lectures and then escaped military life to do as he pleased for five glorious days.

What usually pleased him was good food, hot showers, sightseeing, and—especially—liquor and girls. In fact, GIs had another, less formal name for R&R: "I&I," or, intoxication and intercourse.

Particular cities were known for certain diversions: Tokyo for its culture and modern ways, Hong Kong for its shopping, Bangkok and Taipei for their large contingents of professional girlfriends. From wholesome tourist spots and expensive restaurants to the most squalid back streets and brothels, metropolitan Asia offered the young American a world that seemed, for once, devoted solely to his pleasure.

Soldiers, peddlers, and pleasure seekers stroll along the beach and wade in the surf at the U.S. military's in-country R&R center, Vung Tau, South Vietnam, January 1970.

129

Above. *Bar girls of the Rainbow Bar in Hong Kong's Wanchai District dance with sailors on liberty after patrol duty off the coast of Vietnam, December 1967.*

Left. *Sailors due for a few precious days of shore leave line a ship's deck as the Seventh Fleet enters Hong Kong harbor in December 1967.*

Specialists Ron Klausing and Tom Kienan wear traditional dress for a tour of Hakone, a popular hot-spring resort located at the foot of Mount Fuji in Honshu, Japan.

Marine Corporal Allen Bailey, 21, enjoys the ministrations of bath attendants at Peitou, a hot-sulphur spa twenty minutes from Taiwan's capital city of Taipei.

A young American relaxes with an acquaintance at the Vung Tau in-country R&R center, September 1967.

Catching up on some light reading, Vung Tau, 1967.

A bikini-clad stroller obliges an American soldier's photographic interests on the beach at Vung Tau.

forces move back into the area after the Americans left. For the average U.S. soldier, friendship and camaraderie provided the only relief from the horrific task of combat.

"Yes Sir, Yes Sir, Three Bags Full"

from *F.N.G.*
by Donald Bodey

In this excerpt from **F.N.G.**, *"Chieu Hoi" Sauers's squad is ordered to perform a dangerous and appalling task after they have successfully ambushed an enemy patrol.*

Blood.

Like cottage-red paint shot from a fire hydrant, blood everywhere: sprayed all over the leaves and rocks and running in the rainwater that trickles off the rocks. *Jesus-fuckinchrist.*

"Oh, muthafucker, they're dead."

"We musta got 'em all."

"Let's go. We're lucky this didn't draw a tiger last night."

As we came up, some rodents scampered away and as we are standing there I look away and meet two little eyes looking at us from under a rock. I feel like I hate the goddamn rodent. I hate everything. There are four dinks. Two of them were cut in half by our claymores. *How goddamn much blood is there in a person?* I might faint. It seems like everything should be still but there are flies by the hundreds and the birds in the canopy are squawking. There must be an animal in the matted grass behind the bodies because there is noise there too. At first I can't identify the other sound I hear; then I realize it is the static of the radio.

I have been breathing fast and I'm sweating, but I can't turn away. The rain is drizzle now, but it seems like it would have washed more blood away. I smell something besides wet jungle, but it doesn't smell dead. *Does blood have a smell of its own? Is that what the vultures smell?* I feel faint again: like my mind is swinging up there in the canopy, like *I'm a vulture seeing us look at the bodies. I see Pops break the silence.*

"Four of 'em. That's all we want to know. Let's go back to the top and call it in. I don't want to stand around here. Pick up the rifles." *And I can see me pick up a gun. When I feel it my mind comes back to earth.* We go back up where our rucks are.

The rifle is an AK. I can't forget the sound after the day Chickenfeed got hit. The rifle is beat to pieces. It only has half the original stock; the back half is a piece of wood with twig marks on it still, carved on the end to fit a shoulder. *Which of the four did it come from?*

"Greenleaf, this is Titbird. How's your copy?"

Pops has the radio up on a rock, and the way he is standing there talking makes me flash on a cop, *downtown Cincinnati,* calling in from a beat box. I feel fuckin' drugged. OK, *this is war, man. This ain't Cincinnati. You're part of this, Gabriel. Everybody looks the same—*

empty. Muthafucker, *can this be?* I smell the rifle to see if it was fired last night but there isn't any smell but metal. This ain't the fuckin' movies; you ain't John Wayne. I wonder if it had shot any GIs. It's heavier than my rifle. The ammo clip is curved. The more I stare at the gun the more it looks unreal, toy-like. No, it actually looks more real than my plastic M-16 but there is something childish about it. *The fucking thing looks homemade. That carved butt piece, the way it's wired together. Homemade.*

Pops is scooting the radio up the rock now. It occurs to me that I haven't been watching the bush. Eltee gets up and goes to help Pops. He seems to have regained his composure but his face is tight-looking. Peacock is picking his nose with one hand and toothbrushing the feed mechanism of the Sixty with his other.

"We got four rabbits out here. Coming back to your position. Over."

"Titbird, Greenleaf."

"Stand by."

"Them dinks caught our claymores letters-high," Pea says, to nobody in particular.

"Think of how much dinky damage they musta done to the Z."

"Titbird, how's your copy? Over."

"Good copy. Go ahead, dammit."

"Titbird, Higher says cut a chimney, they'll be out. Over."

Prophet angrily slams his hat on his thigh and Pops bangs the microphone with his free hand.

"No way," Pops says to Eltee. "Fuck those lifers. You tell 'em, we can't cut a chimney through that canopy. All they want to do is make sure we counted right, and I ain't fuckin' doing it."

I can't imagine how we could cut a hole, big enough to let a Loach down, and I can't imagine why.

Pops reads my mind.

"They wanna bring a Chieu Hoi out here and see if he can tell what unit the dinks are from."

"There isn't enough left of the four dinks to tell anybody jack-shit."

"Eltee, tell the fuckers to walk out here. We did," Prophet says.

Lieutenant Williams is standing up with his arms folded across the radio. He is rocking back and forth on his heels and toes. He never looks our way. The radio is low-volume static. If I can read Eltee's mind, I know he is torn, tortured, confused. He's going to be caught in the middle.

"Well, do something, for chrissakes. We can't cut 'em a hole, and we sure as fuck don't want to stay here much longer. Charlie is gonna be looking for these guys."

"Greenleaf, Titbird. Code name William."

"Go, Titbird."

"Greenleaf, too much canopy, too high. We'll bring captured weapons to your papa. These rabbits are in parts. Repeat, in parts. Not enough left for ID. Copy?"

"Code name William, code name Beaver. Wait one."

Pops flips through the code book.

"It's that short red-haired fucker, Billingham."

I didn't know his name, but I figured that's who it was. He's some kind of aide to the colonel and he carries a Car-15. A few days ago I saw his radioman taking his picture. He had a flak jacket and helmet on then, and the asshole probably hasn't ever been to the Bush. This is beginning to get real shitty. I'm becoming afraid again. We blew these guys away and their pals must be around here somewhere. If we don't get going we'll be sitting ducks. I feel my anger and fear mount together. I have a quick fantasy of taking a swing at that fat little fucker.

"Titbird, Greenleaf."

Even the radio seems alive and against us. It must be my fear that makes me think that way all of a sudden. Unfuckin' fair to be out here in the middle of nowhere and scared, talking long-distance and visualizing Billingham sitting in a sandbagged conex telling us to do something we already told him we can't fuckin' do.

"Titbird, it is essential that you provide us a way of identifying your rabbits. Many lives may depend on it."

"Many lives! Our lives are the only ones relevant to them dead dinks; where does he get off giving us a lecture like we're still in The World? This ain't practice. There ain't enough of them dinks left to tell anything. Make the fucker understand they're using us for bait."

Peacock is standing beside Williams now, struggling to keep his voice under control. Eltee looks at him blankly, puts a hand on his back, then pushes his own helmet back on his head. Eltee looks five years older than he did yesterday, and he looks confused.

"Oh, fucker . . . " Callme moans.

Prophet has been sitting with his elbows on his knees, looking away from us. Now he looks up at the canopy and shakes his head.

"Greenleaf, code name William, over."

"Go."

"I repeat. No can do."

"Titbird, that's affirm. Transport your rabbits to Checkpoint Bravo. Out."

No! *Bullshit.* I'm dreaming. Or is this a movie?

Peacock slumps down into the mud and begins stabbing at it with his knife. He is soon using both hands to stab with. He's nuts. I feel crazy too. Everybody else *looks* crazy. Eltee lets the microphone drop against the rock and stands staring at us. He looks like he's trying to get his mind to work.

"OK——" he starts.

"OK, so let's go to Bravo and they can fuckin' walk back up here without us. We'll tell 'em right where the ambush is."

"Listen up," Eltee says. "This is some real bullshit, but there's no alternative."

"No alternative? Let's just fuckin' refuse to do it."

"Pops, you're a short-timer. If we don't do it we're all guilty of disobeying a direct order and we're all going to get court-martialed. You know that. Not just me. They'd bust us, send us all to jail, then send us back out here, and that jail time is bad time. You won't rotate out of here until *next* year. Think about it."

Pops's face is stretched round with red anger. He looks like he's ready to explode. I expect an outburst, but instead he slumps down to his knees and turns his face upward to let the silent rain hit him. He sighs.

"Eltee is right," Peacock says.

"If we're gonna do it, let's do it. We'll get even with them fuckin' Higher-highers," Prophet says.

Lieutenant Williams looks at him and opens his mouth but doesn't say anything.

"You never heard me say that, Eltee, for your own good. We like you and I know what you're thinking, but just forget it. You're one of us, for now."

Jesus, this is escalating. I don't know for sure what Prophet is saying, but his tone is severe and he isn't about ready to back down from anything the Eltee can offer.

"I won't hump no dead guy," Callme says.

"Dinks don't weigh much," Pea says.

Callmeblack makes his big black hand into a big black fist and drives it into his wadded-up poncho. Then he half buries his face in the poncho and either sobs or sighs.

Dear Dad: You won't believe this. Dear Brother Bob: Go to Canada. Dear President Johnson: Could you do this? Dear God: For my mother's sake, numb me. (Fucking jail! . . . Everybody knows the horror stories about military prisons, especially in The Nam.) There's nothing fair about some Army officer three kilometers away telling us to obey this insane order or go to jail. But why should I expect fairness? I'm in the Army, and the Army is in a war. It's simple. I don't have any choice.

So I'm the first one to move. I stand up and unroll my poncho. I'm conscious of the rest of them watching me but I don't look at them.

"Are we supposed to call 'em when we get there?"

"Yeah," Prophet says, "call 'em and say send a taxi after we dragged the muthafuckin' corpses all the way through this damn jungle while they meanwhile sit back there getting dug in, then fly out to meet us."

He stands and is talking loud but not yelling.

"Then, goddammit, then they'll turn that helicopter around and we'll goddamn have to walk back too!"

"Those hardcore Shake-and-Bake officers don't even think about us killing these poor bastards, let alone have to haul around what's left. They probably can't think of it, just have wet dreams about being a hero when they get home."

We're psyching ourselves up. Everybody but Peacock is getting ready now. Eltee already has his ruck on. He goes over to Callme and squats alongside him. They don't even say anything but I can see Callme's courage—or whatever it is—coming back. I feel a little jealous of Eltee right now.

I'm ready. My ruck doesn't feel so heavy and I'm not as tired as I was before it got light.

"Pray for luck," Peacock says. "If Charlie is around here close and sees this mess, you know he ain't gonna goddamn worry about big guns out here. He's gonna have our shit on a stick. He'll be hawking my goddamn watch in Hanoi if he knows what we're carrying and just happens to see us clod-hoppin' American boys here in his jungle. Them lifers think about the wrong things, that's all. They call the war by numbers. They're gonna say them four dinks only had one arm anyway, so we really blew eight away."

"Peacock," Pops says, "I never heard you be so right."

"Man, I'm just talking to keep from seeing, because seeing is believing."

"That's more like your old self, you asshole. That doesn't make any sense."

Jesus the flies.

We have two sets of ponchos snapped into pairs and are going to gather the bodies onto the ponchos, then split the weight up so four guys can carry the two slings. Even then, two guys will have to hump the radio, the machine gun, and the extra weapons, so really we'll be fuckin'-A useless if anything happens. Prophet goes to look for the best way by himself; we want to keep him as light as we can because he will be walking point. When he leaves, the rest of us go back to the site together. The flies are so loud I hear them from behind the first set of rocks, ten meters away.

We spread the ponchos out. Nobody talks. At first we all stand still. Then Callmeblack begins humming "Swing Low, Sweet Chariot" and Pops drags most of a body onto one of the ponchos. The guts drag along between the body's legs. The flies swarm in one extra-loud sound and land again when the body is on the poncho. Pops goes off from us a bit.

Right at my feet is an arm. It's short but it looks like what there is is almost all of what there ever was, like it came off at the shoulder. There are green flies around its bloody end. Callme is still humming and has tossed a couple pieces onto the poncho. I pick the arm up by the unbloody hand and it is like shaking hands with a snake. I'm careful not to touch the fingers. I fling the arm onto the pile that must be most of two guys now. Or women. Pops is back, white and old-looking.

Callmeblack sits down and spits a lot between his boots, but doesn't puke. The head that had been hanging by a thread of skin onto the body Pops carried is between Callmeblack and me and we both see it at the same time. It is most of a face, but half of it is turned into the muddy trail so it looks like a mask except for the flies. Callmeblack and I both look at it and then at each other and he looks back between his boots and half spits, half retches. I kick the head good; the face sails a foot off the ground and lands at the top of the pile, then rolls over the top. I'm glad it doesn't end up looking at me.

Eltee and Pops are about to fold the poncho over their pile and tie it shut.

"Let's be damn sure they're about the same weight."

"I pretended I was splitting a hundred pounds of Cambodian Red weed, man. I eyeballed it like I didn't know which half was mine, I——"

"OK, OK, OK. Shut up."

Peacock looks hurt. His tattoo is showing. I don't think it's raining. I think what is coming down is dripping off the canopy. Peacock's face is an eggshell color. In fact the light is all like that, the color of a dirty white dog.

I take as much air into my lungs as I can. I walk second, behind Prophet, who is carrying one of the captured rifles. Peacock has the other end of the poncho; then Pops and Callmeblack carrying the other sling, and Eltee is walking last. We tried slinging the weight on vines, in hopes that it would be easier carrying, but that didn't work because the trail is so sharp in places that the vines were too long to turn without the lead guy having to stop and turn around. So I twist the corners of the poncho together and use both hands to shoulder my end. Prophet helped me sling my rifle with shoelaces so it at least hangs in front of me and will be possible to get at, if it comes to that.

Eltee stays quite a ways back from the rest of us. Incredibly, he has the radio, the Sixty, and an extra rifle, and he has to pull rear security. I can't breathe normally—it's more like taking a gulp of air in and walking until it's used up, then gasping again, like I've swum too far away from shore. The going is slow and seems noisy. For a while we walk on a fairly level trail and our footing is solid, but the weight gets to us and we have to rest. When we set the poncho down the flies all seem to catch up and swirl into the holes between the snaps on the ponchos. The blood still isn't dried, so when I pick up the knot that makes my handle the blood squeezes out, and some runs down my arms.

After fifteen minutes my back begins to throb. Trying to walk mostly downhill now and still trying to keep the poncho fairly level to make it easier on Peacock strains my muscles and makes me aware of the spots I slept on last night. I'm constantly gasping for breath, and the bag keeps swinging, so I have to struggle to keep my balance. I come to the edge of my endurance. I want to cuss and throw something. I want to destroy. Finally, the slippery knot comes out of my grasp and the sling falls. Without looking back, because I am so goddamn out of touch, I keep walking, dragging the poncho behind me. It slides easily enough through the mud and makes a small sound like a brake rubbing against a bicycle tire. We don't go on like that very long before Prophet stops us and points at a swale below: Checkpoint Bravo. I simply fall down, gasping so hard I wonder if it's possible to catch up on the air I'm missing. I lie there with my eyes closed, listening to the others catching their breath and the buzzing of the flies.

Waiting for signs of the enemy, an infantryman in the central highlands cradles an M79 grenade launcher.

It is almost as though I am asleep, momentarily, because the sound of the flies begins to sound like a song. Honest to God: song. I hear snatches of nursery rhymes, and church choirs and classical music, and the ditty that is the commercial for life insurance. . . . When my breathing gets closer to normal the smell of reality fights its way back, and once again the predominant sound is that of the bloodthirsty flies swarming. I could puke in my own lap and it wouldn't make any difference right now.

From a sitting position I can see cleanly through the foliage. Checkpoint Bravo is a small, almost round, hollow. It looks marshy. Instead of jungle it looks like tall grass. I wonder how deep the water is. My breath has come back now. I see that one of the arms has worked its way partly out from the bundled poncho. I'll be damned if I'm going to touch it again to shove it back in. I don't care if it gets lost.

Eltee is making radio contact; otherwise there isn't any sound except for the goddamn flies. It takes skill to use an Army PRC-25 radio so that it isn't like hearing a supermarket speaker, and Williams is good enough that I can barely hear the transmissions from five meters away. I semi-want to smoke a cigarette, but my hands smell like the blood that is drying black now. I try to think of what it resembles, having squeezed out of the poncho, but it doesn't look like anything but what it is. Thinking about carrying these pieces of dinks to a helicopter landing in a small clearing makes the fear come hard, but who is there to tell I'm scared, and what good would it do?

"Wait till we hear the birds coming," Eltee says. "Pass it on."

We whisper it ahead and Prophet nods. His face is rock-hard and dirty. The way the light is hitting his face I can see the rivulets of sweat running over the wax we use to camouflage our faces. He must have mostly used the stick of green. I used brown. The camo sticks are precious; it is one more thing the Army never has enough of. Prophet sits quietly looking around all 360 degrees, spitting silently between his teeth. I'm glad the rain has quit, at least for now; I'm still cold, or shivering from fear. It isn't long before we hear the helicopters coming. We don't want to give our position away any sooner than we absolutely have to, so we don't move until the birds are in sight. As high up as they stay, their sound is no louder than the noise of the flies. Everybody chambers a round, ready to pick up the ponchos for the last time.

"Pray, baby," Peacock whispers. I nod. I do. I breathe as deeply as I can.

The clearing is a shade different in color than everything else around, darker green. From this distance, it looks like briars, but I've never seen briars over here. I can tell the grass is too tall for a bird to come down in, that we'll have to hack some of it away. My question is what we're going to do with these fucking bodies in the meantime.

Eltee is working his way up the line, whispering to everybody as he goes by. It strikes me as absurd, although not stupid, for him to be whispering. I don't know, maybe he isn't whispering: it's as though all I can hear are the goddamn flies, like a radio station off the air for the night—a low *hummmzaat*. As Williams moves up he walks hunchback to carry the weight of the radio and his ruck. My ruck straps cut into me all the way down the trail but I didn't notice the ache much until now. Fuck it. All we have to do is get these slings another thirty meters, cut a hole, and catch a ride back to the LZ.

Before I know it Eltee is at my side.

"We're about ready to move," he says. His face is like a clock, so exact is the intensity of his expression. I notice his nose looks wider on one side than the other. I listen to what he says, and it seems to echo through my mind even after he's gone. We'll be up and move fast. We're dropping the ponchos on signal. Three of us go out for security and the other three hack a hole in the weeds, good enough for a bird to come down long enough to pick up the pieces; when that bird is gone another will come in to get us. I'm going to be one who cuts.

My mouth feels like I've been sucking a rubber band. The nylon pads in my shoulder straps look freshly painted, and I feel conscious of every one of the five hundred more seconds we sit there. Eltee is still up front with Prophet. I can see them both through a hole in the trees. Eltee is talking on the radio some of the time. First one of their faces shows in the hole, then the other—like watching TV.

We're up. I get the signal from Prophet and pass it on to Peacock, who passes it on. Now we pick up the sling. Heavy. This time I'm very conscious of my rifle swinging in front of me. I've gotten used to having it in my hand when I want it, and right now I want it.

We hustle. Everything hurts—my back, my head where the steel pot has bounced, my arms from having the sling behind me, my feet, my chafing asshole, even my goddamn eyes from sleeplessness. I hurt inside too. I feel like a piece of shit, like nobody. But on we go. In five minutes we're into the swamp. The water is quickly up to my shins, finally up to my balls. It doesn't feel warm or cold, not thick or clean, just wet and one more thing to fight against. We drop the poncho and it half sinks. The flies are there, like they're pissed off. They swirl in a wave like paint flung off a roller. I hate them. Air escapes from the poncho and comes to the surface, and the water turns the color of aged leather from the mud we stir up and the blood.

By pure luck, we stumble upon a hard bottom so we can stand up and hack away at the bushes exactly at water level. It's me, Prophet, and Peacock. We don't speak. We give it hell, our machetes swirling. The bushes are mostly easy to cut, and it doesn't take long to hack a ten-foot by ten-foot hole down to the waterline, and it isn't long after that that the bird arrives.

Combat assault: Operation Paul Revere IV, fall 1966.

It comes over the tree line like a hotrod cresting some country hill, then settles over us with the motion that only helicopters have, a gliding sort of motion, with its tail swerving from side to side. The machine gunners give us a long peace sign. We half carry, half float the ponchos over. It takes four of us to get them out of the water and into the bird. As we're loading the second, trying to keep the chopped-up grass and water out of our eyes and struggling to keep our footing, rounds begin pelting the windshield of the helicopter and either the pilot or the copilot gets hit. I dive into the water and weeds and futilely try to keep my rifle up.

Rounds begin to ricochet all over hell. The gunners open up, firing directly over our heads into the tree line. The shell casings come off the gun in a perfect arc, and some of them land on the grass we have cut that floats on the water. I'm disoriented and afraid to fire because I don't know where anybody else is, but I get my safety off and try to be careful to keep the barrel pointed up while I work my way, staying oh-so-low, away from where the bird is. I glance quickly at it and I can see the gunner taking the vibration of his gun with exact concentration. There is scurrying behind him and either the other gunner or a crew chief is leaned into the cockpit, probably aiding the pilot. I catch sight of Peacock, who has his Sixty at shoulder height. He is pouring rounds out toward the tree line.

The helicopter gets up and hovers for only an instant before it banks slightly and takes off away from the tree line we're facing. It circles and comes back over, low, stirring up the water and cut weeds. It passes over the tree line and both gunners fire continually. Then it comes back again and keeps a steady stream of rounds slashing into the tree line.

Eltee is yelling and signaling to make a circle. He has the radio mike in his hand. His rifle is slung downward and the AK is strapped to the radio. Prophet and Callme come out of the weeds behind him and run as best they can through the water until they reach the edge of our cut. Pops and I begin making it toward the cleared spot from opposite sides. Pops's face is covered with blood. I can't tell if he has been hit or not. Just as I get to where I intend to stop there is an explosion a few meters on the other side of Peacock, then another one, then two more. Mortars. The bursts hit the swamp in tandems now. First, two beyond us; then two in front of us. Peacock is trying to move back to our position but he has to get down every time a mortar lands. They bracketed, and have the range on those tubes now, so I expect the next rounds to come right on top of us. The helicopter is still hanging above the tree line, blasting it.

Four more mortars. The first two are off target but the second ones land almost right on top of Lieutenant Williams, maybe twenty meters away from me on the other side of the clearing. He screams. The wave of water from the mortar's concussion passes by me and there is still shit in the air. Pops slips out of his ruck and begins to work his

way toward Eltee. Everybody else begins to pump rounds into the tree line. I fire about where the helicopter is working out because I thought I saw a muzzle flash come from somewhere near there. As I am looking I see one for sure, a few feet off the ground. I squeeze three or four rounds off at where I saw it, then have to change magazines and when I look up again, the spot is being torn apart by the bird's Sixties. I cheer to myself. *Kill the fuckers.* I expect more mortars any time.

Pops is coming back toward us. He has the radio in one hand and is dragging Eltee behind him in a sort of backward-walking fireman's carry. Eltee is no longer screaming. A second helicopter comes over the opposite tree line. Eltee is dead.

The first helicopter continues working on the tree line and the second one comes at us rapidly. We all make a break for it. I go to Pops to help him. Together, we manage to get to the bird with our gear and the body. He didn't live past the scream. More than half of that handsome black face has been ripped back toward his skull. As long as the body was in the water the blood didn't show much, but when we are loaded and drag the body in after us, a pool of blood the color of fire spreads across the floor. We're all in, we're up, we head away from the tree line, high above which the bird with the ponchos full of bodies now hovers. Exhaustion hits and my body feels like a wet paper bag.

Jesus, there's no way to describe the ride. We get up fast, over a set of mountains, then up again. Riding along on the vibration of the bird is like being wind-rocked in a hammock. The five of us are sitting toward the front. I am leaning against the aluminum wall that defines the cockpit; the machine gunner is between me and the open door; past him I can see a patch of sky and beyond that mountains, mountains, mountains.

The sound of the rotor is steady: *rum thump thump rum thump thump.*

God, I stink. I've been sweating into these same clothes for at least ten days; I've been wallowing around in swamp water.

My mind just roams around like my eyes. The door gunner on my side is dark-complexioned and stocky. His mustache is trimmed and just a dab of black hair shows below the headset helmet. The back of his helmet has something painted on it but I can't read it. Across from me, against the wall on the other side of the doorway to the cockpit, Pops is slumped in a heap. He's filthy. There is a line of mud that runs from the top of his head, over his face and through his mustache, through the hair on his belly, and down to his pants. His shirt is unbuttoned and his flak jacket isn't hooked. Just a trace of a paunch hangs over the belt loops. He looks thinner now than he did just a month ago.

The others are leaning against whatever there is to lean against, and toward the back is Eltee's body. I stare at it, and it doesn't seem like he could be dead. I can't see his head that is half mincemeat now and I can't really believe he will never move again. Dead. Goddamn dead. It could've been anybody. He got a mortar; the dinks weren't going for the radio and they weren't going for him because he was an officer. They were just going for anybody and trying to disable the helicopters. I wonder who will have to write a report up on this mission, and I wonder what Lieutenant Williams's family will find out.

Thump rump kathump kathump. We are descending. I have to sit up straight to see the Z below us and I feel so tired. As we come down we scoot toward the door. It isn't easy because the bird isn't level and the ruck seems to weigh more than ever. I'm so tired. I just want to lie down. It seems like there should be more waiting for us than this goddamn hill full of holes. This, my man, is home for now. Eltee doesn't even have this.

Fifty feet up, then thirty. It's like working on a high, high ladder. The guys on the ground all move away from the pad and cover their eyes. Parts of C-ration cartons whirl up as high as we are and dive through the crazy air currents like bats going after insects in a porch light. All the dudes on the ground are wearing flak jackets, and a lot of them have helmets on. The landing pad is built out of sandbags, and from a few feet up it reminds me of a caned chair seat. We settle between two big slings of ammunition. After the bird shuts down to a low speed, guys start again at unloading the slings and carrying the ammo away. Most of it is for our mortars and artillery. The rounds come in wooden boxes about two feet long.

Over by the big guns are stacks of ammo crates, and guys are carrying these empties away to fill full of sand and build hooches.

The CO comes over to the bird with his face down. He is a stern-looking guy, maybe thirty years old. His expression isn't mean-looking but it sure as hell isn't joyful. He reaches up and helps us off the bird, just puts his hand under our rucks. When he helps me off he is already looking at whoever is behind me.

"There's coffee over there," he says to all of us. "I want to see the whole squad in a few minutes."

We all drop our rucks as soon as we're far enough away from the pad. Getting the ruck off is like taking a good shit. It's cloudy and there's dust in the air from something. Since we've been out, there has probably been a couple thousand sandbags filled. Some are laid into flat parapet walls and some of the hooches are getting to be deep enough for roofs. Ammo crates and full sandbags make squat, solid walls.

Most of three companies are on the Z now and it has spread out like a carnival parking lot. When we started to dig in, we were on the outside of the perimeter but now the perimeter has moved out in all directions.

There are two guys sitting near the coffeepot smoking and waiting for us. They have been humping ammo from the pad. "Hey, what it is."

"It is a muthafucker," Pops says. It seems like a long time since I have heard his voice.

"You guys the squad that got some dinks last night?"

"Yeah, four. How bad was it here?"

"Bad, man. Mostly incoming, but they almost broke through on the other side of the hill. Over there." The guy points to our right.

"Charlie put some shit in here last night," the other guy says. He emphasizes "put" by pounding his rifle's butt plate against the ammo crate he has his feet resting on.

"Eighty-twos?"

"Mostly."

"He was keying on that side of the hill. We were over there, the other side, and everything went over us, wounded one guy out on LP. Alpha Company got it the worst. I heard six KIAs and twenty wounded."

"Our Eltee ate an eighty-two round."

"Dead?"

"Fuckin'-A dead."

"Anybody else get hit?"

"Nope. Freaky. We were loading those goddamn dinks and Charlie walked about a dozen rounds in."

"Bravo Company is going to move out that direction."

"You guys from Bravo?"

"Yeah. We aren't even dug in, but they keep trying to stick us on ammo detail."

"Well, man, Charlie's out there. Even though it musta been bad here last night, I'd rather be here tonight."

"Dig it, but at least our whole company's going out."

I'm surprised the coffee tastes good. C-ration coffee sucks; this came from a big urn shaped like a fire hydrant. There are some shit-green food cans lined up behind the coffee, but it looks like the food must have come in sometime yesterday because some of the cans have shrapnel in them. After I get my coffee I sit down on a pile of sandbags that have been filled but not tied off yet. I can see the bad side of the Z, where there must be twenty shallow craters. The thing I didn't expect to see is the shrapnel holes everywhere and even a few pieces of shrap. There's none nearby but I can see it glint in the sun in a few paths.

Big guns sound somewhere. I wonder what time it is. The sun is still a little above the west ridge of mountains. I'd guess it will be dark in four hours. I wonder if these guys from Bravo are going to try to get dug in tonight. I look at them and try to see the fear that I know is somewhere in their faces.

One guy is Italian-looking. He is sitting on one of the melomite cans, sipping coffee from his canteen cup.

"Eltee didn't have a shot at it," Callme says.

I don't feel like saying anything. I helped float his body through the water. I flash on the body over there in the bird in a pool of blood. The CO is just starting back from the pad. Even though there isn't any dust flying now, he still walks with his face down. Somebody is leaning into the helicopter. Slowly, the rotor starts to turn, and when the

Men of the 173d Airborne land in War Zone C, 1965.

CO gets to us the bird is starting off. We all have to shield ourselves from the shit that flies around. When I look up, the CO is looking at Peacock, who's still looking down. So the CO looks right at me.

"What's your name, soldier?"

"Gabriel Sauers, sir."

"Tell me about it."

"About the patrol?"

"Yeah, from the time you made contact."

"Well . . ." I don't know what to say. Talking to an officer always bothers me. Eltee was an officer though, too. "Well," I say again, "it all happened awful fast. We were set up on a trail, and me and Callme were pretty close together and the rest of them were spread out. Peacock was ahead of us with the Sixty. We heard them coming and somebody blew the claymores. I could see the explosion and action. I emptied a clip and reloaded. That's all I know."

"Did you hear anything afterwards?"

"Nothing, sir."

"Who's the squad leader?"

"I am," Pops says. He doesn't add "sir."

"What's your name, Sergeant?"

"Pops," he says. He has undone his pants and is standing there talking to the CO with his dick out, rubbing one finger all around the jungle rot on his balls. I notice the CO has rot too, on his neck.

"You have anything to add, Pops?"

"I don't think Eltee Williams should be dead."

"What are you saying, soldier?"

"I think somebody fucked up back here. Those dinks were in pieces no bigger than these damn sandbags and there was no reason to bring 'em back here, but we hadda goddamn carry 'em down the fuckin' hill and into that clearing. Any-fuckin'-body woulda known the dinks were gonna drop some shit in there, but if we coulda got right in and right out of the edge of it, then Eltee wouldn't have gotten fuckin' killed. They walked 'em right in on us."

"Sergeant, your squad killed four enemies who might be responsible for killing ten GIs. That's what you have to think of. And"—he puts his hand on Pops's hand, which is still on his nuts, and looks around at all of us—"I understand how you feel. There's nothing I can do about it. Echo Company didn't make the decision, you know that. Listen, I *know* how you feel."

The way he says it, the way he looks around at all of us with a tiny little frown, the way he gives Pops's ball-handling wrist an additional shake . . . something makes me think he *does* know how Pops feels, and probably how I feel even if I don't. I feel something in my throat. Prophet spits, Callme spits, Peacock spits. The CO turns to leave and spits. I spit.

145

Mailer at the Pentagon

In October 1967 writer Norman Mailer joined poet Robert Lowell, critic Dwight Macdonald, and tens of thousands of peace activists in Washington, D.C., for a three-day protest of the Vietnam War. The demonstrators gathered in front of the Lincoln Memorial on Saturday, October 21, then marched across the river to the Pentagon. In his Pulitzer-prize-winning account *The Armies of the Night*, Mailer described the events of that weekend, including his own arrest at the Pentagon.

It was not much of a situation to study. The MPs stood in two widely spaced ranks. The rank was ten yards behind the rope, and each MP in that row was close to twenty feet from the next man. The second rank, similarly spaced, was ten yards behind the first rank and perhaps thirty yards behind them a cluster appeared, every fifty yards or so, of two or three U.S. Marshals in white helmets and dark blue suits. They were out there waiting. Two moods confronted one another, two separate senses of a private silence.

It was not unlike being a boy about to jump from one garage roof to an adjoining garage roof. The one thing not to do was wait. Mailer looked at Macdonald and Lowell. "Let's go," he said. Not looking again at them, not pausing to gather or dissipate resolve, he made a point of stepping neatly and decisively over the low rope. Then he headed across the grass to the nearest MP he saw.

It was as if the air had changed, or light had altered; he felt immediately much more alive—yes, bathed in air—and not yet disembodied from himself, as if indeed he were watching himself in a film where this action was taking place. He could feel the eyes of the people behind the rope watching him, could feel the intensity of their existence as spectators. And as he walked forward, he and the MP looked at one another with the naked stricken lucidity which comes when absolute strangers are for the moment absolutely locked together.

The MP lifted his club to his chest as if to bar all passage. To Mailer's great surprise—he had secretly expected the enemy to be calm and strong, why should they not? they had every power, all the guns—to his great surprise, the MP was trembling. He was a young Negro, part white, who looked to have come from some small town where perhaps there were not many other Negroes; he had at any rate no Harlem smoke, no devil swish, no black power for him, just a simple boy in an Army suit with a look of horror in his eye, "Why, why did it have to happen to me?" was the message of the petrified marbles in his face.

"Go back," he said hoarsely to Mailer.

"If you don't arrest me, I'm going to the Pentagon."

"No. Go back."

The thought of a return—"since they won't arrest me, what can I do?"—over these same ten yards was not at all suitable.

As the MP spoke, the raised club quivered. He did not know if it quivered from the desire of the MP to strike him, or secret military wonder was he now possessed of a moral force which implanted terror in the arms of young soldiers? Some unfamiliar current, now gyroscopic, now a sluggish whirlpool, was evolving from that quiver of the club, and the MP seemed to turn slowly away from his position confronting the rope, and the novelist turned with him, each still facing the other until the axis of their shoulders was now perpendicular to the rope, and still they kept turning in this psychic field, not touching, the club quivering, and then Mailer was behind the MP, he was free of him, and he wheeled around and kept going in a half run to the next line of MPs and then on the push of a sudden instinct, sprinted suddenly around the nearest MP in the second line, much as if he were a back cutting around the nearest man in the secondary to break free—that was actually his precise thought—and had a passing perception of how simple it was to get past the MPs. They looked petrified. Stricken faces as he went by. They did not know what to do. It was his dark pinstripe suit, his vest, the maroon and blue regimental tie, the part in his hair, the barrel chest, the early paunch—he must have looked like a banker himself, a banker, gone ape! And then he saw the Pentagon to his right across the field, not a hundred yards away, and a little to his left, the marshals, and ran on a jog toward them, and came up, and they glared at him and shouted, "Go back."

He had a quick impression of hard-faced men with gray eyes burning some transparent fuel for flame, and said, "I won't go back. If you don't arrest me, I'm going on to the Pentagon," and knew he meant it, some absolute certainty had come to him, and then two of them leaped on him at once in the cold clammy murderous fury of all cops at the existential moment of making their bust—all cops who secretly expect to be struck at that instant for their sins—and a supervising force came to his voice, and he roared, to his own distant pleasure in new achievement and new authority—"Take your hands off me, can't you see? I'm not resisting arrest," and one then let go of him, and the other stopped trying to pry his arm into a lock, and contented himself with a hard hand under his armpit, and they set off walking across the field at a rabid intent quick rate, walking parallel to the wall of the Pentagon, fully visible on his right at last, and he was arrested, he had succeeded in that, and without a club on his head, the mountain of air in his lungs as thin and fierce as smoke, yes, the livid air of tension on this livid side promised a few events of more interest than the routine wait to be free, yes he was more than a visitor, he was in the land of the enemy now, he would get to see their face.

Step Lightly

from *If I Die in a Combat Zone*
(Box Me Up and Ship Me Home)
by Tim O'Brien

If I Die in a Combat Zone is Tim O'Brien's autobiographical account of his combat service in Vietnam. This chapter recounts a particularly terrifying and unpredictable danger: Even with no enemy in sight, the enemy is there—underfoot.

The Bouncing Betty is feared most. It is a common mine. It leaps out of its nest in the earth, and when it hits its apex, it explodes, reliable and deadly. If a fellow is lucky and if the mine is in an old emplacement, having been exposed to the rains, he may notice its three prongs jutting out of the clay. The prongs serve as the Bouncing Betty's firing device. Step on them, and the unlucky soldier will hear a muffled explosion; that's the initial charge sending the mine on its one-yard leap into the sky. The fellow takes another step and begins the next and his backside is bleeding and he's dead. We call it "ol' step and a half."

More destructive than the Bouncing Betty are the booby-trapped mortar and artillery rounds. They hang from trees. They nestle in shrubbery. They lie under the sand. They wait beneath the mud floors of huts. They haunted us. Chip, my black buddy from Orlando, strayed into a hedge-row and triggered a rigged 105 artillery round. He died in such a way that, for once, you could never know his color.

He was wrapped in a plastic body bag, we popped smoke, and a helicopter took him away, my friend. And there was Shorty, a volatile fellow so convinced that the mines would take him that he spent a month AWOL. In July he came back to the field, joking but still unsure of it all. One day, when it was very hot, he sat on a booby-trapped 155 round.

When you are ordered to march through areas such as Pinkville—GI slang for Song My, parent village of My Lai—the Batangan Peninsula or the Athletic Field, appropriately named for its flat acreage of grass and rice paddy, when you step about these pieces of ground, you do some thinking. You hallucinate. You look ahead a few paces and wonder what your legs will resemble if there is more to the earth in that spot than silicates and nitrogen. Will the pain be unbearable? Will you scream or fall silent? Will you be afraid to look at your own body, afraid of the sight of your own red flesh and white bone? You wonder if the medic remembered his morphine. You wonder if your friends will weep.

It is not easy to fight this sort of self-defeating fear, but you try. You decide to be ultracareful—the hard-nosed, realistic approach. You try to second-guess the mine. Should you put your foot to that flat rock or the clump of weed to its rear? Paddy dike or water? You wish you were Tarzan, able to swing with the vines. You try to trace the footprints of the man to your front. You give it up when he curses you for following too closely; better one man dead than two.

The moment-to-moment, step-by-step decision-making preys on your mind. The effect sometimes is paralysis. You are slow to rise from rest breaks. You walk like a wooden man, like a toy soldier out of Victor Herbert's *Babes in Toyland*. Contrary to military and parental training, you walk with your eyes pinned to the dirt, spine arched, and you are shivering, shoulders hunched. If you are not overwhelmed by complete catatonia, you may react as Philip did on the day he was told to police up one of his friends, victim of an antipersonnel mine. Afterward, as dusk fell, Philip was swinging his entrenching tool like a madman, sweating and crying and hollering. He dug a foxhole four feet into the clay. He sat in it and sobbed. Everyone—all his friends and all the officers—were very quiet, and not a person said anything. No one comforted him until it was very dark. Then, to stop the noise, one man at a time would talk to him, each of us saying he understood and that tomorrow it would all be over. The captain said he would get Philip to the rear, find him a job driving a truck or painting fences.

Once in a great while we would talk seriously about the mines. "It's more than the fear of death that chews on your mind," one soldier, nineteen years old, eight months in the field, said. "It's an absurd combination of certainty and uncertainty: the certainty that you're walking in mine fields, walking past the things day after day; the uncer-

tainty of your every movement, of which way to shift your weight, of where to sit down.

"There are so many ways the VC can do it. So many configurations, so many types of camouflage to hide them. I'm ready to go home."

The kid is right:

The M-14 antipersonnel mine, nicknamed the "toe popper." It will take a hunk out of your foot. Smitty lost a set of toes. Another man who is now just a blur of gray eyes and brown hair—he was with us for only a week— lost his left heel.

The booby-trapped grenade. Picture a bushy shrub along your path of march. Picture a tin can secured to the shrub, open and directed toward the trail. Inside the can is a hand grenade, safety pin removed, so that only the can's metal circumference prevents the "spoon," or firing handle, from jumping off the grenade and detonating it. Finally, a trip wire is attached to the grenade, extending across the pathway, perhaps six inches above the dirt. Hence, when your delicate size-eight foot caresses that wire, the grenade is yanked from its container, releasing the spoon and creating problems for you and your future.

The Soviet TMB and the Chinese antitank mines. Although designed to detonate under the pressure of heavy vehicles, the antitank mine is known to have shredded more than one soldier.

Specialist 4 James Sullivan carefully cuts away the boot of a comrade standing on a "Bouncing Betty" mine.

The directional-fragmentation mine. The concave-faced directional mine contains from 450 to 800 steel fragments embedded in a matrix and backed by an explosive charge—TNT or petnam. The mine is aimed at your anticipated route of march. Your counterpart in uniform, a gentle young man, crouches in the jungle, just off the trail. When you are in range, he squeezes his electronic firing device. The effects of the mine are similar to those of a twelve-gauge shotgun fired at close range. United States Army training manuals describe this country's equivalent device, the Claymore mine: "It will allow for wider distribution and use, particularly in large cities. It will effect considerable savings in materials and logistics." In addition, they call the mine cold-blooded.

The corrosive-action-car-killer. The CACK is nothing more than a grenade, its safety pin extracted and spoon held in place by a rubber band. It is deposited in your gas tank. Little boys and men of the cloth are particularly able to maneuver next to an unattended vehicle and do the deed—beneath a universal cloak of innocence. The corrosive action of the gasoline eats away the rubber band, releasing the spoon, blowing you up in a week or less. Although it is rarely encountered by the footborne infantryman, the device gives the rear-echelon mine finder (REMF) something to ponder as he delivers the general's laundry.

In the three days that I spent writing this, mines and men came together three more times. Seven more legs were out on the red clay; also, another arm.

The immediacy of the last explosion—three legs, ten minutes ago—made me ready to burn the midsection of this report, the flippant itemization of these killer devices. Hearing over the radio what I just did, only enough for a flashing memory of what it is all about, makes the *Catch-22* jokes into a cemetery of half-truths. "Orphan 22, this is . . . this is Yankee 22 . . . mine, mine. Two guys . . . legs are off . . . I say again, legs off . . . request urgent dust-off, grid 711888 . . . give me ETA . . . get that damn bird." Tactical Operations Center: "You're coming in distorted . . . Yankee 22? Say again . . . speak slowly . . . understand you need dust-off helicopter?" Pause. "This is Yankee 22 . . . for Chri . . . ake . . . need chopper . . . two men, legs are . . . "

But only to say another truth will I let the half-truths stand. The catalog of mines will be retained, because that is how we talked about them, with a funny laugh, flippantly, with a chuckle. It is funny. It's absurd.

Patent absurdity. The troops are going home, and the war has not been won, even with a quarter of the United States Army fighting it. We slay one of them, hit a mine, kill another, hit another mine. It is funny. We walk through the mines, trying to catch the Viet Cong Forty-eighth Battalion like an unexperienced hunter after a hummingbird. But he finds us far more often than we do him. He is hidden among the mass of civilians or in tunnels or in

Soldiers dispose of a mine and evacuate a wounded buddy.

jungles. So we walk to find him, stalking the mythical, phantomlike Forty-eighth Battalion from here to there to here to there. And each piece of ground left behind is his from the moment we are gone on our next hunt. It is not a war fought for territory, not for pieces of land that will be won and held. It is not a war fought to win the hearts of the Vietnamese nationals, not in the wake of contempt drawn on our faces and on theirs, not in the wake of a burning village, a trampled rice paddy, a battered detainee. If land is not won and if hearts are at best left indifferent; if the only obvious criterion of military success is body count and if the enemy absorbs losses as he has, still able to lure us amid his crop of mines; if soldiers are being withdrawn, with more to go later and later and later; if legs make me more of a man, and they surely do, my soul and character and capacity to love notwithstanding; if any of this is truth, a soldier can only do his walking laughing along the way and taking a funny, crooked step.

After the war, he can begin to be bitter. Those who point at and degrade his bitterness, those who declare it's all a part of war and that this is a job which must be done—to those patriots I will recommend a postwar vacation to this land, where they can swim in the sea, lounge under a fine sun, stroll in the quaint countryside, wife and son in hand. Certainly, there will be a mine or two still in the earth. Alpha Company did not detonate all of them.

"Going Crazy"

from Michael Herr, **Dispatches,** (New York: Alfred A. Knopf, 1968)

After enough time passed and memory receded and settled, the name itself became a prayer, coded like all prayer to go past the extremes of petition and gratitude: Vietnam Vietnam Vietnam, say again, until the word lost all its old loads of pain, pleasure, horror, guilt, nostalgia. Then and there, everyone was just trying to get through it, existential crunch, no atheists in foxholes like you wouldn't believe. Even bitter refracted faith was better than none at all, like the black Marine I'd heard about during heavy shelling at Con Thien who said, "Don't worry, baby, God'll think of something."

Flip religion, it was so far out, you couldn't blame anybody for believing anything. Guys dressed up in Batman fetishes, I saw a whole squad like that, it gave them a kind of dumb esprit. Guys stuck the ace of spades in their helmet bands, they picked relics off of an enemy they'd killed, a little transfer of power; they carried around five-pound Bibles from home, crosses, St. Christophers, mezuzahs, locks of hair, girlfriends' underwear, snaps of their families, their wives, their dogs, their cows, their cars, pictures of John Kennedy, Lyndon Johnson, Martin Luther King, Huey Newton, the Pope, Che Guevara, the Beatles, Jimi Hendrix, wiggier than cargo cultists. One man was carrying an oatmeal cookie through his tour, wrapped up in foil and plastic and three pair of socks. He took a lot of shit about it ("When you go to sleep we're gonna eat your fucking cookie"), but his wife had baked it and mailed it to him, he wasn't kidding.

On operations you'd see men clustering around the charmed grunt that many outfits created who would take himself and whoever stayed close enough through a field of safety, at least until he rotated home or got blown away, and then the outfit would hand the charm to someone else. If a bullet creased your head or you'd stepped on a dud mine or a grenade rolled between your feet and just lay there, you were magic enough. If you had any kind of extra-sense capacity, if you could smell VC or their danger the way hunting guides smelled the coming weather, if you had special night vision, or great ears, you were magic too; anything bad that happened to you could leave the men in your outfit pretty depressed. I met a man in the Cav who'd been "fucking the duck" one afternoon, sound asleep in a huge tent with thirty cots inside, all empty but his, when some mortar rounds came in, tore the tent down to canvas slaw and put frags through every single cot but his, he was still high out of his mind from it, speedy, sure and lucky. The Soldier's Prayer came in two versions: Standard, printed on a plastic-coated card by the Defense Department, and Standard Revised, impossible to convey because it got translated outside of language, into chaos—screams, begging, promises, threats, sobs, repetitions of holy names until their throats were cracked and dry, until some men had bitten through their collar points and rifle straps and even their dog-tag chains.

Varieties of religious experience, good news and bad news; a lot of men found their compassion in the war, some found it and couldn't live with it, war-washed shutdown of feeling, like who gives a fuck. People retreated into positions of hard irony, cynicism, despair, some saw the action and declared for it, only heavy killing could make them feel so alive. And some just went insane, followed the black-light arrow around the bend and took possession of the madness that had been waiting there in trust for them for eighteen or twenty-five or fifty years. Every time there was combat you had a license to go maniac, everyone snapped over the line at least once there and nobody noticed, they hardly noticed if you forgot to snap back again.

One afternoon at Khe Sanh a Marine opened the door of a latrine and was killed by a grenade that had been rigged on the door. The Command tried to blame it on a North Vietnamese infiltrator, but the grunts knew what had happened: "Like a gook is really gonna tunnel all the way in here to booby-trap a shithouse, right? Some guy just flipped out is all." And it became another one of those stories that moved across the DMZ, making people laugh and shake their heads and look knowingly at each other, but shocking no one. They'd talk about physical wounds in one way and psychic wounds in another, each man in a squad would tell you how crazy everyone else in the squad was, everyone knew grunts who'd gone crazy in the middle of a firefight, gone crazy on patrol, gone crazy back at camp, gone crazy on R&R, gone crazy during their first month home. Going crazy was built into the tour, the best you could hope for was that it didn't happen around you, the kind of crazy that made men empty clips into strangers or fix grenades on latrine doors. That was *really* crazy; anything less was almost standard, as standard as the vague prolonged stares and involuntary smiles, common as ponchos or 16's or any other piece of war issue. If you wanted someone to know you'd gone insane you really had to sound off like you had a pair, "Scream a lot, and all the time."

Raid over North Vietnam

from *Flight of the Intruder*
by Stephen Coonts

Stephen Coonts flew A-6A Intruder aircraft from the carrier U.S.S. Enterprise *from 1971 to 1973. His best-selling novel about carrier-based air missions over Vietnam was praised for its technical accuracy and accessibility to those unfamiliar with combat aircraft.*

The starboard bow catapult fired, and the A-6A Intruder accelerated down the flight deck with a roar that engulfed the aircraft carrier and reverberated over the night sea. The plane's wings bit into the air, and the machine began to climb into the blackness. Fifteen seconds later the bomber was swallowed by the low-lying clouds.

In a few minutes the climbing Intruder broke free of the clouds. The pilot, Lieutenant Jake Grafton, abandoned the instrument panel and contemplated the vaulted stars. A pale slice of moon illuminated the cloud layer below. "Look at the stars tonight, Morg."

Lieutenant (junior grade) Morgan McPherson, the bombardier-navigator, sat on the pilot's right, his face pressed against the black hood that shielded the radar screen from extraneous light. He straightened and glanced up at the sky. "Yeah," he said, then readjusted the scope hood and resumed the never-ending chore of optimizing the radar presentation. He examined the North Vietnam-

ese coastline a hundred miles away. "I've got an update. I'm cycling to the coast-in point." He pushed a button on the computer, and the steering bug on the pilot's visual display indicator (VDI) slipped a quarter-inch sideways, giving the pilot steering information to the point on the coast where the Intruder would cross into North Vietnam.

Grafton turned the aircraft a few degrees to follow the steering command. "Did you ever stop to think maybe you're getting too wrapped up in your work?" he said. "That you're in a rut?"

Morgan McPherson pushed himself back from the radar hood and looked at the stars overhead. "They're still there, and we're down here. Let's check the ECM again."

"The problem is that you're just too romantic," Grafton told him and reached for the electronic counter-measures panel. Together they ran the equipment through the built-in tests that verified the ECM was working. Two pairs of eyes observed each indicator light, and two pairs of ears heard each beep. The ECM gear detected enemy radar emissions and identified them for the crew. When the ECM picked up radar signals it had been programmed to recognize as threatening, it would broadcast false images to the enemy operator. Satisfied all was working properly, the airmen adjusted the volume of the ECM audio so that it could be heard in their earphones yet would not drown out the intercom system (ICS), over which they talked to each other, or the radio.

The two men flew on without speaking, each listening to the periodic bass tones of the communist search radars sweeping the night. Each type of radar had its own sound: a low beep was a search radar probing the sky; higher pitched tones were fire-control radars seeking to acquire a target; and a nightmare falsetto was a locked-on missile-control radar guiding its weapon.

Fifty miles from the North Vietnamese coast, Jake Grafton lowered the nose of the Intruder four degrees, and the A-6 began its long descent. When he had the aircraft trimmed, Jake tugged all the slack from the harness straps securing him to his ejection seat, then exhaled and, like a cowboy tightening a saddle girth, pulled the straps as snugly as he could. That done, he asked for the combat checklist.

Leaving nothing to chance or memory, McPherson read each item off his kneeboard card and both men checked the appropriate switch or knob. When they reached the last detail on the checklist, Jake shut off the aircraft's exterior lights and turned the IFF to standby. The IFF, or "parrot," radiated electronic energy that enabled an American radar operator to see the aircraft as a coded blip he could readily identify as friend or foe. Grafton had no desire to appear as a blip, coded or uncoded, on a North Vietnamese radar screen. In fact, he hoped to escape detection by flying so near the ground that the radar return reflected from his plane would merge with the radar energy reflecting off the earth—the "ground return."

The pilot keyed his radio mike. The voice scrambler beeped, then Jake spoke: "Devil Five Oh Five is strangling parrot. Coast-in in three minutes." "Devil" was the A-6 squadron's radio call sign.

"Roger, Five Oh Five," responded the airborne controller circling over the Gulf of Tonkin in an E-2 Hawkeye, a twin engine turboprop with a radar dish mounted on top of the fuselage. The Hawkeye also had launched from the carrier.

The Intruder was going on the hunt. Camouflaged by darkness and hidden by the earth itself from the electronic eyes of the enemy, Jake Grafton would fly as low as his skill and nerves allowed, which was very low indeed.

The pilot cast a last quick look at the distant stars. Flying now at 450 knots, the bird plunged into the clouds. Jake felt the adrenaline begin to pump. He watched the pressure altimeter unwind and shot anxious glances at the radar altimeter, which derived its information from a small radar in the belly of the plane that looked straight down and measured the distance to the ground or sea. He briefly wished that he could turn it off because he knew its emissions could be detected, but he needed this device. The pressure altimeter told him his height above sea level, but tonight he would have to know just how high he was above the earth. As he passed 5000 feet, the radar altimeter began to function and matched the readings of the pressure altimeter perfectly, just as it should over the sea. The pilot breathed deeply and forced himself to relax.

Dropping below 2000 feet, he eased the stick back and slowed the rate of descent. With his left hand he advanced the throttles to a high-cruise power setting. The airspeed stabilized at 420 knots, Grafton's preferred speed for tree-top flying. The A-6 handled very well at this speed, even with the drag and weight of a load of bombs. The machine would fly over enemy gunners too fast for them to track it even if they should be so lucky as to make out the dark spot fleeting across the night sky.

Jake Grafton's pulse pounded as he brought the plane down to 400 feet above the water. They were below the clouds now, flying in absolute darkness, not a glimmer of light visible in the emptiness between sea and sky. Only the dimmed lights of the gauges, which were red so as not to impair the night vision of the crew, confirmed that there was a world beyond the cockpit. Jake peered into the blackness, trying to find the telltale ribbon of white sand that marked the Vietnamese coast on even the darkest nights. Not yet, he told himself. He could feel the rivulets of sweat trickle down his face and neck, some running into his eyes. He shook his head violently, not daring to take his stinging eyes from the red gauges on the black panel in front of him for more than a second. The sea was just below, invisible, waiting to swallow the pilot who failed for a few seconds to notice a sink rate.

There, to the left . . . the beach. The pale sand caught his eye. Relax. . . . Relax, and concentrate. The whiteness flashed beneath them.

"Coast-in," Jake told the bombardier.

McPherson used his left hand to activate the stop-clock on the instrument panel and keyed his radio mike with his left foot. "Devil Five Oh Five is feet dry. Devil Five Oh Five, feet dry."

A friendly American voice answered. "Five Oh Five, Black Eagle. Roger feet dry. Good hunting." Then silence. Later, when Devil 505 returned to the coast, they would broadcast their "feet wet" call. Grafton and McPherson knew that now they were on their own, because the Hawkeye's radar could not separate the A-6's image from the earth's return without the aid of the IFF.

Jake saw moonlight reflecting faintly off rice paddies, indicating a break in the overcast ahead. The weather forecasters were right for a change, he thought. Out of the corner of his eye the pilot saw flashes: intermittent flashes in the darkness below.

"Small arms fire, Morg."

"Okay, Jakey baby." The bombardier never looked up from his radar scope. His left hand slewed the computer cross hairs across the scope while his right tuned the radar. "This computer is working great, but it's a little . . ." he muttered over the ICS.

Jake tried to ignore the muzzle flashes. Every kid and rice farmer in North Vietnam had a rifle and apparently spent the nights shooting randomly into the sky at the first rumble of jet engines. They never saw their targets but hoped somewhere in the sky a bullet and an American warplane would meet. Big morale booster, Jake thought. Lets every citizen feel he's personally fighting back. Jake saw the stuttering muzzle flashes of a submachine gun. None of these small arms fired tracer bullets so the little droplets of death were everywhere, and nowhere.

Patches of moonlight revealed breaks in the clouds ahead. The pilot descended to 300 feet and used the moonlight to keep from flying into the ground. He was much more comfortable flying visually rather than on instruments. With an outside reference he could fly instinctively; on instruments he had to work at it.

Off to the right antiaircraft artillery opened fire. The tracers burned through the blackness in slow motion. The warble of a Firecan gun-control radar sounded for a second in his ears, then fell silent.

A row of artillery fire erupted ahead of them. "Christ, Morg," he whispered to the bombardier. He picked a tear in the curtain of tracers, dipped a wing, and angled the jet through. McPherson didn't look up from the scope. "You got the river bend yet?" Jake asked as the flak storm faded behind them.

"Yep. Just got it. Three more minutes on this heading." McPherson reached with his left hand and turned on the master armament switch. He checked the position of every switch on the armament panel one more time. The dozen 500-pound bombs were now ready to be released. "Your pickle is hot," he told the pilot, referring to the red button on the stick grip which the pilot could press to release the weapons.

Again and again fiery streams of antiaircraft shells spewed forth like projectiles from a volcano. The stuff that came in the general direction of Devil 505 seemed to change course and turn behind them, an optical illusion created by the plane's 700-feet-per-second speed. The pilot ignored the guns fired behind or abreast and concentrated on negotiating his way through the strings of tracers that erupted ahead. He no longer even noticed the flashes from rifles and machine guns, the sparks of this inferno.

A voice on the radio: "Devil Five Oh Eight is feet dry, feet dry."

There's Cowboy, Jake thought. Cowboy was Lieutenant Commander Earl Parker, the pilot of the other A-6 bomber launched moments after them. Like Jake and McPherson, Cowboy and his bombardier were now racing across the earth with a load of bombs destined for a target not worth any man's life, or so Jake told himself as he weaved through the tracers, deeper and deeper into North Vietnam.

"Two miles to the turnpoint," the bombardier reminded him.

An insane warble racked their ears. A red light labeled "MISSILE" flashed on the instrument panel two feet from the pilot's face. This time McPherson did look up. The two men scanned the sky. Their best chance to avoid the surface-to-air missile was to acquire it visually, then outmaneuver it.

"There's the SAM! Two o'clock!" Jake fought back the urge to urinate. Both men watched the white rocket exhaust while Grafton squeezed the chaff-release button on the right throttle with his forefinger. Each push released a small plastic container into the slipstream where it disbursed a cloud of metallic fibers—the chaff—that would echo radar energy and form a false target on the enemy operator's radar screen. The pilot carefully nudged the stick forward and dropped to 200 feet above the ground. He jabbed the chaff button four more times in quick succession.

The missile light stopped flashing and the earphones fell silent as death itself.

"I think it's stopped guiding," McPherson said with relief evident in his voice. "Boy, we're having fun now," he added dryly. Grafton said nothing. They were almost scraping the paddies. The bombardier watched the missile streak by several thousand feet overhead at three times the speed of sound, then he turned his attention to the radar. "Come hard left," he told the pilot.

Jake dropped the left wing and eased back slightly on the stick. He let the plane climb to 300 feet. The moonlight bounced off the river below. "See the target yet?"

"Just a second, man." Silence. "Steady up." Jake leveled the wings. "I've got the target. I'm on it. Stepping into attack." The bombardier flipped a switch, and the computer calculated an attack solution. The word "ATTACK" lit up in red on the lower edge of the VDI, and the computer-driven display became more complex. Symbols appeared showing the time remaining until weapons release, the relative position of the target, the drift angle, and the steering to the release point.

Jake jammed the throttles forward to the stops and climbed to 500 feet. The Mark 82 general-purpose bombs had to fall at least 500 feet for the fuses to arm properly; they were equipped with metal vanes that would open when the weapons were released and retard them just long enough to allow the plane to escape the bomb fragments.

The needle on the airspeed indicator quivered at 480 knots. The stick was alive in the pilot's hand. Any small twitch made the machine leap. Jake's attention was divided among the mechanics of instrument flying, the computer-driven steering symbol on the VDI, and the occasional streams of yellow and red tracers. He felt extraordinarily alive, in absolute control. He could see everything at once: every needle, every gauge, every fireball in the night. With his peripheral vision, he even saw McPherson turn on the track radar.

Inside the cockpit of an A-6A Intruder.

"Ground lock." The bombardier noted the indication on the track radar and reported it to the pilot with an affectation of amazement. The damn track radar often failed. McPherson was glued to the radar screen, his entire world the flickering green light. "Hot damn, we're gonna get 'em."

He feels it too, Jake thought. With the track radar locked on the target the computer was getting the most accurate information possible on azimuth and elevation angle.

On this October night in 1972, Devil 505 closed on the target, a "suspected truck park," jargon for a penciled triangle on a map where the unknown persons who picked the targets thought the North Vietnamese might have some trucks parked under the trees, away from the prying eyes of aerial photography. Trucks or no trucks, the target was only a place in the forest.

The bomb run was all that existed now for Jake Grafton. His life seemed compressed into this moment, without past or future. Everything depended on how well he flew Devil 505 to that precise point in space where the computer would release the bombs to fall upon the target.

The release marker on the VDI marched relentlessly toward the bottom of the display as the plane raced in at 490 knots. At the instant the marker disappeared, the

500-pound bombs were jettisoned from the bomb racks. Both men felt a series of jolts, a physical reminder that they had pulled a trigger. The attack light was extinguished when the last weapon was released, and only then did Grafton bank left and glance outside. Tracers and muzzle flashes etched the night. "Look back," he told the bombardier as he flew the aircraft through the turn.

Morgan McPherson looked over the pilot's left shoulder in the direction of the target, obscured by darkness. He saw the explosions of the bombs—white death flashes—twelve in two-thirds of a second. Jake saw the detonations in his rear-view mirror and rolled out of the turn on an easterly heading. Without the drag of the 500-pounders, the two engines pushed the fleeing warplane even faster through the night, now 500 knots, almost 600 miles per hour.

"Arm up the Rockeyes, Morg."

The bombardier reset the armament switches that enabled the pilot to manually drop the four Rockeye cluster bombs still hanging under the wings. "Your pickle is hot," he told Grafton. He put his face back against the scope hood and examined the terrain ahead.

Grafton kept the engines at full throttle as he scanned the darkness for an antiaircraft artillery piece he could destroy with the waiting Rockeyes. It would have to be fairly close to his track and firing off to one side so that he could approach it safely. He referred to this portion of the mission as "killing rattlesnakes."

Somewhere below, a North Vietnamese peasant heard the swelling whine of jet engines approaching, first faintly, then rapidly increasing in intensity. As the whine quickly rose to a crescendo, he lifted an ancient bolt-action rifle to his shoulder, pointed it at a 45-degree angle into the night above, and pulled the trigger.

The bullet punched a tiny hole in the lower forward corner of the canopy plexiglas on the right side of the plane. It penetrated Morgan McPherson's oxygen mask, deflected off his jawbone, pierced the larynx, nicked a carotid artery, then exited his neck and spent itself against the side of the pilot's ejection seat. Reflexively, Morgan keyed his ICS mike with his right foot, gagged, and grabbed his neck.

Jake Grafton looked at the bombardier. Blood, black in the glow of the red cockpit lights, spurted from between McPherson's fingers.

"Morg?"

McPherson gagged again. His eyes bulged and he stared at the pilot. His eyebrows knitted. He spat up blood. "Jake," he gurgled. He coughed repeatedly with the ICS mike keyed.

Jake tore his eyes from McPherson and thought furiously as he checked the instrument panel. What could have happened? Without noticing he had drawn the stick back and the aircraft was up to 700 feet over the delta tableland and exposed on every enemy radar screen within range. He shoved the stick forward. "Don't try to talk, Morg. I'll get you home." He leveled the plane at 300 feet and was once again hidden amid the ground return.

Jesus! Jesus Christ! Something must have come through the canopy, a piece of flak shrapnel or a random bullet.

A whisper: "Jake . . ." McPherson's hand clutched Jake's arm, then fell away. He raised his hand and again clutched at Jake, this time more weakly. Morgan slumped over, his head resting on the scope hood. Blood covered the front of his survival vest. Holding the stick with his left hand, Jake struggled to unfasten McPherson's oxygen mask. Blood spilled from the rubber cup. Black stains covered the sleeve of his flight suit where McPherson's hand had seized him.

A battery of guns opened up ahead with short bursts of orange tracers that floated aloft: 37 millimeter. They were shooting generally off to the right, so Jake Grafton turned the plane slightly to fly directly over the muzzle blasts. He guided the plane into a gentle climb and as the guns disappeared under the nose, he savagely mashed the bomb-release pickle on the stick. Thump, thump, thump, thump; the Rockeyes fell away a third of a second apart.

"Take that, you motherfuckers!" he screamed into his mask, his voice registering hysteria.

He looked again at McPherson, whose arms dangled toward the floor of the cockpit. Blood still throbbed from his throat.

With one hand on the stick, Jake pulled the bombardier upright where the shoulder harness engaged and held him. He searched for the wound with his fingers. He could feel nothing with his flying glove on, so he tore it off with his left hand and probed for the hole with his bare fingers. He couldn't find it.

He glanced back at the instruments. He was rapidly becoming too busy, an error that he knew would be fatal for both himself and McPherson. The plane would not fly itself and certain death was just below. Raise the left wing, bring the nose up, climb back to 500 feet, then attend to the wounded man. He felt again in the slippery, pulsing blood of McPherson's neck. Finding the wound, he clamped down with his fingers, then turned back to flying the plane. Too high. Flak ahead. Trim the plane. He jerked his left hand from the stick to the throttles, which he pushed forward. They were already hard against the stops. He could feel the throbbing of the flow from McPherson's neck noticeably lessening. He felt elated as he wrestled the plane, thinking that the pressure on the wound might be effective, but the euphoria faded quickly. How could he possibly land the plane like this?

His head swiveled to the unconscious man beside him, taking in the slack way his body reacted to each bump and jolt of the racing aircraft. Jake pressed harder on the wound, pressed until his hand ached from the unnatural position and the exertion.

He remembered the hot-mike switch that would allow him to talk to the bombardier without keying the ICS each time. He released the stick momentarily and flipped it on with his left hand. "Hey, Morgan," he urged, "hang in there, shipmate. You're going to make it. I'll get you back. Keep the faith, Morg."

He could feel nothing now, no pulse, no blood pumping against his fingers. Reluctantly, he pulled his hand away and wiped it on his thigh before grasping the stick. He found the radio-transmit button and waited until the scrambler beeped. "Black Eagle, Devil Five Oh Five, over."

"Devil Five Oh Five, this is Black Eagle, go ahead."

"My bombardier has been hit. I'm declaring an emergency. Request you have the ship make a ready deck for recovery on arrival. I repeat, my bombardier has been shot." His voice sounded strong and even, which surprised him as he felt so completely out of control.

"We copy that, Five Oh Five. Will relay." The radio fell silent.

As he waited he talked to McPherson. "Don't you give up on me, you sonuvabitch. You never were a quitter, Morg. Don't give up now."

More flak came up. He pushed at the throttles again,

unconsciously trying to go faster. They were already traveling at 505 knots. Perhaps he should dump some fuel. He still had 10,000 pounds remaining. No, even with the fuel gone the old girl would go no faster; she was giving her all now, and he might need the fuel to get to Da Nang if the ship couldn't recover him immediately.

Finally, the white-sand beach flashed beneath. Grafton turned the IFF to Emergency. "Devil Five Oh Five is feet wet." McPherson had not moved.

"Black Eagle copies, Devil Five Oh Five. Wagon Train has been notified of your emergency. Do you have any other problems, any other damage, over?" Wagon Train was the ship's radio call sign.

Jake Grafton scanned the instruments, then stole another look at Morgan McPherson. "Just a BN in terrible shape, Black Eagle."

"Roger that. We have you in radar contact. Your steer to the ship is One Three Zero degrees. Squawk One Six Zero Zero."

"Wilco."

The pilot settled on the recommended course, then flipped on the TACAN, a radio navigation aid that would point to the carrier's beacon. As the needle swung lazily several times he turned the IFF to the requested setting,

the "squawk." The TACAN needle stopped swinging, steady on 132 degrees. Jake worked in the correction. He leveled off at 5000 feet and kept the engines at full throttle. The TACAN distance-measuring indicator finally locked in, showing ninety-five miles to the ship.

The overcast hid the moon and stars. Inside the clouds he felt as though he were the only human being alive on earth. He kept glancing at McPherson, whose head rolled back and forth in rhythm to the motion of the plane. He squeezed McPherson's hand tightly, but there was no response. Still he held on, hoping McPherson could feel the presence of a friend. He tried to speak on the ICS but found his voice merely a croak.

The commanding officer of the USS *Shiloh* was on the bridge when news of Devil 505's emergency reached him. Captain Robert Boma had spent twenty-seven years in the navy and wore pilot's wings on his left breast. Tall, lean, and greying, he had learned to live on three hours sleep with occasional catnaps; he was in his elevated easy chair on the bridge every minute that the carrier had aircraft

---

A sailor on the carrier U.S.S. Midway *charts aircraft as they fly bombing missions over North Vietnam.*

aloft. "How far is it to Da Nang?" he asked the officer-of-the-deck (OOD) as he weighed the options. Da Nang was the nearest friendly airfield ashore.

"Nearly two hundred miles, sir."

"We'll take him aboard." The captain leaned over and flipped a few switches on the intercom. "This is the captain. Clear the landing area. Make a ready deck. We have an emergency inbound."

Within seconds the flight deck became organized bedlam. Arming and fueling activities ceased, and the handlers began respotting aircraft forward on the bow, clear of the landing area on the angled deck. Five minutes after the order was given, the carrier's landing area was empty and the ship had turned into the wind. The duty search-and-rescue helicopter, the Angel, took up a holding pattern off the starboard side. The crash crew, wearing asbestos suits, started the engine of the flight-deck fire truck. A doctor and a team of corpsmen appeared from deep within the ship and huddled beside the island, the ship's superstructure.

Grafton's roommate, Sammy Lundeen, was smoking a cigar in the A-6 squadron's ready room when the news came over the intercom mounted on the wall at the duty officer's desk. The squadron skipper, Commander Frank Camparelli, put down his newspaper as he listened to the squawk box. Lundeen drew his cigar from his mouth and fixed his eyes on the metal intercom.

"Sam, you go up to the LSO's platform and stand by on the radio." Camparelli looked at the duty officer. "Hargis, I'm going to CATCC. Get the executive officer and tell him to come to the ready room and stand by here."

Commander Camparelli strode out of the room, headed for the Carrier Air Traffic Control Center with Sammy Lundeen right behind on his way to the landing signal officer's platform. Lundeen's cigar smoldered on the deck where he had dropped it.

"How badly is the BN hit?" the air operations officer asked the strike controller over a hot-line telephone. In the next compartment the controller, focusing on a small green dot moving slowly toward the center of his radar screen, stepped on his microphone switch.

"Devil Five Oh Five, Wagon Train Strike. State nature and extent of BN injuries, over."

Jake Grafton's voice came over the public-address system in the control center. "Strike, Five Oh Five, I think my bombardier's been shot in the neck. It's hard to tell. He's unconscious now. I want a Charlie on arrival."

"Devil Five Oh Five, Strike. Your signal is Charlie on arrival." Charlie was the command to land.

"Roger that."

"Five Oh Five, switch to Approach on button three, and squawk One Three Zero Zero, over."

"Switching and squawking."

At the next radar console the approach controller noted

the blip on his screen that had blossomed with the new IFF code. When the pilot checked in on the new frequency, the controller gave him landing instructions.

The air ops boss turned to the A-6 skipper who had just entered the compartment. "Frank, looks like your boy must be hit pretty badly. He should be at the ramp in six or seven minutes."

Commander Camparelli nodded and sat down in an empty chair beside the boss's chair. The room they sat in was lit entirely by dim red light. On the opposite wall a plexiglas status board seven feet high and twenty feet long listed every sortie the ship had airborne and all the sorties waiting on deck to be launched. Four enlisted men wearing sound-powered telephone headsets stood behind the transparent board and kept its information current by writing backwards on the board with yellow greasepencils. A black curtain behind them and the red light made the men almost invisible and caused the yellow letters to glow.

Commander Camparelli stared at the board. "505, Grafton, 9.0," it read. Camparelli's thoughts began to drift. Grafton and McPherson. Morgan's married to that dark-haired stewardess with United and has a two-year-old boy. Christ, he thought, I hope I don't have to write and tell her she's a widow.

"What kind of pilot is this Grafton?" the air ops boss asked.

"He's on his first tour, second cruise over here. Steady," said Camparelli. He added, "Good driver," but the ops officer had already turned away, trying to sort out what flights could be launched after Grafton had been recovered.

Frank Camparelli breathed deeply and tried to relax. Twenty years of fast planes, stormy nights, and pitching decks had given him a more than casual acquaintance with violent death. And he had found a way to live with it. Eyes open, half listening to the hushed voices around him, he began to pray.

The wind on the landing signal officer's platform tore at Sammy Lundeen's hair and clothing and roared in his ears as he stood on the lonesome perch jutting out from the port side of the landing area. He saw the Angel, the rescue helicopter, circling at 300 or 400 feet off the starboard side. Looking aft he could see the ship's phosphorescent wake and the running lights of the plane guard destroyer bobbing along a mile astern, waiting to rescue aircrews who ejected on final approach to the ship—if the chopper couldn't find them and if the destroyer crew could. Too many ifs. Small clusters of lights several miles away on either beam revealed the presence of two more destroyers.

"Here's a radio, Lundeen." The landing signal officer on duty tonight, Lieutenant Sonny Bob Battles, handed him a radio transceiver, which looked like a telephone, and then turned to the sound-powered telephone operator, an enlisted airman called a "talker." "Where is he?" Battles asked.

The talker spoke into the large microphone held by a harness on his chest. "Twelve miles out, sir. Level at twelve hundred feet."

"What freq?"

"Button three."

The LSO bent and twirled the radio channelization knob on the large control console mounted level with the deck edge. He and Lundeen held their radio transceivers up to their ears and heard the approach controller talking. "Five Oh Five, hold your gear until eight miles."

"Wilco." Jake sounded tired.

The LSO was an A-7 pilot, but like most aviators who acquire the special designation of landing signal officer, he was qualified to "wave" aboard all the types of aircraft the ship carried. He was prepared to talk a pilot aboard using only his eyes and the experience he had acquired observing more than ten thousand carrier approaches and almost as many simulated approaches at runways ashore. He had various sensors arrayed in a panel at his feet, but he rarely had time to glance at them.

"Who's driving Five Oh Five, Sam?"

"Grafton."

"Flies with McPherson?"

"Yeah."

Sonny Bob nodded. Both men heard Grafton give his gear-down call. The approach controller started Devil 505 descending on the glide slope. "Five Oh Five, call your needles."

"Up and right."

"Concur." A computer aboard ship located the A-6 and provided a glide slope and azimuth display on an instrument in the cockpit. But Jake would have to fly the jet down the glide slope and land it manually, a task that was as nerve-racking and demanding as any aviation had to offer.

On the LSO's platform Battles and Lundeen searched the darkness. The LSO keyed his mike. "Lights."

Jake Grafton had forgotten to turn on the aircraft's exterior lights when he crossed the Vietnamese coastline on his way out to sea. Now the lights came on, making Devil 505 visible. Lundeen thought that if Jake had forgotten the lights perhaps he had also failed to safe the weapons-release circuits. "Check your master arm switch," he told Jake. He heard two clicks of the mike in reply, a pilot's way of responding when he was too busy to speak.

"Green deck," the telephone operator shouted.

"Roger green deck," Battles replied. The landing area was now clear and the arresting gear set to receive an A-6.

The Intruder moved up and down on the glide slope and shifted left of centerline, to Battles's right. The LSO keyed the mike. "Paddles has you now, Five Oh Five. Watch your lineup."

The A-6 turned toward the centerline, where it should be.

"Just settle down and keep it coming. How do you feel?"

"Okay." The voice was thin. Tired, very tired.

"Easy on the power. Call the ball." The ball call was essential. It told the LSO that the pilot could see the light, the "meatball," presented by the optical landing system that was located on the port side of the landing area. This device used a yellow light arranged between two green reference, or datum, lights to give the pilot a visual indication of his position in relation to the proper glide path. If he kept the ball centered in the datum lights all the way to touchdown, he would catch the third of four arresting-gear wires rigged across the deck.

"Intruder ball, Six Point Oh."

Down in CATCC the invisible men behind the status board erased the last fuel state for Devil 505 and wrote "6.0" beside the pilot's name. Six thousand pounds of fuel remaining. Commander Camparelli and the air ops boss checked the closed-circuit television monitor that gave them a picture from a camera buried under the flight deck and aimed up the glide slope. They waited.

From his perch on the flight deck, beside the landing area, the LSO could see the lights of the approaching plane grow brighter. In CATCC and in every ready room on the ship, all eyes were fixed on the television monitor with its picture of the glide slope and centerline cross hair and, just visible, the lights of the approaching plane.

Lundeen heard the engines. The faint whine grew louder, and he could hear the compressors spooling up and down as the pilot adjusted the throttles to keep the machine on the glide slope.

Battles's voice: "You're starting to go low." The engines wound up slightly. "Little more power." The engines surged. "Too much, you're high." A whine as the power came off, then a swelling of sound as Jake added power to stabilize his descent.

The A-6 approached the end of the ship, its engines howling. Battles was six feet out into the landing area, braced against the thirty-knot wind, concentrating on the rapidly approaching Intruder. He realized the plane was about three feet too high even as he heard the throttles come back and saw the nose of the machine sag slightly. He's going for the deck, the LSO told himself as he screamed into the radio, "Attitude!"

The Intruder flashed by, a gigantic bird feeling for the deck with its tailhook and main landing gear, its wingtip less than fifteen feet from the LSO's head. Battles sensed, rather than saw, Jake pull the stick back in response to his last call. The A-6 slammed into the deck, and the tailhook snagged the number-two arresting cable, whipping it out. As the plane raced up the deck, the engines wound up toward full power with a blast of sound and hot fury that lashed the two unprotected men. Lundeen almost lost his footing, as he had already begun running up the flight deck the instant he saw the hook pick up the arresting wire.

An A-6 snags a carrier deck's arresting cable.

Training and reflex action had caused Jake Grafton to slam the throttles forward and retract the speed brakes the moment the wheels hit the deck in case the hook failed to snag a wire and he ran off the end of the deck, a "bolter." As he felt the arresting gear slow the plane, he slapped the throttles to idle, flipped the external-light master switch off, and raised the flap handle. The A-6 jerked to a halt and rolled backwards. The pilot pushed the button to raise the hook, then applied the brakes. The Intruder stopped with another jolt, this time remaining at rest.

Jake could see people running toward the plane from the island. He chopped the right engine and opened the canopy. A corpsman in a white shirt scrambled up the ladder on the BN's side of the plane and reached for McPherson. He raised the bombardier's head, looked at his neck, then motioned to the overhead floodlight switch on the canopy bow, the steel longitudinal frame that split the top of the canopy plexiglas. Turning it on, the pilot squinted and blinked as naked white light bathed the cockpit.

Rich red blood was everywhere. Blood covered McPherson and coated the panels on his side of the plane. Grafton's right hand was covered with it, as was the stick grip and everything else he had touched. The cockpit was a slaughter house.

More men draped over and on the cockpit. They flipped up the ejection seat safety latches to prevent the seat from firing accidentally, then released the fastenings that held the bombardier to the seat. They lifted his body out of the cockpit and passed him to the waiting hands below.

Fighting for self-control, Jake folded the wings and switched off the electronic gear. He became aware of Sammy standing on the ladder beside him. Lundeen reached into the cockpit and pulled the parking brake handle, then shut down the left engine. Grafton unlatched his oxygen mask and removed his helmet. His eyes were riveted on the stretcher bearing Morgan McPherson to the island superstructure until it disappeared behind a swinging metal door.

Silence descended on the cockpit. The wind down the flight deck dried the sweat coating Jake's hair and face. He began to chill. He looked again at the blood, on his hand, on the stick, blood everywhere under the harsh white light. The clock in the instrument panel was one of the few things not smeared with blood. The pilot looked up into the face of his friend.

"Sammy——" He felt the burning vomit coming up his throat and caught it in his helmet.

Combat Assault

from *The 13th Valley*
by John M. Del Vecchio

*Thirteen days into a combat patrol of the Khe Ta Laou Valley, Alpha Company closes in on a large concentration of NVA troops as **The 13th Valley** nears its climax. Sergeant Daniel Egan leads First Platoon; "Cherry" Chelini is his radioman; First Lieutenant Rufus Brooks commands Alpha Company.*

The sky is no longer black yet the brightest stars are visible. The earth is dark. In the hour before sunrise everything, everyone—the foliage, the earth, the mountains—takes on a blue-black tint, almost transparent. The wind is steady. The last remnant of fog has dissolved. It is the 13th day of the operation.

Egan leads 1st Plt. He is ecstatic. He is higher than he has ever been and he is at peace within. He has forgotten he is alive. He moves spirit-like, stealing along softly. His mission is to clear and secure the high feature, to cut an LZ on the knoll and to establish a base from which to support and reinforce 2d and 3d Plts if necessary. Behind him twenty-three boonierats advance cautiously. They are on a well-used trail, beneath canopy cover. Everything they see appears permanent. Everything is vacant.

No, Thomaston cries inside. No, we aint really doing this. I'm down to sixteen and a wake-up. Sweat rolls from his forehead into his eyes. Sixteen and a wake-up, he repeats. I'm a lieutenant. I'm not supposed to be in the bush with sixteen and a wake-up.

One mo step, Jax says to himself. One mo little step. His right hand twitches toward his pocket wanting to grab his hair pick. He resists. The ol right in front a the lef, he tells himself. Yo jest keep yo fuckin eyes all over the mothafuckin jungle. Jackson studies the trail briefly. His eyes dart up to the canopy. He keeps his head as still as possible moving only his eyes. A tree there, he says. Bush there. Grass there. If they opens up from the lef I jumps to that bush an do em a damn-damn. If they opens from the right I get in that depression. Jax, yo gotta git a job in comp'ny supply. What yo dowin fightin a white man's war? If they opens from the lef I can make that clump. If they opens from the right I goes back ta the depression.

1st Plt reaches a point approximately 100 meters in from the river at the knoll base. 3d Sqd breaks off and begins climbing. Cherry joins them, leads them. They form a three-man point with Cherry at center, Harley to the left and Hill to the right. Centered behind them is Frye with the new XM-203, then in column, Andrews with the radio, Kirtly, Mullen and Lt. Thomaston at drag. They advance very slowly, letting the other squads continue across the base of the knoll. After 10 meters 2d Sqd breaks off and heads uphill into the knoll. 1st Sqd continues then turns. 1st and 2d form advancing arrows similar to 3d's. These three-man points have the machine gunners at center, riflemen to each side, grenade launcher just behind ready to lob rounds over the point. Now all three squads advance, begin the sweep up the knoll.

Brooks thinks, this is the last time. This is the last time I will lead an infantry company. Three and a wake-up. He leads 2d and 3d Plts in an arc away from the river, behind the knoll, behind 1st Plt. Their mission is to find, enter and destroy the NVA headquarters. Brooks thinks now without speech. He hears, feels, sees inside his thoughts, without words, the bunkers are west, northwest, at the base of the knoll. He leads the boonierats through brush and grass and into a nearly impenetrable bamboo forest. Brooks works slowly, quietly, patiently. He slithers with the patience of a hunter, the natural patience of a cat stalking prey, waiting for the moment to strike.

Behind Brooks no thoughts enter Pop Randolph's mind. He is part of the machine. He is a machine. He is an acute sensor with the responsibility of protecting the point, taking the shock when it comes.

At the middle of the column Doc Johnson's mind is full of thoughts, full of words. He is angry. They got no right, he thinks. No right. The oppressor got no rights the oppressed got to respect. Jax right. Cleaver right. They got no business sendin us down here ta be butchered. This aint a mission; this is suicide. Doc hears a twig snap. His heart freezes then beats one immense pulse which he feels throb down through his abdomen and up to his shoulders and on, building, surging, splashing up behind his eyes. He winces. He does not locate the origin of the sound.

Brooks breaks out of the bamboo thicket and leads them across a red ball. Bamboo frames an arch over the road concealing it from above. The platoons move into a mix of brush and bamboo and grass. 3d Plt begins spreading right, 2d left, the CP remains at middle. Nahele moves to the far right flank. He moves easily, cautiously. His M-60 machine gun seems to pull at his finger as if the weapon wants to be fired, wants to fire. He fights the gun's desire. He pulls his squad, now his squad without Ridgefield or Snell, right. Then he turns and advances and begins the sweep northeast toward the river at the west base of the knoll.

On the knoll 1st Plt reaches the mid-point of their ascent. Every step has been quiet yet they feel a presence, are oppressed with apprehension. They slow further. Cherry smells the air. He smells them. Egan smells them. Cherry looks left right. He drops to one knee and across the sweep they all drop into the brush vegetation. 1st Plt's three prongs have closed from a thirty meter width to a twenty. Cherry smells again. He looks up. The massive tree is 250

meters ahead, 50 meters up. Its colossal spreading limbs seem to stretch over him. He searches the boughs and leafage. He becomes aware of warmth on the back of his arms and neck. The sun is up, has crested the eastern ridge. The noise of helicopters comes from the east and west. Medevacs, he thinks. And the C & C. Suddenly pure white flashes cut across his world. He whirls squeezing his 16, firing at the sight before the sound registers, before he knows he is firing. Bursts of AK-47 fire flashing from the right, then the sound erupts in his ears. There is firing to the left, explosions, the crackcrackcrack M-16s returning fire, his 16 barking.

"I'm hit," he hears Hill yell. Cherry and Harley leap, hit the ground firing. They do not pause for Hill. Frye fires from both barrels. He pays no attention to outgoing. Enemy rounds rip up the dirt at his side. Cherry snaps a second magazine into his 16. He is charging, firing. Great whooshing noises tear the air at his ears. RPGs. Rocket Propelled Grenades. Booming. The concussion rocks his eyes. His concentration does not break. He continues firing. Andrews is screaming, "Bravo! Bravo!" Alpha's code for medic.

To the left Egan is screaming, charging into the fire coming down from above. He fires and charges quick, agile. He is everywhere at once firing rounds like walls of lead. He whirls. He kills. He does not linger on the sight of enemy death. He swings firing right left. "For Minh," he screams. He does not know he has yelled it. Marko and Jackson advance with him. Satchel charges explode before them. The concussion dissipates. Their ears ring. They do not know it. "Let um know they fuckin with the Oh-Deuce," Egan screams. Marko shouts his battle cry. No sound leaves his throat. They dive for concealment, reload. Moneski from 2d Sqd dives in behind Egan. Beaford and Smith dive in behind Cherry and Harley. 2d Sqd has split up, five reinforce 3d Sqd, three 1st Sqd. The NVA do not capitalize on the split by driving up the center.

Cherry crashes forward, smashes forward, firing firing. He leaps a meter at a time and crashes down into the brush, the bamboo. Stalks stab him. Sticks rip his fatigues, his skin. Grass and vines trip him. He falls forward. Thorns rip his face. He does not know it, does not feel it.

"My toes! My foot! It's shot away." Hill is screaming. There is enemy fire coming from above and right. 1st Sqd is battling left. They are diverging. Cherry reloads. It is his fifth magazine. Hill crawls inward, toward the center, away from the firing. He slips under a bush for cover. His right leg drags. Blood is spurting from his ankle. "Medic," Andrews screams. "Medic!" Fuck codes. Doc McCarthy is with 1st Sqd. He and Numbnuts are pinned down. They do not fire. They do not move. Andrews lays his rifle down carefully. He strips the pants from Hill's left leg below the knee. Blood is everywhere. It shines brightly on Hill's white skin. It saturates Andrews' pants where it spurts. Andrews rips Hill's battle dressing from the wounded man's web rushes up left. Jax' grenade explodes. Trying to throw a one-pound grenade into a two foot wide slit from thirty feet while taking fire is impossible. Numbnuts with his XM-203 firing grenade rounds would not have been more effective, was he trying, but he had buried his head in a bush with the first volley. He is crying, weeping. "Let me go home. Let me go home." Doc McCarthy raises his eyes. He hears Andrews call. He can't move. He is trembling. An RPG round explodes above him. His stomach twists, he vomits. He tries to move away from his vomit. Machine gun fire cracks over his head. He drops flat, face-down in his own wretchedness. He curses Numbnuts for infecting him with fear. "Medic!" he hears Andrews scream. I can, he says. I can. I got to. Doc McCarthy crawls. "Where ya goin?" Numbnuts cries. "No," his teeth chatter. "No, Doc." He hears, feels a satchel charge erupting up, up there, between Egan and Marko. He flattens, cries. He is sure he is pinned down forever. McCarthy's gone.

"Rover Two," Brooks' voice comes urgently over the radio. "Rover Two, Quiet Rover Four. Over . . . Rover Two, Quiet Rover Four. Over." Marko's firing steady. The barrel of his 60 is burning. Lairds and Denhardt firing bursts alternately. Reloading alternately. Most of 1st Sqd firing, Egan charging. At the bunker. Egan dives into the bunker with his 16 flashing. He sprays downward left right. It is not a bunker. He sees it immediately. Knows it immediately. It is a trench running horizontal, arcing about the knoll. There is no one in this segment. They can be anywhere. Move anywhere. Fighting is raging to the right.

"Rover Two, Quiet Rover Four," Brooks whispers frantic.

"Four, Two. Over." Hoover answers.

"Sit-rep? Over," Brooks asks urgently.

"We got em running. Over."

"How large an element? Over."

"Fifteen. Maybe eighteen. We can kill em. Over."

"What's your position from basket? Over."

"200 . . . maybe 150 mikes. They're running to the sidelines. Can we get ARA on them? Over."

"Affirmative. Will try. Cut to the basket. Direct your niner, cut to the basket. Set up number five. Over."

"Medic," Hoover hears Thomaston scream from the center. Thomaston is with Hill. Hill is still moaning. His dressing is slick with blood. Thomaston grabs him, unfastens his belt, makes a tourniquet about Hill's thigh groin-high. "Keep it tight," Thomaston directs Andrews. He grabs Andrews' radio. He hears Brooks and Hoover.

"Affirmative," Hoover says.

"Negative," Thomaston cuts in. "Right forward engaged. Double whiskey india Alphas. One priority. Over."

"Shoot for the hoop," Brooks comes on the net. "Set-up five. Over. Out."

1st Sqd sprints for the trench, leaps, jumps dives in. Denhardt leaps from the trench uphill, Lairds follows. They rush foot-by-foot, run crouched, meter-by-meter, toward the center. Egan stays in the trench, runs, fires semi-

Soldiers patrol in the rain during Operation Highland in III Corps, north of Saigon.

belt. "My leg," Hill screams. "My foot. It's blown off." "Shut up," Andrews snarls. "Bite your tongue. You want a gook zeroin in here." Andrews slaps the dressing over the now flowing wound and wraps it over the holes. The ankle is shattered. Tendons are broken. The foot flops lifeless. "Aaaaahh," Hill cries, pain firing up his leg as Andrews clamps his hand on the wound. Direct pressure, Andrews thinks. Hill is thrashing, moaning, under the brush.

Fire from bunkers or fighting positions above slices through the brush, shattering it, smashing it. Marko sprays back into the noise, into the streaming lead, his machine gun ripping smashing ferociously. "Keep em down," Egan yells. He throws a frag at the bunker thirty feet away. He runs, dives, advances six feet, crawls. Marko keeps firing. Jax fires. Denhardt fires. "Move yer fuckin ass," Egan screams firing. The grenade explodes harmlessly below the bunker. Jax advances. Marko keeps firing, mixing fire with enemy fire. Jax throws a frag, his last. He fires. Egan automatic, rounds splatting in the trenchwalls before him. Jax and Marko cover the left flank, one above one below the trench. There is no fire from above. There is an explosion in the trench. Egan's legs burn whitehot, his equilibrium lapses, he cascades forward still running. He has triggered a booby trap, a satchel charge, stone shrapnel burns in his legs. He drops his rifle. The sound of the explosion reaches his brain. He feels instant nausea. It is not a big explosion he thinks. RPDs, AKs, RPG fire explode from the trench before him, beyond his sight, around the curve. He hears Harley scream, "Medic." Egan grabs his 16. Carefully now, he checks it. He ejects the magazine and inserts a fresh one. He chambers a fresh round then tries to crawl. His legs burn, his back feels hot, wet, sticky. Egan pulls his knees up under him, rocks back and stands. He charges down the trench.

Cherry charges the trench from below, his eyes blazing. He has enemy soldiers in his sights. He fires killing one. The other is fleeing. Cherry leaps. He is on top of the enemy. The soldier falls. He is small, lean, hard, but no match for Cherry. Cherry is on him gouging his eyes. *"Choui Hoi,"* the enemy yells cries into Cherry's madly punching fists. The man gashes at Cherry defensively. Cherry is infuriated. He digs his fingers into the enemy's face. The soldier bites Cherry's hand. Cherry bites his face, the nose crushes, Cherry bites, mad-dog, bites and rips the soldier's neck simultaneously thrusting his bayonet into the enemy's stomach. Blood explodes in Cherry's mouth. He freezes. He feels Egan standing over him, staring at him.

Firing erupts sporadically all over the valley. The firebase is being mortared, the C & C takes fire. The NVA's coordinated plan is now being implemented. All four US perimeter companies are being attacked at once. It is costly to the NVA. They have at least thirty-six killed. American helicopters are strafing NVA concentrations. Red smoke is billowing from a dozen US marking grenades, marking US front lines or NVA positions. American units do not advance. They are too close to each other for artillery or tactical air support. The NVA are attempting to have them fire at each other. From the C & C bird the GreenMan sees their plan. He also suspects, as does Brooks on the ground, that the NVA plan does not include Alpha Company, that Alpha has indeed lost itself in the valley and the ruse of not resupplying has worked. Only a skeleton crew of enemy soldiers is protecting the headquarters complex.

They are sweeping northwest through the brushforest. The sun is playing in the valley vegetation throwing dappled shadows against vegetation and ground and men. The shadows seem to dance in the stalks and leaves as the men sweep silently. They are in three rough lines, the front line men seven meters apart, too far, they think, yet that is how Brooks ordered it. The second line is three to four meters back, splitting the distance between the men in front, each second row man walking slack for two front row men. Behind the third line are the reinforcers, the reactors, and the co-ordinators. The sweep has advanced 300 meters. They have halted, listening to 1st Plt's fight, waiting to be directed to help.

"Hey, L-T," FO whispercalls. "Hey," he gestures quickly at a camouflaged mound, a swell not eight inches higher than the valley floor around it. "Hey," he whispershouts, "we're on top of a bunker complex."

Brooks looks. He stares. It is not FO's style to conjure up nonexistent bunkers yet Brooks does not see a bunker. The commander and the forward observer are fewer than two meters apart. They are kneeling behind the front two lines. Brooks stares. FO is covering the mound with his 16. He has risen and is advancing on the mound. The immediate area is silent. 1st Plt's battle for the knoll is quieting. Brooks stares, he sees nothing. Then the form emerges from the camouflaging background. It is like an optical illusion which, once seen, one cannot easily reverse. Brooks scans the area. He sees what FO has seen. There are bunkers everywhere, before them and behind. The camouflage seems to melt away, and there is a field of bunkers, a field of low square mounds buried beneath growing layers of brush and vine and some bamboo and some low trees. A few of the bunkers are beneath what appears to be old Montagnard thatch hootches that have collapsed and rotted.

It happens to Pop Randolph at the far left and to Nahele at the far right. Some still see nothing even as others point out mounds to them. Never have any of them seen such perfect camouflage. There seems to be no openings. A spooky feeling sweeps across the invaders. Where are they? Brooks thinks. Where are the little people? Why haven't they hit us? He directs the unit to squeeze in at the flanks and bulge at the sides. "Have them form a perimeter," he tells El Paso. "We'll clear from inside out. Get Nahele up here. And McQueen. And Pop."

The boonierats react as if they were muscles in Brooks' body. They operate silently as if they communicate by telepathy and not by voice. Fear keeps them silent. Nahele is the first underground. He dives into a bunker opening that FO has found, one of only three discovered in all the square mounds Alpha has now investigated. With a .45 and a flashlight Nahele dives in as an underwater demolition expert on patrol might dive into a harbor across from his target. He comes out in only seconds. "It's empty," he whispers. "It's a vacant room. There's three tunnels leading out a it."

Brooks and Pop and McQueen follow Nahele back in. Brooks follows a tunnel south. The tunnel is large enough for him to walk hunched. It curves right then left and opens into a second room larger than the first. There is another tunnel leaving it. The sides are stacked with cases and crates. Holy fucken Christ! Brooks thinks. Pop is behind him. Then Nahele. McQueen has stayed in the empty room to guard against enemy coming from the other tunnels. Brooks comes from the second room with a case of mortar rounds. He pushes it up, out, above ground where FO grabs it and pulls it aside and helps Brooks from the hole. Brooks moves quickly now. He grabs Cahalan, grabs the handset of his radio and calls the GreenMan. In the second-long pause before the battalion commander answers, Brooks directs El Paso to tell Lt. De Barti that he, Brooks, wants Baiez' squad immediately. "Red Rover," Brooks addresses the GreenMan, "we've found it. We're in it." He continues explaining. "The tip of a iceberg," he says. He hears the GreenMan laughing joyously in his C & C bird circling three thousand feet over the valley. He hears the GreenMan laughing and saying, "This is it. Get it all out. I'll get up a back-up element for security. This is what I've been looking for." Brooks hears, feels the Green-Man's enthusiasm. It makes Brooks feel good.

And up it comes. Cases, cartons, crates. Cases of 82mm mortar rounds, each individually wrapped in corrugated cardboard. Cartons of fuses. Boxes of paper-like explosive propellent discs that the NVA mortarmen used instead of the powder bags used by the US and ARVN forces. Baiez and Shaw are grabbing the supplies, stacking them, building piles. They are breathing hard, sweating. The day is becoming a scorcher.

Below ground it is cool. Pop is investigating a third set of rooms. I bet they're all connected, he thinks. I bet they're connected to Whiteboy's Mine up on the ridge. He and McQueen go into a fourth room. It is filled with radios and communication equipment. They take one radio and drag it through the tunnel network to the entry room. Brooks orders four more men below ground. The air is filled with discovery. Never have any of Alpha's boonierats seen such a cache, captured such quantities of equipment. They are smiling, laughing quietly, working eagerly. Brooks thinks, this is an NVA haven, a refuge for their battle weary soldiers. They could crawl into these bunkers and hide here for weeks. And it *is* their command and communication center. We have it. This is what it should be. Brooks is elated. This, he thinks, is the headquarters of the 7th NVA Front.

Jenkins on the right flank discovers another opening. He and Spangler slip in and find an entry room with tunnels leading northeast and south. They investigate moving south. More equipment. The C & C bird is now circling at fifteen hundred feet. Escort Cobras circle above the C & C. The stack of equipment grows. Chi-com claymore mines fill one entire room. Cases of 37mm anti-aircraft rounds fill another. There are RPG rounds and cans of RPD machine gun ammunition and three thousand sachel charges. The GreenMan can see the stacks growing from one thousand feet.

Suddenly fire erupts at the south perimeter. 2d Plt's CP and 2d and 3d Sqds are receiving fire, returning fire. All hell has broken loose. Molino is at the center. He cannot

tell what is happening. He has hit the dirt with the first burst. He hears someone screaming, "Bravo! Bravo!" Then he sees Doc Johnson running across the top of a bunker. Doc is breaking his way through brush and small trees. He carries his medical bag in his left hand and he is firing his .45 pistol with his right. Doc disappears from Molino's vision. Molino cannot see the wounded because of the thick undergrowth. He sees Pop Randalph running. Pop has sprinted from Alpha's center. He is running in the direction Doc ran. He is screaming in his hoarse high voice, yelling at the top of his lungs. He has a grenade in his left hand and grenades strapped to his web gear. He fires his 16 and yells. Molino cannot understand the words. Pop disappears into the foliage. The fighting is building. The noise is fogthick in the steaming air. Molino hears shrapnel slashing into the vegetation to his left. Someone is screaming. Molino looks leftright. He cannot let them go it alone. He hunches his back, brings his legs up under him, his hands are on the earth, his rifle is stuffed in the muck. He is sprinting. He throws a grenade. He did not even know he had prepared one, he did not know he knew the enemy location. He is firing. He is with Doc and Pop and Calhoun. Doc Hayes is wounded. Doc Johnson is applying battle dressings to his chest. A horrible sucking gurgle is coming from Hayes' chest. Blood froths from Hayes' mouth. It disgusts Molino. The NVA disengage, disappear, dissolve. Pop wants to charge them, pursue them. They have wounded his medic.

"Negative that," Brooks is adamant. It has been his most successful move ever. He does not want it ruined, he does not want it to end. "Pop smoke in front of your position," he radios 2d Plt. Calhoun takes over from there. Red smoke is billowing up from a smoke grenade before them. Calhoun is in radio contact with the Cobras. "Dinks at two one zero degrees," he radios and first one Cobra and then a second roll from the sky diving across Alpha unleashing their mini-guns into and south of the smoke, running cutting a swath on the 210° course. The electric Gatling guns fire so quickly they sound like buzz saws. The pilots report no kills. They do not see the enemy.

Woods comes from the bunker opening. He is livid. He wants to go back in. "There's a map room in there, L-T," he says. "I just know there's goina be a full fledged TOC down there." As he speaks firing erupts behind him where Lt. Caldwell and 3d Plt CP are manning the perimeter. Woods drops flat, scrambles to his ruck and slips in. He grabs his rifle and crawls toward the fight. Again the boonierats pop smoke and again the Cobras dive in but Lt. Caldwell has retreated, has ordered his men back and the NVA have followed. The enemy is on Caldwell's side of the smoke. Kinderly is hit in the head by shrapnel from a B-40 rocket. The skin is torn to pieces, the skull is splintered. He is running, retreating. El Paso, Brown, L-T and FO run into the fight. They overtake Woods. They sweep past Caldwell who is still giving ground. They are firing madly. A shot

grazes Brooks biting a skin chunk off his left wrist. He fires. He sees the man firing at him as he fires. The NVA skull bursts, explodes. He is sweating, crawling, calling in air support. A Cobra pilot sees movement toward the bunkers from the east. He dives his ship firing rockets and mini-gun. Other gunships are diving to the west and the south, then rolling, circling above Alpha and diving again. The NVA are pulling back from hitting Bravo, Charlie and Recon. They are falling back to cover their headquarters complex. Brooks looks up and sees the C & C bird at twenty-five hundred feet. Rockets and Cobras and LOHs are everywhere. There is fire spewing from the sky over Alpha in every direction. The sky is darkening with smoke.

At the complex center Nahele is with the stacked munitions and equipment. He rigs two blocks of C-4 explosive to the radios and inserts a blasting cap. He works quickly, forcing his mind to concentrate, forcing his fingers to operate. Alpha is pulling back. Nahele sees Doc Johnson carrying Doc Hayes on his back. Nahele attaches his claymore wire to the blasting cap wire and quickly unrolls.

A machine gunner of the 101st Airborne opens up on enemy positions during a fierce firefight near Chu Lai.

"Fuck that," Caldwell screams at him. "They can blow it with ARA. Dinks are poppin up all over." Caldwell is running, running for the knoll. Nahele checks his claymore firing device, looks once more at the bunker orifice. It is dark, black in the light of the day. The blackness explodes, Nahele's chest explodes with pain. He falls, is thrown backward. His body racks in spasms. He can hear the crunched bones. The pain ends quickly which surprises him. He can no longer feel it. He hears the impact of rounds slamming into his legs, abdomen, chest, but he does not feel it at all.

Brooks and FO, shouting orders that go unheard, try to organize the boonierats. Alpha retreats to the knoll behind a screen of ARA.

Nixon and Agnew Speak Out

On April 30, 1970, President Richard Nixon sent American troops from South Vietnam into the neighboring country of Cambodia. Their purpose was to search out and destroy Vietcong staging areas and "sanctuaries," especially a supposed "key control center" called COSVN (Central Office for South Vietnam). That night he addressed the nation on his purpose and decisions:

Good evening my fellow Americans:

Ten days ago, in my report to the Nation on Vietnam, I announced a decision to withdraw an additional 150,000 Americans from Vietnam over the next year. I said then that I was making that decision despite our concern over increased enemy activity in Laos, in Cambodia, and in South Vietnam.

At that time, I warned that if I concluded that increased enemy activity in any of these areas endangered the lives of Americans remaining in Vietnam, I would not hesitate to take strong and effective measures to deal with that situation.

Despite that warning, North Vietnam has increased its military aggression in all these areas, and particularly in Cambodia.

After full consultation with the National Security Council, Ambassador Bunker, General Abrams, and my other advisers, I have concluded that the actions of the enemy in the last 10 days clearly endanger the lives of Americans who are in Vietnam now and would constitute an unacceptable risk to those who will be there after withdrawal of another 150,000.

To protect our men who are in Vietnam and to guarantee the continued success of our withdrawal and Vietnamization programs, I have concluded that the time has come for action. . . .

Tonight, American and South Vietnamese units will attack the headquarters for the entire Communist military operation in South Vietnam. This key control center has been occupied by the North Vietnamese and Vietcong for 5 years in blatant violation of Cambodia's neutrality.

This is not an invasion of Cambodia. The areas in which these attacks will be launched are completely occupied and controlled by North Vietnamese forces. Our purpose is not to occupy the areas. Once enemy forces are driven out of these sanctuaries and once their military supplies are destroyed, we will withdraw. . . .

My fellow Americans, we live in an age of anarchy, both abroad and at home. We see mindless attacks on all the great institutions which have been created by free civilizations in the last 500 years. Even here in the United States, great universities are being systematically destroyed. Small nations all over the world find themselves under attack from within and from without.

If, when the chips are down, the world's most powerful nation, the United States of America, acts like a pitiful, helpless giant, the forces of totalitarianism and anarchy will threaten free nations and free institutions throughout the world. . . .

Plucked from relative obscurity to become Richard Nixon's vice-presidential running mate in 1968, Governor Spiro Agnew of Maryland was seldom at a loss for words. He first stirred controversy (and embarrassed Republicans) with Agnew-isms such as "fat Jap" and "if you've seen one city slum, you've seen them all." However, with the aid of good speech writers (including William Safire) Agnew soon became a favorite spokesman of conservatives. His sharp attacks on war protesters, the news media, and intellectuals supposedly hostile to America's "silent majority" earned him both adulation and hatred. Two of his most memorable speeches were delivered in autumn 1969, when the vice president responded to recent antiwar "Vietnam Moratorium" protests:

October 19, 1969, New Orleans, Louisiana

Sometimes it appears that we are reaching a period when our senses and our minds will no longer respond to moderate stimulation. We seem to be approaching an age of the gross. Persuasion through speeches and books is too often discarded for disruptive demonstrations aimed at bludgeoning the unconvinced into action.

The young, and by this I don't mean by any stretch of the imagination all the young, but I'm talking about those who claim to speak for the young, at the zenith of physical power and sensitivity, overwhelm themselves with drugs and artificial stimulants. Subtlety is lost, and fine distinctions based on acute reasoning are carelessly ignored in a headlong jump to a predetermined conclusion. Life is visceral rather than intellectual, and the most visceral practitioners of life are those who characterize themselves as intellectuals.

Truth to them is "revealed" rather than logically proved, and the principal infatuations of today revolve around the social sciences, those subjects which can accommodate any opinion and about which the most reckless conjecture cannot be discredited.

Education is being redefined at the demand of the uneducated to suit the ideas of the uneducated. The student now goes to college to proclaim rather than to learn. The lessons of the past are ignored and obliterated in a contemporary antagonism known as the generation gap. A spirit of national masochism prevails, encouraged by an effete corps of impudent snobs who characterize themselves as intellectuals.

It is in this setting of dangerous over-simplification that the war in Vietnam achieves its greatest distortion.

The recent Vietnam Moratorium is a reflection of the confusion that exists in America today. Thousands of well-motivated young people, conditioned since childhood to respond to great emotional appeals, saw fit to demonstrate for peace. Most did not stop to consider that the leaders of the Moratorium had billed it as a massive public outpouring of sentiment against the foreign policy of the President of the United States. Most did not care to be reminded that the leaders of the Moratorium refused to disassociate themselves from the objective enunciated by the enemy in Hanoi.

If the Moratorium had any use whatever, it served as an emotional purgative for those who felt the need to cleanse themselves of their lack of ability to offer a constructive solution to the problem.

Agnew's New Orleans speech delighted his friends and outraged his foes. He responded to the latter eleven days later, at a Republican dinner in Harrisburg, Pennsylvania.

A little over a week ago, I took a rather unusual step for a Vice President . . . I said something. Particularly, I said something that was predictably unpopular with the people who would like to run this country without the inconvenience of seeking public office. I said I did not like some of the things I saw happening in this country. I criticized those who encouraged government by street carnival and suggested it was time to stop the carousel.

It appears that by slaughtering a sacred cow I triggered a holy war. I have no regrets. I do not intend to repudiate my beliefs, recant my words, or run and hide.

What I said before, I will say again. It is time for the preponderant majority, the responsible citizens of this country, to assert *their* rights. It is time to stop dignifying the immature actions of an arrogant, reckless, inexperienced element within our society. The reason is compelling. It is simply that their tantrums are insidiously destroying the fabric of American democracy.

By accepting unbridled protest as a way of life, we have tacitly suggested that the great issues of our times are best decided by posturing and shouting matches in the streets. America today is drifting toward Plato's classic definition of a degenerating democracy . . . a democracy that permits the voice of the mob to dominate the affairs of government.

Last week I was lambasted for my lack of "mental and moral sensitivity." I say that any leader who does not perceive where persistent street struggles are going to lead this nation lacks mental acuity. And any leader who does not caution this nation on the danger of this direction lacks moral strength.

Now let me make it clear, I believe in Constitutional dissent. I believe in the people registering their views with their elected representatives, and I commend those people who care enough about their country to involve themselves in its great issues. I believe in legal dissent within the Constitutional limits of free speech, including peaceful assembly and the right of petition. But I do not believe that demonstrations, lawful or unlawful, merit my approval or even my silence where the purpose is fundamentally unsound. In the case of the Vietnam Moratorium, the objective announced by the leaders—immediate unilateral withdrawal of all our forces from Vietnam—was not only unsound but idiotic. The tragedy was that thousands who participated wanted only to show a fervent desire for peace, but were used—yes, used—by the political hustlers who ran the event. . . .

Now, we have among us a glib, activist element who would tell us our values are lies, and I call them impudent. Because anyone who impugns a legacy of liberty and dignity that reaches back to Moses, is impudent.

I call them snobs for most of them disdain to mingle with the masses who work for a living. They mock the common man's pride in his work, his family and his country. It has also been said that I called them intellectuals. I did not. I said that they characterized themselves as intellectuals. No true intellectual, no truly knowledgeable person, would so despise democratic institutions.

America cannot afford to write off a whole generation for the decadent thinking of a few. America cannot afford to divide over their demagoguery . . . or to be deceived by their duplicity . . . or to let their license destroy liberty. We can, however, afford to separate them from our society—with no more regret than we should feel over discarding rotten apples from a barrel.

167

Homeward Bound

A soldier's trip home from Vietnam was an abrupt mirror image of his trip in-country one year before: Get processed, get on the plane, get out. In a span of hours he could go from fighting in the jungle to sitting at his old dinner table. There was no decompression period, no long voyage on a troopship with other soldiers, no time to sort it all out.

Some men adjusted well. The sheer relief of making it back home was a powerful healer. But for many, relief was tangled up in other emotions: bewilderment at a culture suddenly hostile to them; anger at the absence of welcome-home parades and praise; sorrow and guilt for the dead. It seemed as if America lost the war, then in its shame tried to lose the men, too. The Freedom Bird could take a veteran back to "The World" in two days; the real trip home sometimes took much longer.

Preceding page. A wounded veteran comes home, Sioux Falls, South Dakota, August 13, 1966.

Don't I Know You?

from *If I Die in a Combat Zone*
(Box Me Up and Ship Me Home)
by Tim O'Brien

The flight home.

The air is still, warm. Just at dusk, only the brightest stars are out. The Southern Cross is only partly there.

The curved bosom, a long, sterile tunnel, opens, and a man rolls a gate open and you walk carefully onto a sheet of tar. You go up eighteen steps.

The airplane smells and feels artificial. The stewardess, her carefree smile and boredom simmering like bad lighting, doesn't understand. It's enraging, because you sense she doesn't want to understand.

The plane smells antiseptic. The green, tweedy seats are low-cost comfort, nothing at all like sleeping in real comfort on top of the biggest hill in the world, having finally climbed it. Too easy. There is no joy in leaving. Nothing to savor with your eyes or heart.

When the plane leaves the ground, you join everyone in a ritualistic shout, emptying your lungs inside the happy cave of winners, trying to squeeze whatever drama you can out of leaving Vietnam.

But the effort makes the drama artificial. You try to manufacture your own drama, remembering how you promised to savor the departure. You keep to yourself. It's the same, precisely the same, as the arrival: a horde of strangers, spewing their emotions and wanting you to share with them.

The stewardess comes through the cabin, spraying a mist of invisible sterility into the pressurized, scrubbed, filtered, temperature-controlled air, killing mosquitoes and unknown diseases, protecting herself and America from Asian evils, cleansing us all forever.

The stewardess is a stranger. No Hermes, no guide to anything. She is not even a peeping tom. She is as carefree and beautiful and sublime as a junior-high girl friend.

Her hair is blond; they must allow only blonds on Vietnam departures—blond, blue-eyed, long-legged, medium-to-huge-breasted women. It's to say we did well, America loves us, it's over, here's what you missed, but here's what it was good for: my girl friend was blond and blue-eyed and long-legged, quiet and assured, and she spoke good English. The stewardess doesn't do anything but spray and smile, smiling while she sprays us clean, spraying while she smiles us back to home. Question. Do the coffins get sprayed? Does she care if I don't care to be sterilized, would she stop?

You hope there will be time for a last look at the earth. You take a chance and try the window. Part of a wing, a red light on the end of it. The window reflects the cabin's glare. You can't even see darkness down below, not even a shadow of the earth, not even a skyline. The earth, with its little villages and bad, criss-crossed fields of rice paddy and red clay, deserts you. It's the earth you want to say good-bye to. The soldiers never knew you. You never knew the Vietnamese people. But the earth, you could turn a spadeful of it, see its dryness and the tint of red, and dig out enough of it so as to lie in the hole at night, and that much of Vietnam you would know. Certain whole pieces of the land you would know, something like a farmer knows his own earth and his neighbor's. You know where the bad, dangerous parts are, and the sandy and safe places by the sea. You know where the mines are and will be for a century, until the earth swallows and disarms them. Whole patches of land. Around My Khe and My Lai. Like a friend's face.

The stewardess serves a meal and passes out magazines. The plane lands in Japan and takes on fuel. Then you fly straight on to Seattle. What kind of war is it that begins and ends that way, with a pretty girl, cushioned seats, and magazines?

You add things up. You lost a friend to the war, and you gained a friend. You compromised one principle and fulfilled another. You learned, as old men tell it in front of the courthouse, that war is not all bad; it may not make a man of you, but it teaches you that manhood is not something to scoff; some stories of valor are true; dead bodies are heavy, and it's better not to touch them; fear is paralysis, but it is better to be afraid than to move out to die, all limbs functioning and heart thumping and charging and having your chest torn open for all the work; you have to pick the times not to be afraid, but when you are afraid you must hide it to save respect and reputation. You learned that the old men had lives of their own and that they valued them enough to try not to lose them; anyone can die in a war if he tries.

You land at an air-force base outside Seattle. The army feeds you a steak dinner. A permanent sign in the mess hall says "Welcome Home, Returnees." "Returnees" is an army word, a word no one else would use. You sign your name for the dinner, one to a man.

Then you sign your name to other papers, processing your way out of the army, signing anything in sight, dodging out of your last haircut.

You say the Pledge of Allegiance, even that, and you leave the army in a taxicab.

The flight to Minnesota in March takes you over disappearing snow. The rivers you see below are partly frozen over. Black chunks of corn fields peer out of the old snow. The sky you fly in is gray and dead. Over Montana and North Dakota, looking down, you can't see a sign of life.

And over Minnesota you fly into an empty, unknowing, uncaring, purified, permanent stillness. Down below, the snow is heavy, there are patterns of old corn fields, there are some roads. In return for all your terror, the prairies stretch out, arrogantly unchanged.

At six in the morning, the plane banks for the last time and straightens out and descends. When the no-smoking lights come on, you go into the back of the plane. You take off your uniform. You roll it into a ball and stuff it into your suitcase and put on a sweater and blue jeans. You smile at yourself in the mirror. You grin, beginning to know you're happy. Much as you hate it, you don't have civilian shoes, but no one will notice. It's impossible to go home barefoot.

Homebound soldiers board a "Freedom Bird" in Vietnam.

Just Back from Vietnam

from *Vietnam-Perkasie: A Combat Marine Memoir*
by W.D. Ehrhart

W.D. Ehrhart's thirteen-month tour of duty with the Marines in Vietnam ended on February 28, 1968, after he spent three weeks fighting in Hue City. His difficult adjustment to "The World," as Americans in Vietnam called home, was typical of many veterans' stories. The young woman he calls Jenny had written him a "Dear John" letter while he was in Vietnam.

The taxi maneuvered through a thick white unbroken cloud that reduced visibility to the red taillights of the automobiles immediately in front of us. I had imagined the sparkling waters of San Francisco Bay dancing in the early morning sunshine and playing off the skyline of the City by the Bay. I had even been prepared to break down with joy and relief at my first daylight glimpse of America in thirteen months. But now I could barely see the heavy steel suspension cables of the Oakland Bay Bridge as we drove across it. I sat in the back seat absently measuring the empty space between my lower ribs, feeling puzzled and vaguely cheated.

"You just back from Nam?" asked the taxi driver.

"Huh?"

"You just back from Vietnam?"

"Uh, yessir."

"I guess you're glad to be home, huh?"

"You can say that again."

"Pretty rough over there?"

"Bad enough. I sure won't miss it any."

"Where you from?"

"Little town near Philadelphia."

"Oh, yeh? Where?"

"Perkasie. 'Bout thirty-five miles north of Philly."

"No, never heard of it. Must be pretty small."

"It is."

"I grew up near Philly," the cabbie explained. "Right across the river in Marlton, New Jersey. Got discharged out here after the war—right there at Treasure Island where I picked you up—just never got around to goin' back East."

"Which war?" I asked.

"World War Two," the cabbie replied, emphasizing the 'two' as though I had failed to recognize the obvious. "The big one. Vietnam and Korea, they ain't really wars. You know that? Congress never declared war. They're police actions, they call 'em."

"No kidding? Coulda fooled me."

"I was in the Navy. Pacific. Earned a Purple Heart at Midway. Jap dive bomber hit our tin can. Yeh, we didn't do none of this one-year-and-come-home stuff like you guys got nowadays. You went in then, you stayed in till the war was over. They oughta do that with this Vietnam thing. Make you guys fight a little harder, wouldn't it?"

"Thirteen months," I corrected. "Marines do thirteen months. I didn't make the rules. I just did what I was asked to do."

"Sure, buddy, sure. Don't get me wrong. You done your duty, and I appreciate that. I just don't understand how come this thing ain't over yet, that's all. I mean, what the hell, just a bunch of slopeheads with chopsticks. It's the damn politicians' fault, ain't it. They don't let you guys get the job over with. Bunch of bleedin' hearts, I'll tell ya; I don't know what this country's comin' to." The cabbie tossed his remarks back over his shoulder casually without turning his head, his attention riveted to the freeway ahead of him where the red and white lights of cars and trucks flashed in and out of the fog.

"You get to the airport, you go find a bar and have a drink on me," he continued. "Welcome home. You've earned it, that's for sure. Least you done your duty. I don't know *where* we'd be without fellas like you."

I thought about fellows like me. I thought about the six-year-old boy with the grenade, about the old man with his hands tied behind his back and the neat little hole in the back of his head, about the woman in the 60-millimeter mortar pit in Hue. I thought about my parents. What would I ever be able to say to them? I pretended to doze off so I wouldn't have to talk, or listen. We rode the rest of the way to the airport in silence. When we arrived, I paid the cabbie. He didn't mention the drink I was supposed to have on him, and didn't kick back anything on the fare. I didn't give him a tip.

Once inside the terminal, I immediately purchased a one-way ticket to Philadelphia and checked my heavy seabag. "Would you like to check that, sir?" asked the TWA clerk, pointing tentatively to the captured rifle I carried slung over my shoulder by a worn leather strap.

"No, ma'am, I'll carry it on if you don't mind. I've got papers for it. It can't fire. I took the bolt out. It's in the seabag." I showed her the empty space where the bolt should have been.

She looked at the rifle, then took the papers I was holding and looked at them carefully. "Okay," she said hesitantly. "Your flight leaves at eleven forty-three; concourse D. The gate should be posted about an hour before take-off. Have a good flight."

Eleven forty-three a.m. It was now just eight forty-five. I had three hours to kill. I'd arrived at Travis Air Force base before dawn on a military charter flight from Vietnam by way of Okinawa. From there, the Marines and sailors aboard the flight had been bussed to Treasure Island Naval Base in the middle of San Francisco Bay to await discharge or, as in my case, processing of their leave papers and travel orders to their next assignment.

The bus ride had been a nightmare. I'd ridden in nothing but jeeps and trucks for more than a year, bumping along pitted dirt roads at twenty-five or thirty-five miles an hour tops, and when that bus had hit the freeway and cranked up to sixty or sixty-five, I'd thought for sure we were going to crash. It felt like we were doing a hundred and ten. I'd ridden the whole way expecting to die like a crushed sardine at any moment, and by the time we'd arrived at Treasure Island, my uniform was drenched with nervous perspiration.

After two more hours of waiting in a transient barracks, I was finally able to get my leave papers and travel orders when the administrative office opened at 0800: twenty-five days' leave, then report to the Marine Corps Air Station at Cherry Point. But I couldn't get my travel money yet because the disbursing office didn't open until 0900. I didn't want to wait another hour. I didn't want to wait another minute. After thirteen months of waiting, my patience was at an end. I'd checked my wallet, decided that I had enough money to get home on, and hopped into one of the taxis waiting at the front gate of the base. Now I had three hours to kill.

I bought a magazine at a newsstand and sat down in the middle of San Francisco airport. It was bustling with people. Men in business suits carrying briefcases. Women in skirts and matching jackets, many of the skirts short like the ones Dorrit had worn in Hong Kong. And now here was an airport full of them. I sat there drooling.

There were also a number of people, most of them more or less my age, dressed in faded blue jeans and denim workshirts and pieces of green utility uniforms with rank insignia on the sleeves. A young couple sat nearby on the floor against the wall, backpacks and rolled-up sleeping bags gathered around them like a fortress. Both had very long hair held out of their faces with brightly colored headbands, and strings of beads hung from their necks. The man was bearded, and held a guitar lightly across his knees. When the woman moved, her breasts swung pleasantly beneath the loose-fitting workshirt. Her nipples poked at the faded blue material. She was obviously wearing no bra. I'd read about free love.

So these were the hippies, I thought. I couldn't remember ever having seen one before I'd left for Vietnam. Like the whole antiwar movement, the hippies and flower people seemed to have materialized out of nowhere during my absence from The World. In high school, I'd been reprimanded by the principal for allowing my hair to grow down over my ears and the collar of my shirt. There had been no hippies in Perkasie. It had never occurred to Jenny *not* to wear a bra, nor had it occurred to her to allow me to remove it, and the hem of her skirt had always reached her knees. When I'd enlisted, my picture had appeared in the local newspapers: the recruiter and I standing by the front door of Pennridge High School shaking hands. Nearly every teacher in school had taken the trouble to congratulate me, or pump my hand and wish me luck.

Words at War

The Vietnam War generated numerous slogans, mottoes, and memorable phrases from both proponents and opponents. Here is a brief selection:

"Hell no, we won't go."—*antiwar slogan*

"War is not healthy for children and other living things."—*poster*

"My solution? Tell the Vietnamese they've got to draw in their horns . . . or we're going to bomb them back into the Stone Age."—*General Curtis E. LeMay, chief of staff, U.S. Air Force, May 6, 1964*

"Grab 'em by the balls, and their hearts and minds will follow."—*American officers summing up pacification*

"Hey, hey, LBJ,
How many kids did you kill today?"
—*antiwar chant*

"I just had the greatest brainwashing that anybody can get when you go over to Vietnam. Not only by the Generals, but also by the diplomatic corps over there, and they do a very thorough job."—*Michigan governor George Romney, during his 1968 presidential campaign*

"It became necessary to destroy the town to save it."—*U.S. Army major describing Ben Tre, South Vietnam, after the town was reduced to rubble, February 7, 1968*

"I was a very inadequate leader, I think."—*Lieutenant William Calley, convicted of premeditated murder at My Lai in 1968*

"Bomb Saigon Now"
"Bomb Hanoi Now"
"Bomb Disneyland Now"
"Bomb Everything"
—*Stickers on a Cobra gunship pilot's helmet*

"There's two million men have fought out there, and their performance has been magnificent. Mention a battle they've lost in Vietnam."—*General Maxwell Taylor, July 4, 1971*

"Nail the coonskin to the wall."—*President Lyndon Johnson's advice to U.S. troops at Cam Ranh Bay, South Vietnam, October 25, 1966*

"I can't get out. I can't finish with what I've got. So what the hell can I do?"—*Lyndon Johnson*

"U.S.A. Love it or leave it."—*pro-war slogan*

"If he's dead and Vietnamese, he's VC."—*commander quoted in Philip Caputo's* A Rumor Of War

"What if they gave a war and nobody came?"—*poster*

"We have reached an important point when the end begins to come into view."—*General William Westmoreland, U.S. commander in South Vietnam, November 1967*

"What the hell is going on? I thought we were winning the war!"—*Walter Cronkite reacting to news of the 1968 Tet offensive*

I wondered if there were any hippies in Perkasie now. All through the long scorching dry season of Vietnam and into the monsoons, I'd read about the hippies and their protest movement in almost every issue of *Stars 'n' Stripes* and *Time:* "Hippies Drop LSD at Haight-Ashbury Be-In"; "Black Panthers Shoot It Out with Cops in Berkeley"; "23 Draft Cards Burned at Yale Rally." As the months had worn on, the antiwar movement—like the Vietcong—had only seemed to get stronger: "VC Flags Festoon Times Square"; "100,000 March on Pentagon"; "Actress Visits Hanoi."

"What the hell do *these* fuckin' people know anyway?" I thought, addressing myself to the hippies in particular and to everyone else in general. "What right do they have?"

Immediately, the other side of the question popped into my head: What right did *I* have? What had I done in the past thirteen months to be proud of? My stomach suddenly felt as though it was being squeezed by an iron fist. Hunched down behind my magazine, I watched the people in the airport coming and going, half-expecting a band of placard-carrying flower people to surround me at any moment, drowning me in flowers and chants of "Baby Killer."

I looked at my watch: nine a.m. "You oughta call Mom and Dad," I thought. My stomach wrenched even harder. In the two days I'd been at Battalion Rear in Phu Bai, I'd put off writing to let them know I was coming home until it had been too late to write from there. I'd had three more days of processing on Okinawa, but I still hadn't written. Every time I'd thought about it, I'd gotten scared. I'd see myself standing over the old woman at the edge of the ricefield; I'd see the old man with his hands tied behind his back going down in a lifeless crumple; I'd put the pen in my hand, but my hand wouldn't move across the paper.

And now I was only a few hours from home, and they still didn't know. "You better go call 'em," I thought, but I didn't get up. I tried to light a cigarette, but I couldn't hold the match steady and finally gave up, angrily crushing the unlit cigarette into an ashtray. "This is ridiculous," I thought. "It's over. Forget it. What about that Coca-Cola? I wonder if anyone drinks Coke at nine in the morning."

I thought of the vision I'd carried for months: me and a pretty American girl sitting at a booth drinking Coke, smiling and smiling, a simple welcome home from the alien ricefields and sand barrens and jungles of Asia. I'd rehearsed the scene a thousand times through the endless days and nights alone: the Coke, the smiles, perhaps a brief touching of hands before we went our separate ways. I looked around furtively at the women passing by, trying to determine which one might be safe to approach. "You chicken," I kept telling myself as opportunity after opportunity walked by. "How long you been waiting for this? If the guys could see you now, they'd laugh their asses off." I tried to screw up my courage, but the threads kept slipping.

And then I saw her: the lovely young blonde in a short pale green skirt and ruffled white long-sleeved blouse. She was walking right toward me; there was something in her face, in the magic twinkle of her mouth, that suddenly made it possible. "Looks kinda like Dorrit," I thought. She was almost in front of me. Was she looking at my uniform? At the three red sergeant's stripes on my arm? "Asshole," I thought. "Now's your chance! Get up and ask her."

"Excuse me, miss," I blurted out, popping to my feet directly in her path, "this must sound really odd, but would you have time to let me buy you a coke. I know it's kind of early, but I've been away for a long time and—"

The woman went white. You could see the color drain right out of her face like somebody had pulled a plug in the bottom of her stomach. She looked as though she was about to scream.

"Wait, please, you don't understand. I don't mean any harm. Really. I've been in Vietnam, you know? I just got back from Vietnam. I'd just like to celebrate with someone a little, you know? I mean, just drink a coke and talk a little. Coca-Cola, you know; it's so *American.* Like it means I'm back, you know? I'm finally home."

The woman backed up a few steps, and began to swivel her head nervously from side to side as though she were looking for an exit sign.

"Honestly, listen, wait," I went on, talking as fast as I could. "I don't mean to—it's just, you know, something I've dreamed about for a long time. Like a little fantasy, you know? I just wanna buy you a Coke, that's all; just sit and talk for a little—"

"I'm glad you're back," the woman stammered, interrupting me. "Look, I've got—"

"Sure. Just a minute or two, that's all I'm asking, okay?" I pointed to a nearby snackbar, and reached out to take her arm.

"Don't!" she almost shouted, pulling away sharply.

"Jesus, lady, all I'm asking—"

"Please! I'm sorry! Leave me alone!"

Abruptly, I was standing there by myself, the blood pounding in my temples. I could feel beads of sweat popping out along the hairline of my forehead, and I found myself almost unconsciously blinking hard against a rising wave of salt. People seated nearby were staring at me. I tried to smile as I sat down again. I accidentally knocked the captured rifle leaning against the chair, and it clattered loudly as it struck the bare tile floor. I picked up the rifle, opened the magazine, took out my cigarettes, dropped the pack, knocked the rifle as I reached for the pack, dropped the magazine as I grabbed unsuccessfully for the rifle, took a deep breath, picked up all three items and sat there staring straight ahead, the whole ungainly pile stacked up on my lap.

"Goddamn bitch," I muttered.

"Goddamn bitch. Couldn't even wait a lousy goddamned year. I'm puttin' my life on the line, and she's out flyin' around in private airplanes and goin' to proms." The thought startled me; I realized that I had been sitting there for some time thinking not about the woman in the green skirt, but about Jenny.

"I don't know; musta been tough on her. She's only eighteen; all her friends doin' stuff and all, goin' on dates and stuff. Once she sees me again—it's *me;* I'm really home—if I can just talk to her, touch her . . . "

"You're settin' yourself up, pal. How long's it been since you heard from her? She tried to get her roommate to be your pen pal, for chrissake!"

"But she loved me, damn it! That just doesn't go away!"

"Just shut up. Don't think about it. Don't think."

Nine forty-five. "Jesus Christ, two more hours. Lemme outta here. I wanna be home." I opened the magazine and stared at the page: an article about Senator Eugene McCarthy, the Democrat bucking his own party to run against President Johnson on a promise of ending the war. American boys were dying in Asia for no good reason, he was saying; the war must be stopped. I thought about Rowe and Calloway, about Roddenbery and Aymes and Stemkowski and Frenchy and all of the others. How many? All for nothing? Was it possible?

Out of the corner of my eye, I noticed a skinny bearded young man in blue jeans and an embroidered denim jacket. He wore a headband, and carried a brightly colored shoulderbag. I glanced up. He seemed to be headed straight for me. "Oh, no," I thought, "please don't. Go away; just leave me alone."

"Peace, brother," he said, smiling broadly. He had freckles all over his face. "How goes it?"

"Look, I don't want any trouble. I'm just waiting for a plane. You come lookin' for trouble, you're gonna get it."

"Hey, be easy, friend," he said, lifting both hands gently away from his sides, palms facing me. "I noticed that rifle there. I'm kind of a gun buff; just wondered what kind it was."

"Oh."

"What kind is it?"

"Oh. MAS-36. French. It's pretty old; not in very good condition. I don't know why I kept it."

"Maybe you could clean it up; get it plated or something. My granddaddy used to have a whole wall full of old guns—rifles and pistols, all kinds—had 'em all fixed up really nice. He owned a ranch in Montana. That's how I know about guns. Used to spend every summer there with him. Punchin' cattle. Playin' cowboy. Used to have the neatest times—like starring in my own TV western. Great place for a kid, Montana. Yippee-i-o-cay-a!" He sat down in the seat next to me and stuck out his hand. "My name's Rex. What's yours?"

"Bill," I said, shaking his hand tentatively.

"You're just back from Vietnam, I guess."

"Yeh. That's where I got the rifle. I guess you could tell that."

"I figured. Well, I'm glad you made it back okay. I guess you are, too! How long were you there?"

"Thirteen months."

"Long time, huh?"

"Seems like forever . . . Rex. I used to dream about today like you dream about bein' a millionaire or winning a gold medal in the Olympics." I shook my head slowly from side to side.

"You get drafted?"

I let out a short snorting grunt through my nostrils. "No. No, I enlisted. Right outta high school. I volunteered. Seventeen."

"Wow, that's heavy, Bill."

A small wild laugh escaped from my throat before I even realized it was there. "It certainly is, Rex," I said. We both smiled as if we were sharing a secret, though I wasn't sure what it was.

"Why don't you get lost, freak."

We both looked up to see two middle-aged men in business suits standing right in front of us. They were both glaring at Rex, as though I wasn't even there. "Beat it, freak," said the man on the left, who looked like a retired professional football player. "What are you bothering good people for? You want your slime to rub off on him?"

"He's not bothering me," I said as Rex stood up.

"It's okay," said Rex, addressing himself to me. "I've got a plane to catch, anyway."

"Go catch it," said the linebacker in the three-piece suit.

"He wasn't bothering me," I said.

"Nice talkin' with ya, Bill," Rex called back as he walked away, his body half turned to face us as he went. "I'm really glad you made it. Look out for yourself now, okay? Never know what you're gonna run into."

"You, too," I called, trying to wave around the bulk of the linebacker. The linebacker took a menacing step in Rex's direction.

"Peace, friend, peace," Rex laughed, lifting both hands in a Vee sign. "You're gonna give yourself an ulcer." He turned and skip-walked away, disappearing into the crowd.

"He wasn't bothering me," I said again. "We were just talking."

"They oughta lock up every last one of those scum," said the linebacker. "Makes me sick to see 'em on the same planet with you boys." He turned, finally, and looked at me. "You got time for a drink, Sergeant?"

I didn't think I liked the linebacker or his partner very much, but as soon as he mentioned having a drink, it occurred to me that I really wanted one.

"Yessir," I said quietly, "I've got time."

"No need to call me 'sir,' " said the linebacker as the three of us walked toward the nearest bar. "I'm just an old enlisted man, same as you. Corporal. Marines. Served in the Pacific. You know what they say: 'Once a Marine, always a Marine.' "

I'd heard the expression often enough; I wondered vaguely if it was true. "Maybe the cabbie sent 'em," I thought as we sat down. Both men ordered scotch on the rocks. I didn't like scotch. I liked sweet drinks like singapore slings and sloe gin fizzes and blackberry brandy. I'd only drank scotch because that was all Gunny Krebs had ever carried in his canteen. "Scotch on the rocks," I told the waitress.

"I'm sorry," she said, "but I have to ask. Are you twenty-one?"

"Of course, he's twenty-one," said the linebacker. "Can't you see those stripes all up and down his arm."

"May I see your ID, please?"

"He's old enough to drink, sweetie," said the linebacker, pulling a five-dollar bill out of his wallet and crushing it into her hand. "Just get the drinks; that's a good girl. How old are you, anyway?" he asked when the waitress was out of earshot.

"Nineteen—and a half."

"Goddamned crime; you're old enough to fight, then they try to tell ya you're not old enough to drink," the linebacker snorted. "Nineteen, and you're a buck sergeant—quite a rack of ribbons you got there, too." He pointed to the double row of decorations on my left breast. "You must be one hell of a good Marine." A surge of pride fought its way to the surface and emerged as a smile on my face. It made me uncomfortable. I looked down at the table. "My name's Barton," he said. "This is Davis. You just back from Nam, aren't you?"

"Yessir—uh, yeh. Just got Stateside this morning."

"Well, here's to you," said Barton, lifting his drink. "Take that weapon over there?"

"Yes."

"That musta been worth at least a stripe. You get the bastard that was carryin' it?"

"It was dark. I'm not sure who got him, me or Calloway." I was about to explain, then decided not to. I shrugged my shoulders.

"I know what you mean," said Davis, speaking for the first time. "Back on Iwo Jima—I was in the Marines, too—sometimes things got so wild you couldn't even keep score. Japs used to attack in human waves; suicide charges. Screamin' at the top of their lungs. All you had to do was lay there and mow 'em down. They just didn't care about dyin'. Die for the emperor and bow out smiling. The Vietnamese are like that too, aren't they? Just don't value life, Orientals. One less face they gotta feed."

I tried to remember. It was true. I'd thought it was true, hadn't I? Kharma, nirvana, reincarnation, Banzai charges, Pork Chop Hill. Asians weren't like us. Even after I'd gotten to Vietnam: old women with black teeth and mouths full of betel nut; children with open running sores and flies all over their bodies; men with loose pajama legs pulled up, urinating in full view of the world; the strange clucking tongues; the empty faces.

Then one day on a patrol near Hoi An, we'd come upon a funeral procession: two men carrying a small ornately carved casket, obviously that of a young child; a file of monks with shaved heads and flowing saffron robes, playing reed flutes and tiny cymbals; a dozen peasants behind them, some of them crying, two women wailing as though their insides had been torn out. I'd watched them pass, and later that night, back at the battalion compound, I'd almost thrown up at the memory of it. Their grief had seemed so real.

Now the memory of it made me feel sick all over again. "I don't know," I said. "I really don't know." I wanted to be on the airplane. I wanted to be back home in Perkasie, in my own room, in my own bed. I tried to remember. I looked at my watch: ten twenty.

"They brainwash 'em," said Davis. "The Reds always brainwash their troops. Hop 'em up on dope and get 'em crazy for blood. I hear the VC go into a village and kill off everybody—everyone but the fighting-age men. Take the men and make 'em join the guerrillas. Isn't that right?"

"I never saw anything like that," I said. "I used to read about things like that before I enlisted, but I never saw anything like it while I was there."

"Well, it happens, believe me," said Davis, taking a gulp of his scotch and putting the glass back with a thump. "Happens all the time."

"You Americans are worse than the VC!" Sergeant Trinh had said the morning he'd told the battalion commander that he was through fighting for us. "Take your ignorance and go home!"

"What the hell do you know about it?!" I burst out, half rising to my feet. "You don't have the foggiest notion what's going on over there. None of you do! We're the ones who waste villages! They don't have to twist any arms to get recruits—we do their goddamned recruiting for them!"

The two men stared at me in disbelief. People at tables nearby turned to see what the disturbance was.

"Hey, Sarge, don't get riled," said Barton. "We're on *your* side, remember? There's no call to get mad. Come on; sit down and have another drink. Hey, we appreciate what you been through."

"The hell you say," I spat. "I got a plane to catch." I picked up my handbag and turned to go.

"Hey, your rifle," said Davis. I didn't stop. As I walked away, I could hear the two men talking.

"What'sa matter with him? Wha'd I say?"

"Christ, that kid's got a problem."

I looked at my watch: ten twenty-five. My head was spinning. I ducked into the nearest men's room, barely making it to the first urinal before I threw up. My stomach was empty: dry heaves. The retching tore at my guts like hot jagged steel.

"Are you all right, son?" There was a light touch on my shoulder. I spun around sharply. A stooped-over black man with curly gray hair took a quick step backwards, surprised by my sudden movement. He was dressed in coveralls and carried a pushbroom.

"I'm sorry," I said.

"Didn't mean to startle you. Are you all right?"

"Yeh. Yeh. I guess I ate somethin' bad or something."

"You want me to get a doctor?"

"No. I'm all right now. I'm just . . . " I flushed the urinal.

"You get yourself cleaned up; wash your mouth out. I'll go get you something to settle your stomach. You wait right here now; I'll be right back."

In front of the Arrivals section of the Philadelphia airport it was crowded with cars and taxis and limousines, but I recognized Larry Carroll's beat-up DeSoto right away. I started waving. He spotted me and stopped, and I jumped in, tossing my seabag and handbag into the back seat. We shook hands.

"This old clunker's still running, huh?" I said.

"Like a champ." Larry eased out into the evening traffic.

"What took you so long to get here? Feels like I been waitin' in airports half my life."

"Well, you didn't give me much warning. 'Hey, I'm in Philadelphia; come pick me up.' "

"Yeh, well, sorry about that."

"How come your folks didn't pick you up?"

"They don't know I'm home yet. I was gonna call—I don't know. Thought it would be fun to surprise 'em. Geez, it's good to see you. Thanks for comin' down."

"What are friends for? Good to see you, too, Bill. I thought you might be gettin' home about now. You timed it just right."

"How long you home for?"

"A week. Term break."

"Anybody else around?"

"Jeff's around, but he's down in DC on the senior class trip till Friday. Eric Rogers is home. That's about it. Most of 'em don't get off till around Easter."

"Rogers," I said. "I wrote him three times last spring—never wrote back once. Some friend."

"Yeh, well, I got a letter from Sadie Thompson back in January," said Larry. My stomach tightened at the sound of her name. "She wanted to know if I'd heard from you, if you were all right, when you were getting home, whole list of questions. Said she hadn't heard from you since last April or May. How come you haven't written to her?"

"I don't know, Larry. You know Sadie. Hell, you know what she said to me before I left? 'Try not to kill anyone.' "

"That's Sadie," Larry laughed.

"It ain't funny. That's been banging around in my head for thirteen fuckin' months. What am I supposed to say to her? What was I supposed to write? I'm havin' a picnic?"

"Pretty bad over there, huh?"

"Crazy, man. Jesus. Tell you all about it sometime. I'm *out* of it, that's all that counts. Somebody else's fuckin' problem now."

We rode a long way in silence, passing out of the city into the northern suburbs, and then into the rural country of central and upper Bucks County.

"Pretty shaggy hair you got there," I said finally. "Where's your beads?"

"Just keepin' up with the times," said Larry.

"Somebody oughta tell the commandant of the Corps," I said, running my hand over my bristly short hair. "He ain't heard yet. How do you like Penn State?"

"It's okay. Too much to do, though; I never seem to get around to the books. Damn good parties!"

"Everybody's in college but me," I said.

"Well, you gotta come up sometime—maybe some weekend. Where you gonna be?"

"North Carolina. Gotta report the end of the month."

We crested the long hill on Route 309 just south of Souderton, and Larry turned onto Fairhill Road. Familiar turf. Down in the wide shallow valley off to our left, I could see the lights of the small communities among which I'd grown up: Sellersville, Souderton, Telford, Silverdale, Blooming Glen, Dublin, Perkasie. Between the towns lay the dark patches of woods and the dark farm fields. The car glided along the dark two-lane roads, weaving a path down into the valley toward Perkasie.

"Never thought I'd be so happy to see Perkasie," I said.

"It's still Hicksville," Larry replied with a laugh.

"That's okay by me. I think I'm gonna enjoy a little Hicksville for a change. Hard to believe I couldn't wait to get out of here. God, that wasn't even two years ago."

Larry laughed again. "Hard to believe you're so glad to be back in the old dump."

"You don't know, Larry. Man, you don't know."

"I guess not," said Larry. "Don't think I wanna find—" He stopped abruptly in mid-sentence.

"What?"

"Nothin'."

The car slid up Chestnut Street over the bridge crossing Lenape Creek. We'd all grown up in that creek, storming through the lily pads in our bare feet searching for turtles and snakes and catching golden carp with our bare hands, camping out, ice skating in the winter, a blazing bonfire making our wet skates steam. Just over the bridge, on the right, two three-story apartment buildings and a parking lot filled what had once been a swampy meadow.

A Michigan family welcomes back its veteran son from a tour of duty in Vietnam.

178

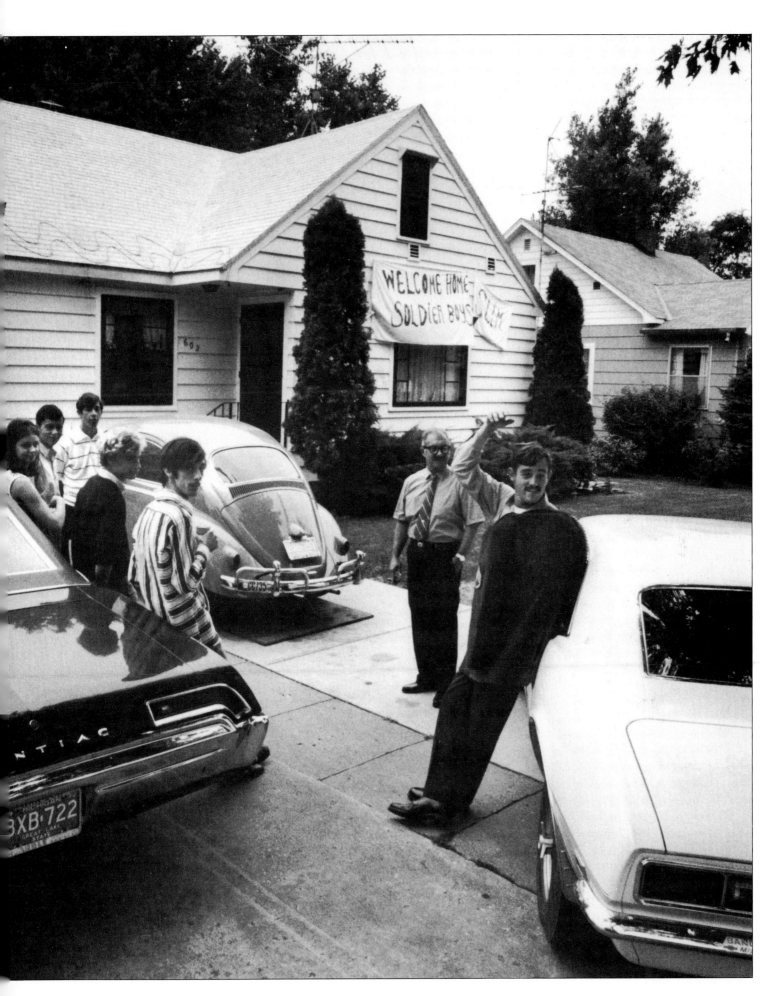

"When'd they build those?" I asked.

"Last summer."

"Suburbia comes to Perkasie."

"Ugly, ain't they?"

The car approached the intersection of Chestnut and Third streets. I pointed up Third Street hill. "'Member the time we trashed Old Man Bowen's garage?" I said. We grinned at each other, then laughed, each of us remembering back ten years.

"*You* got away—and then you came back! Sucker," said Larry.

"Least I didn't get caught red-handed—like you, sucker."

Larry turned the opposite way on Third Street. We passed the Third Street Elementary School. "Ah, the good old days," I said, nodding toward the school.

"Oh, yeh, swell. I always *loved* the nuclear bomb drills," said Larry. The fire bells clanging mercilessly, all of us scurrying out of the classrooms and into the halls where we'd sit facing the walls with our heads tucked between our knees and our hands over our heads, waiting for the Russian Sputnik to come through the roof, newsreels of the mushroom cloud over Hiroshima rising vividly behind my eyes. "I could never get it into my head that they were just drills," Larry went on. "Everytime we had one, I couldn't sleep for a month. Nightmare city. Hell of a trip to lay on a ten-year-old."

I thought of the small boy in the marketplace in Hoi An, and the trip I'd laid on him. My stomach rose, then sank sharply. "He had a grenade, for chrissake," I thought. "What the hell else were you supposed to do?"

The car turned left onto Market Street. I could see a traffic light up at Fifth & Market.

"A traffic light?!" I said. "Apartment buildings. Traffic lights. Whaddaya mean, Hicksville? We're gettin' *civilized*. I go away for a year, and they turn the place into Levittown."

"We got two cop cars now," Larry boasted mockingly. "Two, folks. Count 'em."

We passed only two or three other cars on the way through town. The whole town lay on the edge of sleep, though it was only nine thirty.

"So where's the mayor?" I said. "Where's the majorettes? Where's my white Cadillac convertible? I thought you were gonna take care of everything, Larry. I feel like an ex-con sneakin' back into town in the dead of night."

"It's after six o'clock, buddy," Larry deadpanned. "Come back Memorial Day. You can be in the parade."

He turned the car onto Sixth Street. There was my father's church on the corner of the next block. We pulled up in front of the big stone house beside the church and stopped. Lights burned in the downstairs.

"Home, sweet home," said Larry.

"Yeh," I said. I blinked back tears, embarrassed. "Thanks, Larry. You be home tomorrow?"

"Yeh. Gimme a call."

"So, here I am," I said.

My mother, father, younger brother and I were sitting in the living room. It had taken quite a while to settle them down. My sudden appearance at the door had given them a start. Mom had screamed, almost fainting. I'd hugged my Dad for the first time since I'd been a little boy. Tom, now almost thirteen, had grown several inches.

"Why didn't you tell us you were coming?" Mom asked. "You said you wouldn't be home till the middle of the month."

"Well," I said, staring down at my shoes and fidgeting with my hands, "I figured the last few weeks would be the hardest on you, so I decided to let you think the last few weeks weren't here yet."

"What are the ribbons for?" Tom asked, touching my chest, his eyes wide.

"Nothin'. This one's the Sioux City, Iowa, Occupation Award," I said, pointing to the National Defense Medal. "This here's the Visit Vietnam Award. This one's the Thank-You-For-Visiting-Vietnam Award. This is the Booby Prize."

"That's the Purple Heart, isn't it?" Tom asked excitedly.

"That's what I said—the Booby Prize. All you gotta do is be in the wrong place at the wrong time." I couldn't help feeling the glow of my brother's admiration. It was confusing. "It's no big deal, Tom. I'm not a hero." I didn't want to say that.

"You were wounded?" Mom gasped.

"Just a little. In Hue City, last month. I got caught tryin' to paint the town red."

"Bill! Why didn't you tell us? Your letters said you were—"

"What was the point? You'd just worry. I imagine you did enough of that as it was." I reached into my sock and pulled out a pack of cigarettes. "Mind if I smoke?" I asked. I'd never been allowed to smoke in the house when I was in high school.

"Well, all right," said Mom, "but you know I don't approve."

"I know, Mom," I said, lighting one. "Mom, that letter you sent me . . . " I started laughing. "The one about getting lung cancer in twenty years. You'd have had a heart attack if you could have seen where I was when I got it. Twenty years?!"

Mom turned red, caught between laughter and tears. I looked around the living room. A portrait photograph of me in a dress blue uniform sat on the television set. A map of Vietnam hung on the wall. "Have you heard from Jenny lately?" I asked.

"We got a very nice Christmas card from her," said Dad.

"That's more than I got," I said. An awkward pause followed.

"People grow up, Bill," said Mom. "That's a long time to be apart at that age."

"Wasn't no longer for her than it was for me."

"It wasn't *any* longer," said Mom. "Just be thankful that

you're home safe. Things'll get straightened out for the best. Give yourself some time. You just got home."

"I am, Mom. It's good to be here. Man, I never knew thirteen months could be so long."

"Well, it's good to have you home, son," said Dad. "We're very proud of you."

I winced involuntarily, immediately hoping he hadn't noticed. I wondered if I would ever be able to tell them what had happened in Vietnam. I wasn't sure myself what had happened. Now wasn't the time to try to explain, I decided. I let it go.

"Can I borrow the car for a little while?" I asked. "I'm gonna buy one tomorrow, but I'd sort of like to go somewhere tonight."

"Where?" asked Mom. "You just got home. It's ten thirty."

"Well, I just thought I'd drive over to Trenton."

"Tonight? To see Jenny?"

"If I can just talk to her, Mom," I said, lifting my shoulders in an unfinished shrug. "You know? Once she realizes that I'm home . . ."

"It'll take you an hour to get there," said Dad. "It'll be midnight. You won't even be able to get in the dorm."

"They'll let me in. I'll explain. I'll wear my uniform."

"Why don't you just get a good night's sleep," said Mom. "You've had a long day."

"Mom, I've waited a long time already. Maybe too long."

"At least call first," said Dad. "She'll be asleep by the time you get there."

I went to the telephone in the dining room, then decided to go upstairs instead. I got the main number for the nursing school from the operator, and finally managed to get through to the right dormitory.

"Just a minute," said a sleepy voice, "I'll see if she's up." I hadn't heard Jenny's voice since I'd called her from Pendleton the day before I'd left the States. I tried to remember what it would sound like. The receiver scraped against my ear. I tried to think of a good first line.

"Hello?"

"Jenny?"

"Yes."

"It's me. Bill."

"Oh. Uh, hello. I was asleep."

"Jenny, I'm home. I'm in Perkasie."

"That's wonderful, Bill." There was a pause. "It's good to hear your voice again."

"Yours, too, Jen. Gosh, it sounds good. Just like I remembered."

"How are you?"

"Okay. Fine. I, uh, I got wounded last month . . . but it wasn't too bad." Another pause. "Listen, can I come over to see you?"

"When?"

"Tonight."

"Tonight?"

"Sure. I can be there in forty-five minutes."

"Bill. Uh. It's awfully late. The dorm's locked. They don't allow visitors after ten."

"Oh. Well, look, how about tomorrow? I can drive over first thing in the morning."

"Bill, I've got class all day—"

"Well, tomorrow night then. I'll take you out to dinner; someplace fancy—"

"Bill, I'm sorry, I've got a big test Thursday. I've just got to study for it. I just can't—"

"Well, when then?!" Another pause. "Are you ever gonna see me, for chrissake?"

"Don't swear at me, Bill—"

"I'm not swearing! Don't you even want to *see* me?" There was another long pause. "Jenny?"

"Bill, I just don't think it's a good idea to see each other right now."

"You won't even let me *talk* to you?! Jenny, it's me, Bill! You were gonna *marry* me. Doesn't that count for anything?"

"I'm sorry. I don't want to hurt you. I tried to explain when I wrote. I *tried* to explain. It's not you. I'm just—"

"You can't even *see* me? You can't even *talk* to me?!"

"Bill, please try to understand; it isn't easy—"

"Oh, I understand, all right—"

"—I just don't think it would be—"

"—I understand! You sucker me in; then when things get tough, you dust me off just like that! I'm over there gettin' my ass shot at every goddamned day, and you're back here spreadin' your legs for every rich draft-dodger that comes down the pike! You goddamned whore! You think you can just—" The phone went dead. "Jenny?! Jenny, I'm sorry; I didn't mean to—" I lifted the receiver away from my ear and held it at arm's length. "You don't understand," I said softly. "Jesus fucking *Christ!!*" I slammed the receiver down so hard that the cradle cracked.

I didn't go back downstairs again. I couldn't. I went into my room. On top of the dresser, and on the night stand, and hanging from the ceiling on strings, were the dozens of plastic model airplanes I'd made while I was growing up: P-38 Lightnings; P-51 Mustangs; Spads; Sopwith Camels; B-17 Flying Fortresses; F4U Corsairs with their graceful gull-like wings—each plane carefully hand-painted and carrying the proper military markings. I knew all about each one: its armament, powerplant, top speed and rate of climb and range; which ones could turn tightly in a dogfight; which could take a beating and keep flying. I even knew about the men who'd flown them: Pappy Boyington, Richard I. Bong, Frank Luke, Billy Bishop, Eddie Rickenbacker. Aces. Knights. Heroes.

I took off my uniform and hung it up carefully on the back of the door. I turned out the light, and stretched out face up on the bed, my hands behind my head. Every fifteen minutes, the clock downstairs in the living room chimed. Every fifteen minutes. Far into the night.

Bruckner's Homecoming

from *Dau: A Novel of Vietnam*
by Ed Dodge

*In Ed Dodge's novel **Dau** the protagonist, airman Morgan Preston, finds out about the death of a friend from a newspaper casualty list. This passage recounts his friend's funeral. Almost 58,000 Americans returned from Vietnam this way, the saddest homecoming. The title of the book means "pain" in Vietnamese.*

Relatives and friends gathered at the funeral home, muddying the foyer with slush from the last snowfall of 1968.

A minister who had never known Bruckner delivered the eulogy. He spoke of the vagaries of premature death and about the mysteries of life, mysteries to which God alone had answers. The minister also expressed his own deep-felt conviction that Bruckner had died the most gallant and ennobling death an American man possibly could: on the field of battle in the service of his country, fighting to ensure that the people of South Vietnam who desperately

wanted to live in a democratic nation would be able to do so.

The minister had never served in the military, but he was hawkish on the war, as were the majority of the mourners who listened intently to his every word. They sat on hard folding chairs, their reddened, sniffling noses hidden in handkerchiefs: the four stoic brothers; Bruckner's stone-faced father; Bruckner's mother, slumped against her husband's bony shoulder, her eyes misting; Bruckner's widow, who simply stared at the flag-draped casket.

They listened to the minister and believed his words, believed that Bruckner indeed had died in the cause of furthering democracy. They all had to believe, for to do otherwise—to come to the realization that one they had raised and loved had been killed in a senseless war—would have shattered their faith in the rightness of the war, would have caused them to question the actions of their own government. And these simple and humble people just could not do that. Rather, they chose to believe that Bruckner had died heroically, and for a just cause.

The hearse-led procession of cars, moving slowly under the gray Michigan sky, snaked its way through the streets of Traverse City. This cortege halted at the entrance to the hilltop cemetery. Six solemn pallbearers—classmates of Bruckner's—pulled the casket from the back of the hearse. They grasped the cold brass handles tightly, then started up to the burial site.

The ragged line of mourners followed.

Amid gnarled, bare-limbed trees, the mourners assumed respectful attitudes of attention as two members of the VFW honor guard, chafed by the cold, fumbled with and finally folded the flag that had covered Bruckner's casket. One of them, a World War II veteran, approached Bruckner's widow and offered the flag to her.

She accepted it, her eyes never leaving the casket.

The seven man honor guard fired three salvoes with their old M-1 rifles. The gunfire was briefly carried on, then silenced by, a vicious wind that whipped in off Lake Michigan.

A young soldier wet his lips and raised a bugle to his mouth. The sounds of "Taps" carried sadly across the cemetery.

Shortly after the last bars echoed into silence, the minister had a few last words to say. The mourners, cut to the bone by the weather, impatiently shuffled their feet in the dirty remnants of snow.

In one last, loving gesture, Bruckner's widow walked to his casket. She placed a single red carnation on its lid. The wind toyed with the flower for a moment, then swept it up and deposited it in the freshly turned grave.

With faces aged beyond their years by the harshness of their lives and now by the harshness of Bruckner's death, the mourners walked, huddled and hunched against the cold, back to the cars.

On the back side of the hill, two men emerged from the warmth of the cemetery's toolshed and walked toward Bruckner's burial site. Both men carried shovels, and one of them bore a slender white cardboard box. Inside the box, furled around its pinewood staff, was a miniature replica of the flag of the United States of America.

Shortly, the Bruckner house filled with a large gathering of relatives and friends. Aunts and cousins bustled about the kitchen preparing casseroles and pouring stiff shots of whiskey for the men.

Everyone ate, drank, and laughed too much.

The teenaged cousins grew bored with the gathering and piled into one car, leaving to find a place and a way of their own to pay their last respects to Bruckner.

The younger children played quietly at the feet of their parents, aware of some new and strange current of emotion at this specific gathering, but too young to grasp its significance. After a while the young boys wondered why their fathers were regarding them with such long and thoughtful stares, and became restless.

One by one the friends and relatives paid homage to Bruckner's parents, brothers, and widow—a brief murmuring of sympathetic words, a touching of lips to cheeks. The men firmly took Mr. Bruckner's hand, each man trying to massage into the old man's flesh their own messages of empathy, compassion, and sorrow. They, too, had sons.

By dusk the gathering was over. Bruckner's brothers left en masse, after first kissing their parents and sister-in-law.

There were no more words to be spoken. The three of them stood in the middle of the living room and embraced. Then Bruckner's widow left for her own home.

Mr. and Mrs. Bruckner sat in the living room as the night deepened. Mrs. Bruckner read silently from a well-thumbed Bible, stopping every so often to take off her bifocals and wipe them with Kleenex. Bruckner's father sat in his armchair and stared at a photograph that sat atop an end table.

The photo was of Bruckner at sixteen. He was standing tall and proud, holding a rifle, next to a deer he had killed. The dead animal was dangling from the branches of a pine tree, head down. Its eyes open and glassy—lifeless. But Bruckner's eyes, as shown in the photo, were clear and smiling, alive with the first burst of youth, the intimations of manhood already showing on his face.

Bruckner's father stared at the photograph. Every once in a while the old man cleared his throat.

At 9:00 P.M. Bruckner's father arose from his chair and turned on the radio. He and his wife listened to the news and, after the local weather report, prepared for bed. They performed the same presleep rituals that they had throughout their thirty-seven-year marriage.

They walked through the suddenly too big, too empty living room and up the stairs to their bedroom: Bruckner's father and mother together, alone.

Seven blocks away, Bruckner's widow walked into her bedroom, alone.

In the safety of their room Mrs. Bruckner prayed, petitioning God to take good care of her son.

Mr. Bruckner tried to hold back his tears but, under cover of darkness, surrendered to the pain of the loss of his youngest son. The old man's throat spasmed with hopelessness; his tears began rolling freely down his ruddy cheeks. He tasted his own salt and grief; his chest heaved as he openly expressed his pain. He instinctively reached out toward his wife, as she had to her God. His trembling fingers were met halfway in their search by his wife's careworn hands. They huddled together in their bed of thirty-seven years and held each other tightly, the tears on their seamed faces mingling.

Seven blocks away, Bruckner's widow sobbed as she embraced the pillow which had once cradled her husband's head.

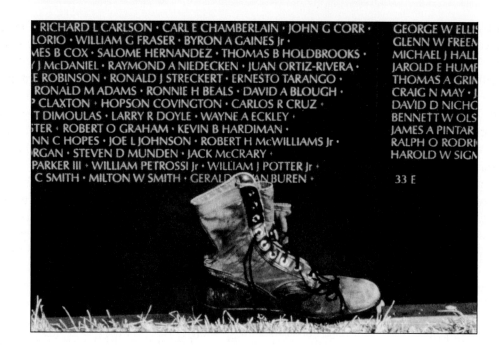

RICHARD L CARLSON · CARL E CHAMBERLAIN · JOHN G CORR ·   GEORGE W ELLI
LORIO · WILLIAM G FRASER · BYRON A GAINES Jr ·   GLENN W FREEM
MES B COX · SALOME HERNANDEZ · THOMAS B HOLDBROOKS ·   MICHAEL J HALL
J McDANIEL · RAYMOND A NIEDECKEN · JUAN ORTIZ-RIVERA ·   JAROLD E HUMP
E ROBINSON · RONALD J STRECKERT · ERNESTO TARANGO ·   THOMAS A GRIN
RONALD M ADAMS · RONNIE H BEALS · DAVID A BLOUGH ·   CRAIG N MAY · J
CLAXTON · HOPSON COVINGTON · CARLOS R CRUZ ·   DAVID D NICHO
T DIMOULAS · LARRY R DOYLE · WAYNE A ECKLEY ·   BENNETT W OLS
TER · ROBERT O GRAHAM · KEVIN B HARDIMAN ·   JAMES A PINTAR
NN C HOPES · JOE L JOHNSON · ROBERT H McWILLIAMS Jr ·   RALPH O RODRI
RGAN · STEVEN D MUNDEN · JACK McCRARY ·   HAROLD W SIGN
PARKER III · WILLIAM PETROSSI Jr · WILLIAM J POTTER Jr ·
C SMITH · MILTON W SMITH · GERALD VANBUREN ·   33 E

A Visit to the Wall

from *In Country*
by Bobbie Ann Mason

Novelist Bobbie Ann Mason's **In Country** *is the story of a young woman, Sam Hughes, whose life has been deeply affected by Vietnam. Her father was killed in the war and her beloved Uncle Emmett, with whom she now lives, suffers from war-related ills. This passage, the novel's conclusion, takes place in summer 1984, when seventeen-year-old Sam, Uncle Emmett, and Sam's grandmother, Mamaw, have driven to Washington, D.C., to visit the Vietnam Veterans Memorial.*

As they drive into Washington a few hours later, Sam feels sick with apprehension. She has kept telling herself that the memorial is only a rock with names on it. It doesn't mean anything except they're dead. It's just names. Nobody here but us chickens. Just us and the planet Earth and the nuclear bomb. But that's O.K., she thinks now. There is something comforting about the idea of nobody here but us chickens. It's so intimate. Nobody here but us. Maybe that's the point. People shouldn't make too much of death. Her history teacher said there are more people alive now than dead. He warned that there were so many people alive now, and they were living so much longer, that people had the idea they were practically immortal. But everyone's

going to die and we'd better get used to the notion, he said. Dead and gone. Long gone from Kentucky.

Sometimes in the middle of the night it struck Sam with sudden clarity that she was going to die someday. Most of the time she forgot about this. But now, as she and Emmett and Mamaw Hughes drive into Washington, where the Vietnam Memorial bears the names of so many who died, the reality of death hits her in broad daylight. Mamaw is fifty-eight. She is going to die soon. She could die any minute, like that racehorse that keeled over dead, inexplicably, on Father's Day. Sam has been so afraid Emmett would die. But Emmett came to Cawood's Pond looking for her, because it was unbearable to him that she might have left him alone, that she might even die.

The Washington Monument is a gleaming pencil against the sky. Emmett is driving, and the traffic is frightening, so many cars swishing and merging, like bold skaters in a crowded rink. They pass cars with government license plates that say FED. Sam wonders how long the Washington Monument will stand on the Earth.

A brown sign on Constitution Avenue says VIETNAM VETERANS MEMORIAL. Emmett can't find a parking place nearby. He parks on a side street and they walk toward the

Washington Monument. Mamaw puffs along. She has put on a good dress and stockings. Sam feels they are ambling, out for a stroll, it is so slow. She wants to break into a run. The Washington Monument rises up out of the earth, proud and tall. She remembers Tom's bitter comment about it—a big white prick. She once heard someone say the U.S.A. goes around fucking the world. That guy who put pink plastic around those islands should make a big rubber for the Washington Monument, Sam thinks. She has so many bizarre ideas there should be a market for her imagination. These ideas are churning in her head. She can hardly enjoy Washington for these thoughts. In Washington, the buildings are so pretty, so white. In a dream, the Vietnam Memorial was a black boomerang, whizzing toward her head.

"I don't see it," Mamaw says.

"It's over yonder," Emmett says, pointing. "They say you come up on it sudden."

"My legs are starting to hurt."

Sam wants to run, but she doesn't know whether she wants to run toward the memorial or away from it. She just wants to run. She has the new record album with her, so it won't melt in the hot car. It's in a plastic bag with handles. Emmett is carrying the pot of geraniums. She is amazed by him, his impressive bulk, his secret suffering. She feels his anxiety. His heart must be racing, as if something intolerable is about to happen.

Emmett holds Mamaw's arm protectively and steers her across the street. The pot of geraniums hugs his chest.

"There it is," Sam says.

It is massive, a black gash in a hillside, like a vein of coal exposed and then polished with polyurethane. A crowd is filing by slowly, staring at it solemnly.

"Law," says Sam's grandmother quietly. "It's black as night."

"Here's the directory," Emmett says, pausing at the entrance. "I'll look up his name for you, Mrs. Hughes."

The directory is on a pedestal with a protective plastic shield. Sam stands in the shade, looking forward, at the black wing embedded in the soil, with grass growing above. It is like a giant grave, fifty-eight thousand bodies rotting here behind those names. The people are streaming past, down into the pit.

"It don't show up good," Mamaw says anxiously. "It's just a hole in the ground."

The memorial cuts a V in the ground, like the wings of an abstract bird, huge and headless. Overhead, a jet plane angles upward, taking off.

"It's on Panel 9E," Emmett reports. "That's on the east wing. We're on the west."

At the bottom of the wall is a granite trough, and on the edge of it the sunlight reflects the names just above, in mirror writing, upside down. Flower arrangements are scattered at the base. A little kid says, "Look, Daddy, the flowers are dying." The man snaps, "Some are and some aren't."

The walkway is separated from the memorial by a strip of gravel, and on the other side of the walk is a border of dark gray brick. The shiny surface of the wall reflects the Lincoln Memorial and the Washington Monument, at opposite angles.

A woman in a sunhat is focusing a camera on the wall. She says to the woman with her, "I didn't think it would look like this. Things aren't what you think they look like. I didn't know it was a wall."

A spraddle-legged guy in camouflage clothing walks by with a cane. Probably he has an artificial leg, Sam thinks, but he walks along proudly, as if he has been here many times before and doesn't have any particular business at that moment. He seems to belong here, like Emmett hanging out at McDonald's.

A group of schoolkids tumble through, noisy as chickens. As they enter, one of the girls says, "Are they piled on top of each other?" They walk a few steps farther and she says, "What are all these names anyway?" Sam feels like punching the girl in the face for being so dumb. How could anybody that age not know? But she realizes that she doesn't know either. She is just beginning to understand. And she will never really know what happened to all these men in the war. Some people walk by, talking as though they are on a Sunday picnic, but most are reverent, and some of them are crying.

Sam stands in the center of the V, deep in the pit. The V is like the white wings of the shopping mall in Paducah. The Washington Monument is reflected at the center line. If she moves slightly to the left, she sees the monument, and if she moves the other way she sees a reflection of the flag opposite the memorial. Both the monument and the flag seem like arrogant gestures, like the country giving the finger to the dead boys, flung in this hole in the ground. Sam doesn't understand what she is feeling, but it is something so strong, it is like a tornado moving in her, something massive and overpowering. It feels like giving birth to this wall.

"I wish Tom could be here," Sam says to Emmett. "He needs to be here." Her voice is thin, like smoke, barely audible.

"He'll make it here someday. Jim's coming too. They're all coming one of these days."

"Are you going to look for anybody's name besides my daddy's?"

"Yeah."

"Who?"

"Those guys I told you about, the ones that died all around me that day. And that guy I was going to look up—he might be here. I don't know if he made it out or not."

Sam gets a flash of Emmett's suffering, his grieving all these years. He has been grieving for fourteen years. In this dazzling sunlight, his pimples don't show. A jet plane flies overhead, close to the earth. Its wings are angled back too, like a bird's.

"The Wall," the Vietnam Veterans Memorial, seen from a nearby grove of trees.

Two workmen in hard hats are there with a stepladder and some loud machinery. One of the workmen, whose hat says on the back NEVER AGAIN, seems to be drilling into the wall.

"What's he doing, hon?" Sam hears Mamaw say behind her.

"It looks like they're patching up a hole or something." *Fixing a hole where the rain gets in.*

The man on the ladder turns off the tool, a sander, and the other workman hands him a brush. He brushes the spot. Silver duct tape is patched around several names, leaving the names exposed. The names are highlighted in yellow, as though someone has taken a Magic Marker and colored them, the way Sam used to mark names and dates, important facts, in her textbooks.

"Somebody must have vandalized it," says a man behind Sam. "Can you imagine the sicko who would do that?"

"No," says the woman with him. "Somebody just wanted the names to stand out and be noticed. I can go with that."

"Do you think they colored Dwayne's name?" Mamaw asks Sam worriedly.

"No. Why would they?" Sam gazes at the flowers spaced along the base of the memorial. A white carnation is stuck in a crack between two panels of the wall. A woman bends down and straightens a ribbon on a wreath. The ribbon has gold letters on it, "VFW Post 7215 of Pa."

They are moving slowly. Panel 9E is some distance ahead. Sam reads a small poster propped at the base of the wall: "To those men of C Company, 1st Bn. 503 Inf., 173rd Airborne who were lost in the battle for Hill 823, Dak To, Nov. 11, 1967. Because of their bravery I am here today. A grateful buddy."

A man rolls past in a wheelchair. Another jet plane flies over.

A handwritten note taped to the wall apologizes to one of the names for abandoning him in a firefight.

Mamaw turns to fuss over the geraniums in Emmett's arms, the way she might fluff a pillow.

The workmen are cleaning the yellow paint from the names. They sand the wall and brush it carefully, like men polishing their cars. The man on the ladder sprays water on the name he has just sanded and wipes it with a rag.

Sam, conscious of how slowly they are moving, with dread, watches two uniformed marines searching and searching for a name. "He must have been along here somewhere," one says. They keep looking, running their hands over the names.

"There it is. That's him."

They read his name and both look abruptly away, stare out for a moment in the direction of the Lincoln Memorial, then walk briskly off.

"May I help you find someone's name?" asks a woman in a T-shirt and green pants. She is a park guide, with a clipboard in her hand.

"We know where we are," Emmett says. "Much obliged, though."

At panel 9E, Sam stands back while Emmett and Mamaw search for her father's name. Emmett, his gaze steady and intent, faces the wall, as though he were watching birds; and Mamaw, through her glasses, seems intent and purposeful, as though she were looking for something back in the field, watching to see if a cow had gotten out of the pasture. Sam imagines the egret patrolling for ticks on a water buffalo's back, ducking and snaking its head forward, its beak like a punji stick.

"There it is," Emmett says. It is far above his head, near the top of the wall. He reaches up and touches the name. "There's his name, Dwayne E. Hughes."

"I can't reach it," says Mamaw. "Oh, I wanted to touch it," she says softly, in disappointment.

"We'll set the flowers here, Mrs. Hughes," says Emmett. He sets the pot at the base of the panel, tenderly, as though tucking in a baby.

"I'm going to bawl," Mamaw says, bowing her head and starting to sob. "I wish I could touch it."

Sam has an idea. She sprints over to the workmen and asks them to let her borrow the stepladder. They are almost finished, and they agree. One of them brings it over and sets it up beside the wall, and Sam urges Mamaw to climb the ladder, but Mamaw protests. "No, I can't do it. You do it."

"Go ahead, ma'am," the workman says.

"Emmett and me'll hold the ladder," says Sam.

"Somebody might see up my dress."

"No, go on, Mrs. Hughes. You can do it," says Emmett. "Come on, we'll help you reach it."

He takes her arm. Together, he and Sam steady her while she places her foot on the first step and swings herself up. She seems scared, and she doesn't speak. She reaches but cannot touch the name.

"One more, Mamaw," says Sam, looking up at her grandmother—at the sagging wrinkles, her flab hanging loose and sad, and her eyes reddened with crying. Mamaw reaches toward the name and slowly struggles up the next step, holding her dress tight against her. She touches the name, running her hand over it, stroking it tentatively, affectionately, like feeling a cat's back. Her chin wobbles, and after a moment she backs down the ladder silently.

When Mamaw is down, Sam starts up the ladder, with the record package in her hand.

"Here, take the camera, Sam. Get his name." Mamaw has brought Donna's Instamatic.

"No, I can't take a picture this close."

Sam climbs the ladder until she is eye level with her father's name. She feels funny, touching it. A scratching on a rock. Writing. Something for future archaeologists to puzzle over, clues to a language.

"Look this way, Sam," Mamaw says. "I want to take your

A visitor points out a name engraved in the highly polished black granite wall of the Vietnam Veterans Memorial in Washington, D.C.

picture. I want to get you and his name and the flowers in together if I can."

"The name won't show up," Sam says.

"Smile."

"How can I smile?" She is crying.

Mamaw backs up and snaps two pictures. Sam feels her face looking blank. Up on the ladder, she feels so tall, like a spindly weed that is sprouting up out of this diamond-bright seam of hard earth. She sees Emmett at the directory, probably searching for his buddies' names. She touches her father's name again.

"All I can see here is my reflection," Mamaw says when Sam comes down the ladder. "I hope his name shows up. And your face was all shadow."

"Wait here a minute," Sam says, turning away her tears from Mamaw. She hurries to the directory on the east side. Emmett isn't there anymore. She sees him striding along the wall, looking for a certain panel. Nearby, a group of marines is keeping a vigil for the POWs and MIAs. A double row of flags is planted in the dirt alongside their table. One of the marines walks by with a poster: "You Are an American, Your Voice Can Make the Difference." Sam flips through the directory and finds "Hughes." She wants to see her father's name there too. She runs down the row of Hughes names. There were so many Hughes boys killed, names she doesn't know. His name is there, and she gazes at it for a moment. Then suddenly her own name leaps out at her.

SAM ALAN HUGHES PFC AR 02 MAR
49 02 FEB 67 HOUSTON TX 14E 104

Her heart pounding, she rushes to panel 14E, and after racing her eyes over the string of names for a moment, she locates her own name.

SAM A HUGHES. It is the first on a line. It is down low enough to touch. She touches her own name. How odd it feels, as though all the names in America have been used to decorate this wall.

Mamaw is there at her side, clutching at Sam's arm, digging in with her fingernails. Mamaw says, "Coming up on this wall of a sudden and seeing how black it was, it was so awful, but then I came down in it and saw that white carnation blooming out of that crack and it gave me hope. It made me know he's watching over us." She loosens her bird-claw grip. "Did we lose Emmett?"

Silently, Sam points to the place where Emmett is studying the names low on a panel. He is sitting there cross-legged in front of the wall, and slowly his face bursts into a smile like flames.

189

Text Credits

Enter Here
pp. 8-10 from *Going After Cacciato* by Tim O'Brien. Copyright © 1975, 1976, 1977, 1978 by Tim O'Brien. Reprinted by arrangement with Delacorte Press/Seymour Lawrence. All rights reserved.
p. 11 from John F. Kennedy's inaugural address, January 20, 1961, and Ho Chi Minh's Declaration of Independence speech, September 2, 1945.
pp. 12-15 from *12, 20, & 5: A Doctor's Year in Vietnam* by John A. Parrish. Copyright © 1972 by John A. Parrish. Reprinted by permission of John A. Parrish.
pp. 16-19 from *The 13th Valley* by John M. Del Vecchio. Copyright © 1982 by John M. Del Vecchio. Reprinted by permission of Bantam Books.

Acts of War
pp. 34-44 from *The Offering* by Tom Carhart. Copyright © 1987 by Tom Carhart. Reprinted by permission of William Morrow & Company.
pp. 45-51 from *Dispatches* by Michael Herr. Copyright © 1977 by Michael Herr. Reprinted by permission of Candida Donadio Association. This work first appeared in a slightly different form in the August 1968 issue of *Esquire* magazine.
p. 52 from the Southeast Asia Resolution, passed by Congress August 7, 1964; President Lyndon B. Johnson's message to Congress, August 5, 1964; and Senator Wayne Morse's comments on the Senate floor, August 5, 1964.
pp. 53-56 from *Brothers: Black Soldiers in the Nam* by Stanley Goff and Robert Sanders with Clark Smith. Copyright © 1982 by Presidio Press. Reprinted by permission of Presidio Press.
p. 57 from "Vietnam: The War Is Worth Winning" by Hedley Donovan. *Life*, February 25, 1966. Copyright © 1966 by Time Inc. Reprinted by permission of Time Inc.

WIA
pp. 60-67 from *Home Before Morning: The Story of an Army Nurse* by Lynda Van Devanter. Copyright © 1983 by Beaufort Books. Reprinted by permission of Beaufort Books.
p. 62 from "Where We Are Now—On the Threshold of a New War" by George Ball. Report to President Lyndon B. Johnson detailing the French experience in Vietnam, June 18, 1965.
pp. 68-69 from "Declaration of Independence from the War in Vietnam" sermon by Dr. Martin Luther King, Jr., April 4, 1967.
pp. 70-81 from *365 Days* by Ronald Glasser. Reprinted by permission of George Braziller, Inc., New York. Copyright © 1971, 1980 by Ronald J. Glasser. All rights reserved.
p. 80 from *Dear America: Letters Home from Vietnam* ed. by Bernard Edelman. Copyright © 1985 by The New York Vietnam Veterans Memorial Commission. All rights reserved. Reprinted by permission of Bernard Edelman and The New York Vietnam Veterans Memorial Commission.

Behind the Lines
pp. 98-103 from *A Rumor of War* by Philip Caputo. Copyright © 1977 by Philip Caputo. Reprinted by permission of Henry Holt and Company, Inc.
pp. 104-109 from *F.N.G.* by Donald Bodey. Copyright © 1985 by Donald Bodey. Reprinted by permission of Viking Penguin, Inc.
pp. 110-111 from "Minutes of a White House Meeting" by James C. Thomson, Jr. Reprinted from the *Atlantic Monthly*, May 1967.
pp. 112-115 from *Vietnam-Perkasie: A Combat Marine Memoir* by W.D. Ehrhart. Copyright © 1983 by W.D. Ehrhart. Reprinted by permission of McFarland & Company, Inc. Publishers, Jefferson, NC.
pp. 116-117 from "Red Gains in Viet Cities Like Last Nazi Spasm at the Bulge " by William S. White, *Washington Post*, February 12, 1968, copyright © 1968 by United Feature Syndicate. Reprinted by permission of United Feature Syndicate; "Who, What, When, Where, Why: Report from Vietnam by Walter Cronkite," aired February 27, 1968, printed by permission of CBS; "'We Have the Enemy on the Run,' Says General Custer at Big Horn" by Art Buchwald, *Washington Post*, February 6, 1968, copyright © 1968 by Art Buchwald, reprinted by permission of the author.
pp. 118-121 from *Dog Soldiers* by Robert Stone. Copyright © 1973, 1974 by Robert Stone. Reprinted by permission of Houghton Mifflin Company.
p. 121 from a speech by Senator George Aiken, October 19, 1966.
pp. 122-127 from *. . . And a Hard Rain Fell: A GI's True Story of the War in Vietnam* by John Ketwig. Copyright © 1985 by John Ketwig. Reprinted with permission of Macmillan Publishing Company.

Acts of War II
pp. 138-145 from *F.N.G.* by Donald Bodey. Copyright © 1985 by Donald Bodey. Reprinted by permission of Viking Penguin, Inc.
p. 146 from *The Armies of the Night* by Norman Mailer. Copyright © by Norman Mailer. Reprinted by arrangement with New American Library, New York, NY.
pp. 147-149 from *If I Die in a Combat Zone (Box Me Up and Ship Me Home)* by Tim O'Brien. Copyright © 1969, 1970, 1972, 1973 by Tim O'Brien. Reprinted by arrangement with Delacorte Press/Seymour Lawrence. All rights reserved.

p. 150 from *Dispatches* by Michael Herr. Copyright © 1977 by Michael Herr. Reprinted by permission of Candida Donadio Association. This work first appeared in a slightly different form in the August 1968 issue of *Esquire* magazine.
pp. 151-159 from *Flight of the Intruder* by Stephen Coonts. Copyright © 1986 by U.S. Naval Institute, Annapolis, MD. Reprinted by permission.
pp. 160-165 from *The 13th Valley* by John M. Del Vecchio. Copyright © 1982 by John M. Del Vecchio. Reprinted by permission of Bantam Books.
pp. 166-167 from a speech by President Richard M. Nixon, April 30, 1970, and speeches by Vice President Spiro Agnew, October 19, 1969, and October 30, 1969.

Homeward Bound
pp. 170-171 from *If I Die in a Combat Zone (Box Me Up and Ship Me Home)* by Tim O'Brien. Copyright © 1969, 1970, 1972, 1973 by Tim O'Brien. Reprinted by arrangement with Delacorte Press/Seymour Lawrence. All rights reserved.
pp. 172-181 from *Vietnam-Perkasie: A Combat Marine Memoir* by W.D. Ehrhart. Copyright © 1983 by W.D. Ehrhart. Reprinted by permission of McFarland & Company, Inc. Publishers, Jefferson, NC.
pp. 182-183 from *Dau: A Novel of Vietnam* by Ed Dodge. Copyright © 1984 by Ed Dodge. Reprinted with permission of Macmillan Publishing Company.
pp. 184-189 from *In Country* by Bobbie Ann Mason. Copyright © 1985 by Bobbie Ann Mason. Reprinted by permission of Harper & Row, Publishers Inc.

Picture Credits

Cover Photo
© 1987 David Burnett/Contact

Enter Here
p. 6, Marc Riboud—Magnum. p. 8, © 1987 David Burnett/Contact. p. 10, © Larry Burrows Collection. pp. 12-13, Mark Jury. p. 14, Bruno Barbey—Magnum. p. 16, © 1987 David Burnett/Contact. p. 18, Donald McCullin—Camera Press Ltd. p. 19, © 1987 David Burnett/Contact.

First Encounters
pp. 20-23, Enrico Sarsini. pp. 24-27, Co Rentmeester—LIFE Magazine, © Time Inc. pp. 28-31, Enrico Sarsini.

Acts of War
pp. 32, 34, 37, UPI/Bettmann Newsphotos. p. 40, © Larry Burrows Collection. p. 43, Bunyo Ishikawa. p. 45, UPI/Bettmann Newsphotos. pp. 46, 49-50, Donald McCullin—Magnum. p. 53, © Larry Burrows Collection. p. 55, Perry Kretz—Black Star.

WIA
p. 58, AP/Wide World. p. 60, Mark Jury. p. 65, Philip Jones Griffiths—Magnum. p. 70, © Larry Burrows Collection. pp. 72, 74, Mark Jury. p. 79, Andrew Schneider—Black Star.

Vietnam on Film
pp. 82-83, © Nancy Moran. p. 84 top, SYGMA; bottom, Ricky Francisco—SYGMA. pp. 85-87, SYGMA. p. 88, Philip Jones Griffiths—Magnum. p. 89, © Nancy Moran. pp. 90-91, C. Milinaire—SYGMA. p. 92, SYGMA. p. 93, Bruce Talamon—SYGMA. p. 94, Gamma-Liaison. p. 95, Steve Schapiro—SYGMA.

Behind the Lines
p. 96, Larry Burrows—LIFE Magazine, © 1965 Time Inc. p. 98, Mark Jury. pp. 100-101, © Larry Burrows Collection. p. 103, Peter Marlow—Magnum. pp. 104-106, Mark Jury. p. 109, UPI/Bettmann Newsphotos. p. 112, © Larry Burrows Collection. p. 114, Mark Jury. p. 118, © 1987 David Burnett/Contact. p. 122, René Burri—Magnum. p. 124, Philip Jones Griffiths—Magnum. p. 127, René Burri—Magnum.

R & R
pp. 128-129, U.S. Army. pp. 130-131, Maynard Frank Wolfe/TIME Magazine. p. 132, T. Tanuma/TIME Magazine. p. 133, Maynard Frank Wolfe/TIME Magazine. pp. 134-135, Martyn Green—Black Star.

Acts of War II
p. 136, Bunyo Ishikawa. p. 138, © 1987 David Burnett/Contact. p. 141, Andrew Rakoczy—Black Star. p. 142, Christian Simonpietri—SYGMA. p. 145, © Tim Page. p. 147, UPI/Bettmann Newsphotos. p. 148, U.S. Army. p. 149, Robert Ellison—Black Star. p. 151, Mark Godfrey—Archive Pictures Inc. p. 154, Courtesy Grumman Corporation. p. 156, Black Star. p. 159, U.S. Navy. p. 160, © Tim Page. p. 162, Ray Cranbourne—Black Star. p. 165, U.S. Army.

Homeward Bound
p. 168, AP/Wide World. pp. 170-172, © 1987 David Burnett/ Contact. pp. 178-179, John Olson—LIFE Magazine, © Time Inc. p. 182, AP/Wide World. p. 184, Peter Marlow—Magnum. pp. 186-187, Sal Lopes. p. 189, Susan Meiselas—Magnum.

Names, Acronyms, Terms

AID—Agency for International Development.

AIT—advanced individual training. Specialized instruction a soldier receives after boot camp to finish his training.

AK47—a Soviet-designed semiautomatic rifle firing 7.62MM ammunition. Accurate and reliable, it was the standard rifle of the North Vietnamese and Vietcong infantry.

AO—artillery observer. Also a military unit's area of operations.

APC—armored personnel carrier. A tracked transport vehicle, usually armed with a .50-caliber machine gun.

ARA—aerial rocket artillery. Rockets fired from a Cobra AG-1H helicopter gunship.

ARVN—Army of the Republic of Vietnam, the South Vietnamese regular army.

AWOL—absent without leave.

berm—the perimeter line of a fortification, usually raised above surrounding area.

B-52—a heavy American strategic bomber, used for high-altitude bombing in the Vietnam War. Also, a military-issue can opener.

B-40—a Communist rocket-propelled grenade launcher. Also designates rockets fired from this launcher.

boonierat—a combat infantryman.

BOQ—bachelor officer quarters.

CA—combat assault.

CAR15—a carbine rifle.

C&C—command and control. The helicopter the unit commander rides in and from which he directs the battle.

C-4—a powerful plastic explosive used in claymore mines and other weapons.

Charlie, Victor Charlie—*see* VC.

cherry—a new troop.

Chieu Hoi—the GVN "open arms" program promising clemency and compensation to VC guerrillas and NVA regulars who defected to live under South Vietnamese government authority. Also, a term of surrender used by Communist troops.

Chinook—a large, twin-rotor cargo helicopter, the CH-47.

claymore mine—antipersonnel mine with a one-pound charge of C-4 behind 600 small steel balls.

click, klick—a kilometer.

CO—commanding officer.

Cobra—an assault helicopter gunship, the AG-1H.

CP—command post.

CP pills—antimalaria pills.

C-rats, Charlie Rats—combat rations.

CS gas—a riot-control gas; tear gas.

D&I—debridement and irrigation. An operation to cut away dead skin, remove fragments, and clean a wound.

DEROS—date of estimated return from overseas. The date a soldier was due to return from Vietnam.

DRV—Democratic Republic of (North) Vietnam. Since 1975, the designation for all Vietnam.

dustoff—the medical evacuation by helicopter of casualties. Also the helicopter that performed such evacuations.

EM—enlisted man.

ER—emergency room.

ETS—estimated termination of service. The scheduled date of getting out of the Army.

expectants—casualties who are expected to die.

FAC—forward air controller. Pilot or observer who directs strike aircraft and artillery.

flack, flak—antiaircraft fire.

FNG—fucking new guy. A new troop.

Freedom Bird—common term for any aircraft used to take U.S. military personnel out of Vietnam.

gook—a derogatory term for Vietnamese people.

grunt—popular nickname for an infantryman. Supposedly derived from the sound one made when lifting up his rucksack.

GVN—U.S. abbreviation for the government of South Vietnam. Also referred to as the Republic of Vietnam.

HE—high explosive. Used to describe a type of bomb dropped by aircraft or shells fired by artillery.

Higher-Higher—the command or commanders.

hooch, hootch—any small shelter, including makeshift bunkers used by U.S. troops as well as native Vietnamese huts.

IG—inspector general.

in-country—in Vietnam.

KIA—killed in action.

LAW—M72 light antitank weapon. A shoulder-fired 66MM rocket with a one-time, disposable, fiber glass launcher.

LCU—large amphibious landing craft used by the Marines.

lifer—a career officer or enlisted man.

LOH (pronounced "loach")—light observation helicopter.

LRRP—long-range reconnaissance platoon or patrol. LRRP troops were known as "lurps."

LSA—lubricant, small arms.

LSO—landing signals officer on a U.S. aircraft carrier.

LZ—landing zone. A "hot" LZ was a landing zone under enemy fire.

MACV—Military Assistance Command, Vietnam. U.S. command for all military activities in Vietnam.

medevac, medivac—medical evacuation of wounded or ill troops from the field by helicopter or airplane. Also name given to the evacuating aircraft.

M14—a wood-stock, semiautomatic U.S. rifle, firing 7.62MM bullets, that was standard issue in the early years of the war. Replaced by the M16.

montagnard—a member of any of the mountain tribes of Vietnam, Laos, or Cambodia.

MOS—military occupational specialty.

MP—military police.

M79—an American single-shot, 40MM grenade launcher. Also called the "thumper."

M16—a gas-operated automatic/semiautomatic assault weapon with a twenty-pound magazine, an effective range of 460 meters, and an effective automatic firing rate of 100-200 rounds per minute. After 1967, the standard American military weapon.

M60—the standard American light machine gun, an air-cooled, belt-fed weapon using 7.62MM ammunition. Also called the "sixty," the "gun," or the "pig."

napalm—a jellied petroleum substance that burns with fierce heat. Used as an antipersonnel weapon.

NCO—noncommissioned officer, usually a squad leader or platoon sergeant.

NLF—National Liberation Front. Officially the National Front for the Liberation of the South.

NVA—North Vietnamese Army. Also called the People's Army of Vietnam (PAVN) and Vietnam People's Army (VPA).

OD—olive drab, the standard U.S. military hue.

PFC—private first class.

pogey-bait—Marine term for snacks, candy, and other nonmilitary-issue food.

point—the lead man of a patrol.

PRC-25, Prick-25—the standard infantry radio used in Vietnam.

PRG—Provisional Revolutionary Government, the political arm of the NLF after 1969.

Pseudomonas—a bluish, foul-smelling bacterial infection common among burn victims.

PSP—perforated steel plate.

PX—post exchange, a small general store at U.S. Army garrisons.

R&R—rest and recuperation.

red ball—a high-speed trail or road used by Communist troops.

REMF—rear-echelon motherfucker. A noncombat troop.

rock 'n' roll—firing a weapon on full automatic.

rotate—to return to the United States at the end of a military tour in Vietnam.

RPD—a 7.62MM Communist light machine gun with a 100-round, belt-operated drum magazine.

RPG—rocket-propelled grenade. Generally used to designate a Soviet-made weapon comparable to the U.S.-made light antitank weapon (LAW).

RTO—radio-telephone operator.

ruck, rucksack—backpack issued to infantry in Vietnam.

RVN—Republic of (South) Vietnam.

sapper—a VC or NVA commando, usually armed with explosives.

Section Eight—a military discharge based on mental illness or instability.

short-timer—soldier nearing the end of his tour in Vietnam.

SI—seriously ill.

sitrep—situation report.

slack—the second man in a patrol. Walking right behind the point man, he gave him immediate support, or "took up his slack."

slick—nickname for UH-1 Iroquois, or "Huey" helicopter.

SOP—standard operating procedure.

strack—a highly proficient soldier. More generally, the best; outstanding.

T&T—through-and-through wound, one in which a bullet or fragment has entered and exited the body.

Tet offensive—a series of coordinated attacks by the VC and NVA against military installations and provincial capitals throughout South Vietnam at the start of the lunar New Year in late January 1968.

top—nickname for a company first sergeant.

VC—an abbreviation for Vietcong, which was, in turn, a contraction of Vietnam Cong San (Vietnamese Communist). Also called Victor Charlie or Charlie.

Vietminh—the coalition founded by Ho Chi Minh that fought the French, then led the DRV. Absorbed by the Lao Dong (Communist) party in 1951.

VSI—very seriously ill.

wake-up—the last day of a soldier's Vietnam tour, as in "seven and a wake-up."

White Mice—the Saigon police.

WIA—wounded in action.

Willie Peter, WP—white phosphorus, a chemical used in high-temperature incendiary bombs and grenades.

World, The—America or anywhere outside Vietnam.

XO—executive officer. Second in command of a military unit.